Gems of Dharma,
Jewels of Freedom

Gems of Dharma,
Jewels of Freedom

*the clear and authoritative, classic handbook of mahâyâna Buddhism
by the great 12th century Tibetan bodhisattva*

Jé Gampopa

a new translation from the Tibetan by

Ken and Katia Holmes

*according to the detailed explanations traditional to
the Karma Kagyü Lineage*

ISBN Hardcover edition — 0 9524555 1 X
ISBN Paperback edition — 0 9524555 0 1

British Library Cataloguing-in-Publication Data. A catalogue record for this book is available from the British Library.

Layout and setting by Kenneth Holmes
Printed by Cromwell Press, Melksham, Wiltshire
Published by Altea Publishing, Parkmount House, St Leonards Road, Forres IV36 0DW, Scotland.

The cover photo is a detail from a major thangka of Gampopa in the Kagyü Samyé Ling temple in Eskdalemuir, painted by master-artist Sherab Palden Beru and his students. Line drawings used throughout the text are by the same artists, from illustrations they have provided for various K.D.D.L. publications: thanks therefore to Dolma Jeffreys, Heinz Hoes, Angelika Schnabel and Carlo Luycxx.

Copyright on all illustrations: Kagyü Samyé Ling Tibetan Centre.

Special recognition to Vita de Waal and the Foundation for Gaia, whose kindness and generosity has enabled this translation to see the light of day. Their profound concern for the well-being of humankind is a moving inspiration in these times of change.

This book is dedicated to Dharma Arya Akong Rinpoche, who made every aspect of this work possible, to all our Kagyü teachers, in particular Khenchen Thrangu Rinpoche and Khenpo Tsultim Gyamtso Rinpoche, for their crystal-clear explanations, and to His Holiness the XVIth Gyalwang Karmapa, who was an inspiration and example for us all.

May Urgyen Tinley, the XVIIth Gyalwang Karmapa, and all those dedicated to bringing truth and peace to our world enjoy long lives, good health and success in their compassionate works.

The Twelfth Tai Situpa

Preface

Gampopa (1079-1153) was one of the greatest masters of Tibetan Buddhism. His classic *thar.pa.rin.po.che'i.rgyen.* is the most well-known text that he wrote.

It is a pleasure to see this new translation, as 'Gems of Dharma, Jewels of Freedom', appear in the English language.

Although no translation can ever match the original Tibetan words of Gampopa, I am sure that this work will carry the blessing of his lineage. Ken and Katia Holmes, who have been my students for more than twelve years, were among the very first Westerners involved in Tibetan Buddhism. During their many years of serving His Holiness the XVIth Gyalwa Karmapa and translating for some of the Kagyu's finest masters, they have encountered the right circumstances for bringing the traditional meaning of this sacred teaching to the Western world.

I sincerely hope and pray that it will bring the light of dharma into the hearts of many.

The Twelfth Tai Situpa
August 1994
Kagyu Samye Ling
Scotland

SHERAB LING
INSTITUTE OF BUDDHIST STUDIES
P.O. BHATTU DISTRICT KANGRA HIMALCHAI. PRADESH 176-125 INDIA

Contents

Contents II

Contents IV

Contents V

Contents VI

Contents VIII

Contents XII

Foreword

The Author and the Text

Gampopa is considered to have been the emanation of a 10th-level bodhisattva[1] who has been manifesting in world after world for endless cosmic ages, in order to help establish the universal teachings of truth we call *dharma*. At the time of Buddha Sakyamuni, he appeared as one of the eminent members of the entourage, as a very holy being, Candraprabhakumâra. It was in response to his questions that the Buddha taught the *samâdhirâjasûtra*, some of his most profound teachings on meditation. In that text, and in other sûtra, the Buddha predicts Candraprabhakumâra's future existence as a physician in Tibet and that he and his fellow bodhisattvas will keep alive vital insight into the real essence of His teachings' meaning.

In the earlier part of his life, Gampopa (1079-1153) mastered his intellectual understanding of Buddhism under eminent scholars of the Khadampa movement. In the later part of his life, Gampopa achieved enlightenment under the guidance of Milarépa — perhaps nowadays the best-known of all Tibetan mystics — from whom he received complete transmission of *mahâmûdra*, and the *Kagyü*[2] teachings of Tilopa and Naropa. The latter were the distilled quintessence of all the powerful techniques of Indian tantric Buddhism. Hence Jé Gampopa's writings are those of a great scholar possessing the most profound insight of a fully-accomplished yogi.

Gampopa, the forefather of the Kagyü traditions of Tibet, incarnated all the major elements of Buddhism: he was a perfect

---

1. see chapter 19, which describes the qualities of these very enlightened beings.

2. Kagyü — The unbroken transmission (*gyu* Tib. *brgyud*) of prowess (ka short for ka-bap (Tib. *bka bab*). *bka bab* means skill passed on from a brilliant teacher to his or her gifted successor. Here the skill lies in four very special areas of practice which are the very essence of the three levels of Buddhism. For a fuller explanation see the XIIth Tai Situpa's "Way to Go", Dzalendara.

monk and Abbot, founder of the first Kagyü monastery; he was master of highly advanced Buddhist meditation and yoga techniques, and in particular of mahâmûdra; he was also a brilliant scholar. Through him, the profound teachings of Tilopa and Naropa became set within the context of both monastic and scholastic mahâyâna Buddhism. In practical terms, this means that, due in part to him, the Kagyü tradition offers its followers every aspect of Buddhist training, from the most basic to the most advanced, according to each of their personal needs, capacities and aspirations. It is not surprising that this exceptional being, a giant in the history of Buddhism, second only to the Buddha, should have been the teacher and guru of the first Gyalwang Karmapa. Through an unbroken line of 17 Karmapas, the teachings and realisation of Gampopa have been kept vividly alive to this day, i.e. for the best part of a millennium.

Lord Buddha's teachings took place in three crucial phases, known as the *three dharmacakra* or *three turnings of the wheel of dharma*. The first *dharmacakra* gave rise to the teachings accepted by all Buddhists throughout the world. These are those of the Four Noble Truths, the Eightfold Path, No-Self, Impermanence etc., through which one can free the mind forever from suffering.

The second *dharmacakra* extended the earlier teachings to embrace both a wisdom which encompasses the voidness of everything and an approach totally rooted in a motivation of universal compassion. Only through such wisdom and compassion can one become a Buddha.

The third *dharmacakra* set all the former teachings into an ultimate context — that of *buddha nature* — in which the unchanging essence of everyone and everything is shown to be enlightenment, endowed with all its illustrious qualities.

These teachings altogether make the *Three Trainings* of Right Conduct, Meditation and Wisdom, explained respectively in the *tripitaka* — the 'triple collection' — of *vinaya*, *sûtra* and *abhidharma*. Lord Buddha also taught the extraordinarily profound and powerful techniques of *tantra*, which can bring these three trainings to their completion with great rapidity, providing that teacher and disciple each have all the appropriate qualities.

The teachings in *Gems of Dharma, Jewels of Freedom* present us with a comprehensive picture of Lord Buddha's teaching, from a viewpoint of one who had the maturity of having understood and practised everything mentioned above. The Buddhism benefiting from the breadth of understanding of the second and third dharmacakra is generally called *mahâyâna* Buddhism. Within mahâyâna there are two main traditions: those of Maitreya/Asanga and of Manjuśri/Nagârjuna. Both are well represented in this work, without any partiality.

This brilliantly-structured analysis of mahâyâna Buddhism will prove of use to many different types of person. In itself, it provides the direct information needed by anyone wishing to acquire an overall view of Buddhism. For scholars, it sets up a comprehensive first framework enabling all further Buddhist study to fall immediately into the right context. For meditators and yogis it constitutes an understanding of dharma that will be essential for the right development of their intense practice.

Background to the Present Translation

Our studies of Gampopa's *Gems of Dharma, Jewels of Freedom*[1] began during His Holiness the XVIth Gyalwang Karmapa's 1977 tour of Europe.[2] We were fortunate enough to travel with him, as part of his staff, for six months, during which time he kindly arranged for Khenpo Tsultrim Gyamtso, who was lecturing professor for the tour, to give us daily instruction in *dharma* (Buddhist teaching).

Over the months, this developed into a travelling dharma class for which, despite the inadequacies in our fledgling Tibetan, we became obliged to assume the roles of interpreters. At the end of the tour His Holiness wished all the students to continue what had been started and a further six months' intensive study was set up. In very memorable days at the château of La Poujade in the

---

1. The title ༄༄། །དམ་ཆོས་ཡིད་བཞིན་ནོར་བུ་ཐར་པ་རིན་པོ་ཆེའི་རྒྱན་ཅེས་བྱ་བ།

This above Tibetan title loses some of its natural flow and power when translated into English, becoming approximately *A Bejewelled Ornament of Liberation, Wish-Fulfilling Gems of Sublime Dharma.* It is said that the title of a Tibetan text can reveal the whole nature of the work's content to someone having sufficient wisdom to understand what the author wished to imply by it. The following is a traditional explanation of the words of this title.

The *sublime dharma* i.e. the discerning exposition of the relative and ultimate natures of all phenomena, is like a *wish-fulfilling gem*, because the wisdom and insight it provides will eventually enable one to achieve profound happiness and to totally transcend suffering. This is what everyone wishes for — yet barely anyone manages to achieve. By applying these teachings one attains *liberation*; not just liberation for oneself but a compassionate liberation which brings benefit to all beings. This is enlightenment, which falls neither into the extreme of worldliness nor into the extreme of meditative escape. These wish-fulfilling gems of sublime dharma have already been expounded by the Buddha in his discourses (sûtra) etc. and explained thoroughly in Buddhist treatises (śastra), by the most renowned Buddhist masters. Although Gampopa has nothing new to add to what they have taught so well, he has taken their gems of truth and set them into a *bejewelled ornament*, arranging them beautifully and meaningfully for the delight of his students' clear appreciation of their value.

2. H H the Gyalwang Karmapa is the Head of the Karma Kagyü tradition of Tibetan Buddhism. The XVIth Karmapa (1924-1981) was deeply revered by Buddhists of all the Kagyü schools. In 1977 he toured Europe for a second time, visiting existing Buddhist centres and founding new ones.

Dordogne, Khenpo shared with a small group of students his clear knowledge of both this text and the *uttaratantrasastra*. This coincided with the arrival in the West of the linguist Dharmacarya Tenpa Negi Gyaltsen — the first Tibetan we had ever met to quote Shakespeare by heart — whose presence completed, with Khempo-la and ourselves, a team well enough equipped to establish a first translation of this text through a reliable, idea-by-idea, explanation of the meaning according to the traditional Karma Kagyü interpretation.

Our personal debt to Khenpo Tsultrim Gyamtso can never be repaid. His patience and almost unparalleled skill in this area of teaching laid the framework for all the translation and study activity that has since followed.

Since then, we have had the opportunity to work several times through this *Dagpo Tarjen*, as it is generally known in Tibetan — yet again with Khenpo Tsultrim Gyamtso and also through two intensive courses given by Khenchen Thrangu Rinpoche, senior tutor of the Kagyü lineage, at Kagyü Samye Ling. The latter's compassion, magnificent erudition and unquestioned authority helped complete our intellectual grasp of this and several other main texts that form the basis of Kagyü training. In particular Khenchen Thrangu Rinpoche clarified points in the *Dagpo Tarjen* that we had come to realise needed further explanation. Since that initial and very intense period of study in the late seventies and early eighties, further light has been thrown onto specific topics of the *Tarjen* by the various teachers who have visited Kagyü Samye Ling, and in particular by the XIIth Tai Situpa and the XIIth Goshir Gyaltsabpa. Besides explaining specific points, each of these great teachers has helped set this work — and indeed all Buddhist study — within perspectives each proper to their own maturity and experience.

Throughout the last 20 years, Dharma-Arya Dr Akong Tulku Rinpoche's constant and unique supervision has also been a guiding light; the light of mahâmûdra[1] which he incarnates. Like Guru Rinpoche enabling dharma to become established in Tibet, he has taken great pains to ensure that the finest Kagyü scholars and meditators come to the West, to set the right examples of how Buddhist understanding and practice should be. In particular, in collaboration with Khentin Tai Situpa and Khenchen Thrangu Rinpoche, he established an "ideal" study programme designed to give those entering long-term meditation retreats an excellent theoretical, as well as experiential, understanding of buddhadharma. The *Tarjen* is a foundation stone of that training.

During that memorable period when the great teachers mentioned above could spend several months giving detailed teachings on these traditional texts, Akong Rinpoche arranged for us to study with them, indicating the importance and necessity of assimilating as much as possible of the heritage of knowledge they had to share. Since then, the number of dharma centres in the West has increased greatly and demands on those teachers' time are such that comparable long courses in just one place are no longer possible. Akong Rinpoche's tremendous foresight in arranging those courses and recording them for history is striking.

In the last twelve years or so, I have had to teach this *Gems of Dharma, Jewels of Freedom* in its entirety on three occasions, each time to prepare people for Kagyü Samye Ling's long-term retreat. As Khenpo Tsultrim once said, there is nothing like having to teach a text to make one study it well. Over the years, this particular text has become very close to my heart. The incomparable greatness of Gampopa — as both a scholar and the meditation heir to Milarepa — make this legacy of his teachings very special. Like an eagle soaring high above the mountains and the plains, he saw the whole of the Buddha's teachings, which he had studied so thoroughly in

---

1. **mahâmûdra** - the ultimate Buddhist teachings, revealing the true nature of all.

his younger life, with the great clarity of, and from the ultimate perspective of, the mahâmûdra he mastered in later years.

In this work, he provides the student with an easy yet masterly frame of reference for approaching dharma study. Gampopa always backs up his statements with key quotations from the major scriptures of the two main mahâyâna traditions. This means that, in one book, he places the quintessence of several hundred scriptures in the palm of one's hands. He himself said that anyone assimilating the meaning of these chapters would be as close to him as if they had met him personally and taken teachings from him. It is the heart and mind of the great father of all the Kagyü traditions.

Unfinished Work

It will, no doubt, take some fifty to a hundred years to establish definitive, authoritative translations of the major Buddhist texts in the Tibetan canon: texts containing teachings which had already made the cultural journey from the civilisation of India to that of Tibet. Although this is not the place to enter into a discussion on the complexities of transferring a body of knowledge richly extant in one culture and language, into another, the following comments may be helpful in understanding our approach in this publication.

As we study all the efforts made, in the 8th century and onwards, by the *rnying.ma* and then *gsar.ma*[1] schools to ensure that both the media and the messages of Indian Buddhism were properly preserved, we come to realise the enormity of the task now in our hands. We do not today dispose of the means that King Trisong Detsen was able to put at the service of dharma in eighth century

---

1. The first real implantation of Buddhism in Tibet came through the *rnying.ma* (earlier) movement in the 8th century (C.E.). Due to many reasons, including the ravages wrought by an anti-Buddhist King of Tibet, there was a need for renewal, brought about by the *gsar.ma* (later) movements of the 11th and 12th centuries.

Tibet and there is certainly a larger ravine to bridge between Western and Tibetan concept structures than there was between Tibetan and Indian ones. Translators such as ourselves can only attempt to do our best now, in the hope that other and better translations will gradually replace these first efforts, as and when the right scholars appear. It seems reasonable to expect the whole process to take the better part of a century. By the time that work is completed, the rustic bridges being built now between Tibetan and Western worlds by this first generation of dharma pioneers will doubtless have crumbled away and perhaps a new, global, Buddhist presence, as yet unimaginable, will be alive and healthy, making current notions of East and West quite redundant.

Words about Words

The reader is asked to accept this translation in the light of the above comments. Feeling tiny and insignificant compared to the lamas who figure in the illustrious history of these teachings, we are very aware that Gampopa deserves better than this and we pray that the better will soon come.

The mark of good translators is that they colour the original as little as possible with the hues of their own personality and reproduce in the listener or reader's mind the imagery in the mind of the original speaker or writer. Translation involves choices of words and words are powerful things. Terms pleasing to some may upset others. Furthermore, there is no one obvious criterion for choice of words: for instance, terms which might win through on a democratic basis (i.e. the terms a majority of translators might vote for) and be approved by the public at large may not necessarily be the ones an omnilingual Buddha, in his profound wisdom, would choose. Buddhist teaching is not a public relations exercise; sometimes it needs to shock or to stimulate reactions.

Without entering further into this huge debate, the essential point we would like to make is that readers should not deprive themselves of the value of Gampopa's teaching simply because one or two terms used in this translation set their teeth grinding. That would be like throwing away a large cheque because one was put off by the squiggles of the signature. The "secret", as in all study, lies in seeing beyond the words to the real meaning. If necessary, one can create one's own, preferred, substitute terms mentally as one reads.

From time to time, footnotes have been added to explain why some obviously controversial terms have been used. Your comments on these or any other terms or styles of expression used in the book are warmly invited.

Criteria Used for Translating

The terms used in this text are those that have grown up to be the dharma language of Kagyü Samyé Ling. Some originally Sanskrit words — such as *buddha, bodhicitta, mahâyâna, jñâna* etc. — have been left as they are, either because they have already officially entered the English language or because no adequate English equivalent has yet been found. It is often necessary to introduce a pronoun in the English translation of a Tibetan phrase which itself has none. Wherever, and particularly in scriptural quotations, we have used *he* as a general reference to a person, the reader should understand that it refers to he or she. To have translated ancient scriptures with modern political correctness of language would have been to impose a nuance and complication upon them which they did not have.

There is a bit of a tendency at present to window-dress Buddhism; the way books and lectures are presented can be almost like a marketing operation, carefully avoiding potentially disturbing notions — like those, for instance, of the hells, which have, until now, been clearly taught for millennia in a carefully-preserved oral and literary tradition. Thus what were explained as being nightmare states of experience that can really happen after death become, overnight, merely allegories for aspects of human experience. This may suit some readers and avoid shocking those who have fled such notions in other faiths, but it corrupts the tradition. Words, too, can be softened beyond recognition, for fear of upsetting. We have tried our best to avoid any such filtration of the original subject-matter.

However, this does not mean that this is a literal translation. Some of our contemporaries are quite keen on extremely literal, word for word, translations, feeling they may enable future generations to reconstruct the Tibetan from the English. They also assume these to be the most faithful translations of the original. As for the first point, it would perhaps be better simply to ensure preservation of the original text using the many technological means now available. As for the second point, who with experience in the wider world of professional translation could ever agree?

In brief, our aim has been to try to reproduce the original concepts (not words) as closely as possible, using a minimum of addition or alteration. English words have been chosen on the basis of matching the feel and power which Tibetan words convey when used by lamas during their explanations. This approach leads to a primary translation, close to the Tibetan mentality, which can serve as a basis for skilful presentations to various audiences.

Gampopa's text is not written in the flowery, versified, ornate style that one finds in certain Tibetan works. Neither does it have the awkwardness of Tibetan texts which are translations from the Sanskrit. It is written in a very direct, clear language that is a delight to read. The feeling one has when reading the text is that of receiving advice from one's own teacher, person to person: only facts, no frills. We have tried our best to reproduce this and sincerely pray that you, the reader, will gain through this present English translation some of the joy and confidence in dharma that we have found through consulting the *Tarjen* in Tibetan.

Ken Holmes,
Kagyü Samyé Ling, May 1994.

AUTHOR'S INTRODUCTION

Prostration

I prostrate to Mañjuśrî, the ever-young[1]!

Commitment

Avowing my sincere respect to the buddhas, to their spiritual descendants, to the sublime dharma and to the gurus, who are the very source of them all, I now write, through the grace and kindness of holy Mila, this "most precious gem of sublime dharma, which is like a wish-fulfilling jewel[2]", for both my own and others' benefit.

Résumé

Generally speaking, all phenomena can be classified as belonging to either samsâra or nirvâna:

samsâra

its **actual nature** is voidness,
the **form it takes** is that of illusion and
its **key characteristic** is to manifest as suffering.

nirvâna

its **actual nature** is (also) voidness,
the **form it takes** is the exhaustion of and disappearance of illusion and
its **key characteristic** is liberation from all suffering.

Whom does this samsaric illusion delude? All sentient beings of the three dimensions[3].

---

1. **ever-young** refers to the fact that Mañjuśrî appears to remain for aeons as a 10th-level bodhisattva, continually helping other beings. It is as though he chooses to remain "young" as a bodhisattva, not maturing into the adulthood of being a buddha.

2. **wish-fulfilling jewel** — a rare gem which, according to legend, makes one's wishes come true by its mere proximity.

3. **three dimensions** — the three main types of existence, in terms of the experience predominant in the life of the being concerned: sensual, conceptual or formless.

What is the foundation (about which there is) illusion? — voidness.
What causes the illusion? — great ignorance.
How are beings deluded? Their illusion takes the form of the six realms,[1] which they experience as objective realities.
What would be a suitable example for this illusion? It is like that of sleep and dream.
How long has this illusion been happening? — since beginningless time[2].
What is wrong with this illusion? They experience nought but suffering.
When will the delusion become ultimate awareness? When highest enlightenment[3] is reached.
Those who think that illusion may be dispelled of its own accord (should be aware that) samsâra is well-known for being endless.

Having thus carefully considered samsâra in terms of it being illusion, tremendous suffering and something which is long-lasting and not self-dispelling, one will strive in all earnestness and with great diligence, from this very moment onwards, to attain insurpassable enlightenment. What exactly is needed to strive towards enlightenment? The answer is given in the synopsis:

"Prime cause, basis, condition, means, result and activity — by these six key terms should the wise[4] know peerless bodhi."

This means that one needs to know:

— the **prime cause** for highest enlightenment.
— which types of existence form a **basis** for achieving it.

---

1. **six realms** — the worlds of gods, demi-gods, humans, animals, spirits and hell-beings.

2. **beginningless time** — tracking back chains of cause and effect, in a chicken-and-egg manner, never reveals a beginning since, however far one goes back, the phenomena of that time must themselves have emerged from previous causes. A second meaning of this phrase is that time is a relative human abstraction, rather than a fixed reality in its own right. Because humans conceive of beginnings does not mean they have to exist as such.

3. **highest enlightenment** — many mahâyâna texts refer to the accomplishments of bodhisattvas as enlightenment. Here it is the total, perfect enlightenment of the Buddha.

4. **wise** — bodhisattvas who have authentic, stable realisation of voidness.

— the **condition** which enables that achievement to occur.
— the **means** by which it is achieved.
— the **results** of it having been achieved.
— the enlightened **activity** of such achievement.

These will be explained, in the above order, as being the following:

The prime cause is the enlightened essence[1] (sugatagarbha). The basis is a most precious human existence. The condition is the spiritual mentors' (help). The means are the instructions they bestow. The results are the embodiments of perfect enlightenment.[2] The activity is to accomplish, non-conceptually, the welfare of sentient beings.

This is just a synopsis outlining the main structure of the text. What follows is a detailed explanation of each point.

---

1. i.e. the essence of "mind", the essence of everything, known as the *sugatagarbha, tathagatagarbha,* buddha nature, voidness etc. according to context.

2. embodiments of perfect enlightenment — see chapter 20: these are *buddhakâya.*

PART ONE:
THE PRIME CAUSE

THE ENLIGHTENED
ESSENCE

As we have seen, we need to gain freedom from the deluded nature of samsâra and to attain highest enlightenment. However, one might well think: "If I or other ordinary people like me try, even very hard, how could we ever possibly attain enlightenment?" In fact, if anyone practises with great effort, he or she cannot fail to reach enlightenment! Why? — because all forms of conscious life, ourselves included, possess its prime cause: within us is the essence of enlightenment. It says in the *samâdhirâjasûtra*[1]:

"The essence of enlightenment (*sugatagarbha*[2]) totally permeates all sentient beings."

In the shorter *mahâparinirvânasûtra* it says:

"All sentient beings possess the enlightened essence (*tathâgatagarbha*[3])."

---

1. **samâdhirâjasûtra** — this sutra has tremendous significance as far as Gampopa's life is concerned, for he is identified as being the bodhisattva (Candraprabhakumara) to whom much of that sutra is addressed and to whom its future perpetuation was entrusted. In that sutra we find predictions of his future appearance (as Gampopa) as a physician excellently versed in dharma.

2. **sugatagarbha** — see note on P. 3

3. **tathâgatagarbha** — see note on P. 3

Further, in the longer *mahâparinirvânasûtra* it says:

"Just as, for example, butter totally permeates milk, so likewise does the enlightened essence pervade all sentient beings."

In the *mahâyâna-sûtrâlankâra* it is also said:

"Suchness (*tathata*) is the same for all and everyone: it is that which is pure. Hence that which is enlightened (*tathâgata*) is the very essence of all beings."

The reasons for all sentient beings having this enlightened essence are the following:

1. *dharmakâya*, voidness, pervades all beings.
2. the universal essence (*dharmata*), suchness (*tathâta*), is without differentiation and
3. all sentient beings possess the potential for enlightenment[1].

This is also stated in the *mahâyanottaratantrasâstra*. It says:

"All living beings at all times possess the essence of enlightenment because of the pervasiveness of the kâya[2] of perfect enlightenment, because of the indivisibility of the true nature of things and because of the existence of a potential."

1. Let us examine the first of these three reasons. It is said that dharmakâya pervades all beings. Buddha is the dharmakâya and the dharmakâya is voidness. Since voidness is something pervading all sentient beings, it follows that all those beings have the essence of buddhahood.

2. The second reason is that the universal essence − the very nature of things − is without differentiation. This means that whether it be in terms of good and bad, great and small or higher and lower, there is no difference between the universal essence in buddhas and the universal essence in sentient beings. Thus sentient

---

1. **potential for enlightenment** (Tib: *rigs*) — a difficult term to translate on account of its various meanings. The term gives the feeling of inherent potential, almost as something genetically present: hence its later division into five categories.

2. an explanation of the kâya is given in chapter 20. See also "Changeless Nature".

beings possess the essence of buddhas.

3. The third point is that sentient beings have the potential to become buddhas. They are found to have five forms of buddha-potential. These are outlined in the synopsis which follows:

"Those with enlightenment potential can be summed up as belonging to five groups: those with switched-off[1] potential, undetermined potential, śrâvaka[2] potential, pratyekabuddha[3] potential and mahâyâna[4] potential."

1. Those with "switched-off" potential

These are characterised by six traits — absence of a sense of dignity or a sense of shame, lack of compassion etc. The great master Asanga has said the following about them:

"Even though they see samsâra's faults, they are not in the least put off by it (1). Even though they know about the qualities of the enlightened, they feel not the slightest faith in them (2). Without self-respect[5] (3) or a sense of shame[6] (4) and devoid of even a little compassion (5), they feel not even a little regret for the unwholesome acts in which they indulge (6). Through these six shortcomings they are far from ready for enlightenment."

It also says, in the *sûtrâlankâra*:

---

1. **switched-off potential**— literally "cut-off". "Switched-off has been used to avoid implying, as is explained in the text, an irreversibly amputated potential for enlightenment.

2. **śrâvaka** (Tib. *nyan.thos*) literally "listeners" — listening to teachings was the main way of learning dharma. These are those who study: see definition which follows in text.

3. **pratyekabuddha** (Tib. *rang.sangs.rgyas*) literally "self-enlighteners". These are sravakas who have greatly developed their understanding and scope of meditation ability: see also definition in text.

4. **mahâyâna** (Tib. *theg.chen*) — "the greater capacity", sometimes called "greater vehicle". This is dealt with at length in later chapters. It is the way followed by those determined to help all conscious life forms to enlightenment.

5. **self-respect:** personal sense of right and wrong vis-a-vis one's actions.

6. **shame:** similar to dignity, above, but vis-a-vis the public aspect of one's actions: their effect upon others.

"It is certain that some are solely engaged in what is harmful. Some are constantly destroying whatever is good. Others lack those virtues conducive to liberation. They are devoid of anything that could in any way be wholesome."

Although those who have the above traits are said to be "of switched-off potential", this refers to them having to pass an exceedingly long time in samsâra but does not mean that they have definitively severed any chance of achieving enlightenment. Provided that they make the effort, they can attain enlightenment. Concerning this, it says in the *mahâkarunâ-pundarîkasûtra:*

"Ananda! Were someone lacking the spiritual maturity to attain nirvâna to cast a flower up in the sky, while simply thinking of buddhahood, that person would be one who possesses the fruit of nirvâna. I declare that person to be one who will reach nirvâna and who will penetrate to its furthest end."

2. Those with undetermined potential

Their lot depends upon circumstances. Those who train under śrâvaka spiritual teachers, become involved with śrâvaka or come across śrâvaka scriptures will place their trust in the śrâvaka way and, by now being the śrâvaka potential, will actually and manifestly become śrâvaka themselves. Likewise those who encounter pratyekabuddha or mahâyâna circumstances will embrace the pratyekabuddha or mahâyâna ways.

3. Those with śrâvaka potential[1]

These are those afraid of samsâra, trusting in nirvâna but having lesser compassion. The scriptures say:

"Seeing samsâra's sufferings, they are afraid. They have manifest trust in nirvâna. They do not enjoy working for the welfare of sentient beings. The śrâvaka potential bears these three marks."

---

1. **śrâvaka potential** This does not mean *potential to be śrâvaka,* It means the universal potential of buddha nature, exploited in the way that śrâvaka exploit it.

4. Those with the pratyekabuddha potential[1]

These are those who, in addition to the above three characteristics, have great self-confidence, keep quiet about their teachers and prefer solitude. It is said:

"Thus should the wise recognise the pratyekabuddha potential: they are disgusted with samsâra, eager for nirvâna, of lesser compassion, exceedingly self-confident, secretive about their teachers and they love staying in solitude."

The above two groups — those with the śrâvaka or pratyekabuddha potential — give rise to two capacities for practice[2] (yâna). Those who develop those capacities will reap their respective results but what they achieve is not actually nirvâna[3]. At the time of their achievement they will, on account of a condition of latent ignorance, inherit and exist in a subtle mental body, brought about by their (former) untainted activity (karma). However, they themselves are convinced that the state of untainted profound absorption they are in is nirvâna and that they have attained nirvâna. In fact, it is not real nirvâna and this may lead some to question the propriety of the Transcendent Accomplished Victorious One[4] teaching those two paths.

It was, in fact, extremely correct of the Buddha to teach them. Let us consider the following example. Some merchants from Jambudvipa[5] set out to the far-off oceans to obtain precious gems. At one point in their journey, while crossing a great wilderness, they felt so tired and exhausted that they started thinking that they would never manage to get the jewels. They felt like turning back.

---

1. idem as for the śrâvaka potential — see note above.

2. **capacity** — (yana) means "ability to carry" or "vehicle for". See note above, p.6.

3. nirvâna—meaning "suffering ended"— refers to not one but a range of liberated states, from the definitive transcendence of suffering and its causes (Arhat state) to that which, besides this, possesses enlightenment's wealth of wisdom and compassion (Buddhahood).

4. **Transcendent Victorious Accomplished One** — a literal translation of the Tibetan *bcom.lden.'das* which is their translation of the Sanskrit *bhagawan.*

5. **Jambudvipa** — the continent to the south of Mt Meru, in the ancient world-picture. This term is used loosely to refer to our planet.

However, through his conjuring powers, their leader created a great citadel where they were able to rest and recuperate their strength.

Like (the merchants in) the example, beings with little strength of resolution will be quite afraid when they learn about the tremendous wisdom of the buddhas and might feel that the task of achieving it is too daunting; far beyond the capacity of the likes of them. On account of the awe they feel, they will either never undertake the task (of enlightenment) or else they will (start out but) give up. By teaching the two paths — of the śrâvaka and pratyekabuddha — the buddha enables them to attain the refreshing, healing state of śrâvaka or pratyekabuddha. In the *saddharmapundarîkasûtra* it says:

"Likewise all the śrâvaka, under the impression that they have attained nirvâna, are told by the buddhas that their 'nirvâna' is in fact a rest."

When the tathâgatas know that those beings have rested and refreshed themselves in the state of being a śrâvaka or pratyekabuddha, they encourage them next to achieve buddhahood. How? They inspire them with their perfect bodies, their pure speech and their noble minds: light rays stream out from their hearts and, by these merely touching the mental bodies of the śrâvaka and pratyekabuddha, they are awakened from their untainted profound absorption. Then the tathâgatas appear with their perfect bodies and say the following with their pure speech:

"O monks. By merely doing what you have done, the task is not being accomplished: the work is not yet done. Your nirvâna is not nirvâna. Monks! Now approach the tathâgata and pay heed to what he says; understand his instruction."

Thus they motivate them. This is also taught in the verses of the *saddharmapundarîkasûtra:*

"O monks! I therefore tell you today that by merely this you will not attain nirvâna and that for you to gain the essence-awareness of the Omniscient One you must give rise to a noble and mighty wave of effort. By so doing you will achieve all-knowing essence-awareness."

Through being exhorted in this way, the śrâvaka and pratyekabuddha will cultivate the mentality of great enlightenment. Having conducted themselves as bodhisattvas for countless[1] ages, they will become buddhas. We find this stated in the *saddharmapundarîkasûtra* in the same way as it is stated in the *lankavatarasûtra:*

"Those śrâvaka who have not attained nirvâna will all, through having practised the bodhisattva way of life, become buddhas."

5. Those with mahâyâna potential

The synopsis is:

Mahâyâna potential is summed up through six topics: its categories, their essential character, its synonyms, the reasons why it is so much better than the others, the forms it takes and its distinctive characteristics.

5A   CATEGORIES

There are two main categories of this potential:

a. the potential as it exists naturally and
b. the potential as something to be most properly attained.

5B   AN ANALYSIS OF THE ESSENTIAL CHARACTERISTICS OF EACH OF THESE

a. the potential as it exists naturally: this is the ability, existing since beginningless time and obtained through the universal essence (dharmatâ), to give rise to enlightened qualities[2].

b. the potential as something which will be most properly attained: is the ability to give rise to enlightened qualities that is obtained through former cultivation of virtue.

---

1. **countless ages** — a term used to describe a long cosmic aeon.

2. **enlightened qualities**: the qualities of enlightened beings are indescribable, being myriad and inconceivable. However, the main ones are usually listed as the 4 fearlessnesses, 18 distinctive qualities, 10 powers and 32 major signs of a perfect being. See mahayanottaratantraśastra ("The Changeless Nature").

Both the above aspects of mahâyâna potential make a readiness for enlightenment.

5C   THE SYNONYMS FOR THIS POTENTIAL

It is called "potential", "seed", "element" and "very nature".

5D   THE REASONS IT SURPASSES OTHER POTENTIALS

The śrâvaka and pratyekabuddha potentials are both inferior because to realise them one only needs to annihilate the defilement obscuration[1]. The mahâyâna potential is superior because its total realisation involves annihilation of both obscurations[2]. This makes the mahâyâna potential peerless; far, far better than all the others.

5E   THE DIFFERENT FORMS OF MAHAYANA POTENTIAL

The potential can be either activated or dormant:

activated potential: its signs are manifest — "the results have been most properly attained."

dormant potential: the signs are not manifest — "the results have not been most properly attained."

What causes the potential to become activated? When there is freedom from adverse conditions and the support of favourable ones, the potential will be activated. When the contrary is the case, it remains dormant. There are *four adverse conditions:*

---

1. **defilement obscuration**—gross and harmful mental conditioning, which obscures mind's true nature; consisting mainly of habitual patterns of desire, aversion, stupidity, jealousy and pride, and all their sub-categories. These arise due to ignorance, ego-illusion and dualism.

2. see note above. The other obscuration is the **cognitive obscuration**: the subtle mental habit of ignoring the true nature of things and instead arbitrarily splitting perception into two—subject and object.

Four adverse conditions:

a.   to have been born in an unfavourable form of existence[1],
b.   to lack habitual tendency[2],
c.   to have become involved in aberrant ways and
d.   to be afflicted by obscurations.

There are *two favourable conditions:*

a.   the external condition (due to others) — in one's life there are dharma teachers.
b.   the inner condition, whereby one has a proper mental attitude; aspiration to the wholesome etc.

5E   THE SIGNS OF THIS POTENTIAL

It says, about the tokens indicating the presence of this bodhisattva potential, in the *dashadharmakasûtra*:

> "The potential of the wise, of bodhisattvas, is detected by its signs, just as fire is recognised through smoke and water detected by the presence of water-fowl."

What are these signs?   (Bodhisattvas) are naturally and uncontrivedly peaceful in what they do and say, their minds have little deceit or hypocrisy and they are loving and joyful in their relations with others. Of this, it says in the *daśadharmakasûtra*:

> "Never rough or rude, beyond deceit and hypocrisy and full of love for all beings: they are bodhisattvas."

Further, as a prelude to any action they do, they give rise to compassion towards all beings; they genuinely aspire to mahâyâna dharma; they will undertake a difficult task with a forbearance that is never put off by its enormity and they practise most properly and excellently those things which are constant sources of virtue, the

---

1. **unfavourable conditions** — see next chapter.

2. **habitual tendency** — a tendency to wholesomeness, compassion etc. that is present due to habits formed in previous existences.

very nature of which is transcendent perfection[1]. It says, in the *mahâyânasûtrâlankâra*:

"The compassion which precedes their actions—and their aspiration, forbearance and practice of most proper virtues—they should be recognised through these signs of their potential."

The above means that of the five types of potential the mahâyâna potential is the most direct cause for buddhahood. The śrâvaka and pratyekabuddha potentials are also causes for attaining buddhahood, but they are more remote causes. The undetermined potential is sometimes a direct cause, sometimes a remote cause. The switched-off potential is considered to represent a very remote cause but not a total amputation of the possibility of enlightenment: it is therefore an exceedingly far-removed cause for it.

Thus we have seen that, on account of having one or another of these types of potential, sentient beings possess the essence of buddhahood and this has also been demonstrated through the above three reasons. The actual way in which they possess it can be exemplified by the way silver is present in silver ore, the way sesame oil is present in sesame seeds or the way butter is present in milk. It is possible to obtain the silver that is in the ore. It is possible to obtain the oil that is in the sesame seeds. It is possible to obtain the butter that is in milk and likewise it is possible to obtain the buddhahood that is in sentient beings.

This concludes the first chapter, on the potential for enlightenment, of this Gems of Dharma, Jewels of Freedom.

---

1. **transcendent perfection** (Skt. *pâramitâ*) covers both that which *has* "reached the other shore" (its literal meaning), i.e. the truly perfected qualities, and that which *will* "carry one to the other shore", i.e. development of those qualities. The other shore is enlightenment.

PART TWO:
THE BASIS

A PRECIOUS HUMAN
EXISTENCE

As all sentient beings possess this enlightened nature, one may wonder whether or not the five (non-human) types of being[1] would be able to achieve buddhahood. In fact they cannot.[2] The best sorts of being, whose existence *does* form a suitable basis for achieving buddhahood, are described as having a *precious human existence*. These are endowed with two types of physical attribute ("freedoms" and "assets") and three kinds of trust as their mental attribute. The synopsis explaining this is:

"The very best basis is summed up in five points: freedoms, assets, conviction, aspiration and clarity. Two of these are physical and three are mental."

1. The Freedoms

These are freedoms inasmuch as one is free from eight unfavourable conditions, which, according to the *saddharma-*

---

1. i.e. gods, demi-gods, animals, deprived spirits and hell-beings.

2. This is a generalisation, based upon the reasons given later in this chapter. It is not totally impossible for some non-humans, e.g. gods, to obtain advanced results, particularly if they practise the profound techniques of vajrayana.

smrtyupasthâna, are:

"The eight unfavourable states are these: to be in a hell-state[1], to be a deprived spirit[2], an animal, a savage, a long-living god[3], to be someone with fixed aberrant views, one born in a time without buddhas[4] or to be a person with a severe understanding impediment[5]."

Why are these states deemed unfavourable (for the attainment of enlightenment)? **Hell**-states are unsuitable because the very character of experience within them is one of constant (totally-preoccupying) suffering, the **deprived spirit** states are unsuitable because of their mental anguish and so is the **animal condition** because animals are subject to a predominant and wide-ranging confusion. These three states are also devoid of self-respect[6] or a

---

1. **hell** — like all relative realities, hell is a state of mind rather than a physical location. This having been said, hell is, in terms of the subjective experience of those who hallucinate the hell states (sometimes for what seems interminable ages), a very real experience. It seems as real and horrible as the frightening images of a nightmare do.

2. **deprived spirit** — a wide-ranging category, stretching from miserable spirits, searching during long periods for food, drink or shelter, to mighty demons, almost gods. It is a form of experience created by a powerful build-up of greed and avarice in the mind.

3. **long-living gods** are those in a long-lasting state within which sense perception is temporarily suspended: this is a product of former intense concentration. This term is used, by extension, to include all gods since they all live much longer than humans.

4. **time without buddhas** Viewed in terms of ultimate truth, the awakened plenitude of mind (buddhahood) is omnipresent. As we saw in chapter one, buddha nature/ dharmakaya /voidness pervades all. Whether this omnipresence is perceived or not, in the relatively-true worlds, depends upon the individual and group karmas of those worlds' inhabitants. It can happen that buddhas are not perceived in worlds for aeons, if the karma of those worlds' beings is so poor or mediocre that their lives are no more than the mundane working-out of results of former actions.

5. **understanding impediment** — the Tibetan word *(lkugs.pa)* means "dumb" — either figuratively or literally. The point is that there is a communication handicap sufficiently marked that is excludes or greatly reduces the possibility of the person getting the advice they will need to be able to work progressively on their mind.

6. **self-respect** — a sense of morality, that works in private, preventing one from committing bad action, by a personal or inner shame.

sense of shame[1]. Beings in these states do not really have any possibility of practising dharma because the aforementioned shortcomings render their lives generally inappropriate for it.

"Long-living gods" are gods without cognition. They do not have the possibility of practising dharma[2] since their mind cannot apply itself to it — the continuity of their consciousness, along with its related mental activities, being suspended. Apart from these gods, sense-dimension[3] gods live long, compared to humans, and so could also be included in this category. In fact, all the gods are in an unfavourable condition on account of the attachment they feel towards the comforts they experience in their worlds. Their attachment makes them unsuitable for a vigorous quest for virtue. In this respect, the relatively limited degree of manifest suffering present in our human lives is a quality, inasmuch as it generates disgust with samsara, quells pride, gives rise to compassion for other beings and makes us shun unwholesome action and appreciate virtue. This is also mentioned in the *bodhicaryâvatâra*:

> "Furthermore, suffering is a quality. World-weariness will remove arrogance, compassion will well up for those caught up in samsâra and, shunning non-virtue, one will delight in virtue."

The above explains why four non-human sorts of existence are quite without the freedom (to work towards enlightenment). But this is also true of some forms of human existence. It is true of:

savages because of the improbability of them communicating with spiritual teachers,

those with fixed aberrant views because of the difficulty they have in understanding virtue to be the cause of rebirth into better

---

1. **sense of shame** — as above but related to one's public life. One would be ashamed of other people's reactions to one's own immorality.

2. **to practise dharma** — this phrase, now more or less universally used, means to apply the Buddha's teachings (dharma); to put them into practice. More generally, it means to apply oneself successfully to the quest for truth and liberation.

3. **sense dimension** — category of beings whose existence is governed by sensory experience. Some analyses of the god realms define 6 main types of sense-dimension god, 17 types of form-dimension god and 4 types of formless dimension god.

states and of liberation,
those born in a world without buddhas because of the absence
of teachings on proper and improper action and
those with severe understanding impediments as these make
them unable to comprehend teachings explaining what is
worthwhile and what is harmful.

The *very best freedom* is to be free from the above eight.

2. The Assets

There are ten: five personal assets and five outwith oneself.

2A THE FIVE PERSONAL ASSETS

These are described as, "to be a human, born in a central place,
with one's faculties complete, not to have deviated into the worst
of actions and to trust that which is appropriate."

To be human means to have been born the same as other humans,
with normal male or female organs.
To have been born in a central place means birth in a land
where there are holy people to guide one.
To have one's faculties complete means that, by not being stupid
or afflicted by a communication impediment, one has the wit
necessary for actually practising virtue.
Not to have deviated into the worst possible action means not
to have committed the "actions of immediate consequence[1]".
To trust in the appropriate means trusting in that which is all
good—the noble dharma declared by the Buddha; the way of (self)-
control.

---

1. **actions of immediate consequence** — very powerful actions which induce bad rebirth
immediately after death, without even having to pass through the inter-life (bardo) state. Five
actions are often cited:
1. to harm a Buddha
2. to kill an Arhat
3. patricide
4. matricide
5. to create a real schism in the sangha during the Buddha's life.

2B   THE FIVE ASSETS OUTWITH ONESELF

**"The Buddha has come to one's world,
the noble dharma has been taught,
the teachings of noble dharma are still extant,
there are those who maintain those extant teachings and
there exist others[1] who inspire love and compassion."**

Someone possessing these ten factors, which relate to their own circumstances and their surroundings, is called "one with the very best assets". A *most precious human existence* is one endowed with these freedoms and assets. Why is it called "very precious"? It is so termed because, being rarely encountered[2] and exceedingly beneficial and useful, its qualities are comparable to those of a wish-fulfilling gem.

"rarely encountered"

It says, in the *bodhisattvapitaka:*

"It is difficult to obtain a human existence and to maintain the human life-force. It is hard to obtain the noble dharma and rare for a buddha to manifest."

It also says, in the *mahâkarunâpundarîkasûtra:*

"It is not easy to come across a human existence. It is rare to encounter the very best sort of freedom and rare for a buddha to appear in the world. It is not easy to aspire after virtuous qualities nor is it easy to encounter most perfect prayers."

It also says, in the *gandavyûhasûtra:*

"It is rare to avoid the eight unfavourable circumstances; rare to be a human; rare too is the very best form of freedom, in all its plenitude. It is rare for a buddha to manifest, rare not to be

---

1. **others** — dharma teachers and sponsors whose love and guidance enables one to practise.

2. **rarely encountered** — both in the sense that it is rare to meet someone in possession of all these factors and in the sense that during interminable rebirths it is rare for an individual to find him or herself equipped with all these conditions.

deficient in one's faculties and rare to be able to study the buddha-dharma; rare too to befriend holy people. Rare are truly-qualified spiritual teachers. It is rare to be able to practise properly the traditional teaching on the most wholesome life; rare to maintain a right livelihood and rare, in the human world, to earnestly enact those things compatible with dharma."

Furthermore, it says in the *bodhisattvacaryâvatâra:*

"These freedoms and assets are exceedingly rare."

What could *exemplify* this rarity, *for whom* is it so rare and *why* is it such a rare thing?

An *example* is given in the *bodhisattvacaryâvatâra:*

"On account of it being like that, the Transcendent Accomplished Victor has said that to be a human is as rare as (the chance of) a turtle putting its neck through the hole of a wooden yoke floating on a turbulent ocean."

From where does this quote come? In the "Most Excellent Scripture" it says:

"Were this vast earth to be transformed into nought but water and were someone to set afloat a single one-holed wooden yoke, to be driven in the four directions by the winds, an injured[1] turtle might take thousands of years (to put its head through it)," etc.

Those *for whom* it is so hard to obtain are those born in the lower states of existence[2]. *Why* is it so rare, in terms of (being a rare result of certain) causes and conditions? The principal cause for obtaining an existence endowed with the freedoms and assets is a former accumulation of virtue[3]. Once born into the lower realms, one constantly does nothing but wrong; one does not know the way to

---

1. **injured turtle** — sometimes described as a blind turtle

2. **lower states of existence** — the "three lower realms" — hell-beings, spirits and animals.

3. a precious human existence being the karmic consequence of a tremendous build-up of goodness in the past.

develop virtue. For this reason only those beings born in the three lower realms who have built up relatively little evil, or those who have created bad karma but will experience its results in some other sequence of existences, can obtain a human rebirth.

"exceedingly beneficial and useful"

It says, in the *bodhicaryāvatāra:*

"A life endowed with the freedoms and assets is called "powerful human potential"[1] on account of it having the strength or ability to attain higher rebirth[2] or ultimate good[3]. Further, since there are three levels of ability—lesser, middling and best—there are three types of powerful human potential—lesser, middling and best."

It also says, in the *bodhipathapradīpa:*

"One should know there to be three types of powerful human potential: lesser, middling and best."

Those with *lesser powerful human potential* are those with the ability to achieve human or divine rebirth, by avoiding falling into the lower states. Thus it says:

"A lesser powerful human potential is explained as being that of someone who strives for his or her own welfare, merely in terms of worldly happiness, by whatever means."

Those with *middling powerful human potential* have the ability to attain a condition of peace and well-being by liberating themselves from samsāra:

"One who turns his back on worldly happiness, turns away from unwholesome action and strives for only his own peace is called

---

1. **"human"** — the Sanskrit word *puruṣa* means *one with power or capabilityĕ*

2. **higher rebirth** *(mngon.mthod)*, literally "manifestly elevated", refers to rebirth as a god, demi-god or human.

3. **ultimate good** i.e. nirvana

a middling human."

Best powerful human potential is that of those with the ability to attain buddhahood for the benefit of sentient beings:

"Those who, through (awareness of) suffering in themselves, are completely dedicated to eradicating totally every suffering in everyone else are known as 'supreme humans'."

Master Candragomin has also commented on the great benefit and use of a precious human existence, saying:

"Whoever longs to reach the end of the ocean of rebirth and, further, plants the virtuous seed of supreme enlightenment—such a person is far, far richer in qualities than a wish-fulfilling gem. Who could deprive such a one of his achievement? The path trodden by a human of such great fortitude of mind is one unattainable by gods, nâga, garuda, vidyâdhara, kinnara or uragas[1].

On account of this human existence endowed with freedoms and assets, there is the ability to give up non-virtue, the ability to cross samsâra's ocean, the ability to tread the path of enlightenment and the ability to attain perfect buddhahood. Therefore such an existence is far better than others—those of gods, nâgas etc. It is something even better than a most precious wish-fulfilling gem. Because this human existence endowed with freedoms and assets is hard to obtain and of such great benefit, it is called 'most precious'."

"so easily destroyed"

Although it is so hard to obtain and of such tremendous benefit, a precious human existence is very easily destroyed, because there is nothing that can perpetuate the life-force, because there are many causes of death and because the flow of instants of time never stops. Thus, it says in the *bodhicaryâvatâra:*

---

1. all various kinds of non-human, endowed with some sort of special power.

"It is inappropriate to dwell in a contented attitude that thinks 'At least I won't die today.' It is without doubt that at one time or another I shall be annihilated."

Therefore, whether it be in terms of its rarity, its fragility or its great purpose, one should consider this physical existence as a *vessel* with which one must do whatever is necessary to escape from the ocean of samsâra. Thus it says:

"Making use of this vessel of powerful human potential, get free from the mighty river of suffering. Since such a craft will be hard to come across in the future, fall not into confusion: sleep not when it is time (to act)."

Considering one's existence as a *steed* to be ridden, one should do whatever must be done to get free from the hazardous path of samsâra and suffering. Thus it says:

"Having mounted the steed of a pure human existence, gallop away from the hazardous paths of samsâra's suffering."

Considering this physical existence as a *servant*, one should make it do wholesome tasks. Thus it says:

"This human existence should be used in service."

the three types of trust

In order to act in such a way, one needs trust: it is said that, without trust, the noble qualities will not develop in someone. Thus the *daśadharmakasûtra* says:

"The noble qualities will not arise in someone without trust, just as a green shoot will not sprout from a scorched seed."

The *buddhâvatamsaka* also says:

"Those of worldly disposition with little trust will be unable to know the buddhas' enlightenment."

Therefore, one should cultivate trust: as the Buddha says in the *lalitavistara:*

"Ananda! develop trust — this is the request of the Tathagata."

What exactly does "trust" mean? Upon analysis, there are three areas of trust: trust as conviction, trust as aspiration and trust as lucidity.

3. Trust as conviction

This is something which occurs due to considering action and its consequences[1]—the Truth of Suffering and the Truth of (suffering's) Origination[2]. Conviction means being convinced that the consequence of virtuous action is to experience well-being in the sense dimension; the consequence of unvirtuous action to experience misery in the sense dimension and the consequence of concentration (meditation) activity is to experience well-being in the two higher dimensions. It means being convinced that through having engaged in the defilements[3] and action, explained through the Truth of all Origination, one will have the five tainted aggregates[4], explained through the Truth of Suffering.

4. Trust as aspiration

Envisioning highest enlightenment as something very special indeed, one devotedly attends to the way to attain it.

---

1. see chapter on action: cause and effect.

2. these are the first two of the "four noble truths" — or, more accurately, the "four truths perceived by the Realised".

3. **defilements** (Skt. *klesa*, Tib. *phung.po*) — the main mind poisons, such as clinging, aggression, ignorance etc., which stem from basic ignorance of the pure nature of mind and which engender action.

4. **five tainted aggregates** (Skt. *skandha*) — the five main areas of worldly experience, called "aggregates" because each is so manifold. They are: forms, feelings, perceptions, mental activities and the consciousnesses. To "have" them means to be reborn as them.

5.   Trust as lucidity

This is the stable trust which emerges towards its object—the Triple Gem[1], being the joyful lucidity of mind which has devotion and respect for the most precious one, the Buddha, as teacher of the path; for the most precious dharma as that which is the path itself and the most precious sangha as the companions who practise the path.

Thus it says, in the *abhidharmakośa:*

"What is trust?   It is confidence in actions, their results, the Truths and the most precious ones. It is aspiration and it is lucidity of mind."

Further, it says in the *ratnâvalî:*

"Whoever, despite temptation, anger, fear or confusion, never strays from dharma is said to possess trust. Such a person is a wonderful vessel for the truly excellent[2]."

~ not to stray from dharma through temptation ~

This means not to give up dharma through craving. For instance, even if one were to be tempted with food, wealth, consorts, kingdoms or whatever enticement may be proffered to persuade one to give up the dharma, one would still not give it up.

~ not to stray from dharma through aggression ~

This means not to give up dharma through anger. For instance, one would not relinquish a dharma way of life in order to (combat) someone who had not only done one a great deal of harm in the past but who is also doing great harm at present.

---

1. **Triple Gem** (Tib. *dkon.mchog.gsum,* Skt. *triratna*) — sometimes called the "three jewels" or the "three rare and sublime" — the Buddha, the dharma and the sangha.

2.   **truly excellent** *(Tib. ngas.legs)* — that which leads to, and that which is, liberation from samsara.

~ not to stray from dharma through fear ~

This means not to give up dharma through fear. For instance, even if threatened that, were one not to relinquish dharma, 300 fearsome warriors would come and cut five ounces of flesh from one's body every day, one would still not give it up.

~ not to stray from dharma through confusion ~

This means not to give up dharma through ignorance. For instance, other people might insist that cause and effect, the three precious Refuges etc. are falsities and throw one's dharma into question — but one would still not relinquish it.

One who can maintain his or her conviction when faced with these four sorts of situation is someone with trust. On account of their trust their state of mind[1] makes them the most suited for the achievement of liberation. Those sorts of trust will give rise to countless benefits. Among the inconceivable qualities that they enable to emerge one might mention that they:

- give rise to the mentality of the best of beings[2],
- eliminate the unfavourable,
- sharpen and brighten the faculties,
- ensure the non-degradation of right conduct,
- remove defilements[3],

---

1. Tib: *snod* — often translated by its literal meaning — "vessel". Such a person is a vessel suitable for attaining enlightenment. Since it is their attitude, rather than their physical situation, which determines this, the implied meaning of the word rather than the literal one has been used.

2. bodhisattvas.

3. Tib: *nyon.mongs* Skt *klesa* – a major Buddhist term, variously translated as canker, defilements, negative affect, disturbing emotion, mind poison etc. The klesa are all the shades of desire, aversion and confusion that stem from basic ignorance of ultimate reality and the ensuing dualistic perception of things.

- take one beyond domains of experience marred by evil[1],
- enable one to encounter the way of liberation,
- gather a vast store of virtue,
- make one see many buddhas and
- cause the buddhas' blessing[2] to be received.

As it says in the *ratnolkâ-nâma-dhâranî:*

> "Trust in peerless enlightenment, i.e. trusting enlightened beings and their teachings and trusting the activity of the buddhas' heirs, gives rise to the mental attitude of a great being."

This and more is said. Further, it is taught that all the buddhas, the accomplished transcendent victors, will appear before one endowed with trust. Thus, it says in the *bodhisattvapitaka:*

> "Thus the buddhas, the accomplished transcendent victors, having recognised them as being worthy vessels of buddhadharma, will appear before them and will most properly teach them the way of the bodhisattva."

Hence a "most precious human existence" — having two (sets of) qualities, i.e. the freedoms and assets, and three mental qualities, i.e. the aspects of trust, — is one which constitutes the proper basis for achieving peerless enlightenment.

This concludes the second chapter, concerning the basis, of this Gems of Dharma, Jewels of Freedom.

---

1. Tib: *bdud* Skt: *mara* — another major Buddhist term, denoting the four chief evils afflicting existence — the defilements (see above), death, the aggregates (*skandha*) and egotistic indulgence: sometimes personified as the four great demons persecuting or tempting beings.

2. **blessing** — not to be taken in too sentimental a way. The real blessing is the transmission, or rather induction, of profound insight, as the mind experiences something of its inherent enlightened nature.

PART THREE:
THE CONDITION

THE GOOD MENTOR

It was said, "The special condition is the good mentor." This means that even if one has the very best *basis* but lacks the encouragement of good mentors[1], who represent the *condition*[2] (for enlightenment), it will be very difficult to progress along the path to enlightenment. This is because of unwholesome tendencies, due to former bad actions, and the power of conditioning. Therefore the support of good mentors is a necessity. The synopsis is:

"The support of good mentors is treated through six points: justification, the different kinds, the specific characteristics of each kind, how to relate to them skilfully and the benefits of so doing."

---

1. good mentor — the Tibetan term *dge.ba'i.bshen.gnyen* is very evocative, meaning *friend and relative in virtue*. It gives feelings of closeness, goodness and the guidance, in something noble, of one with whom there exists a profound link (hence "relative"). This has sometimes been translated as "spiritual friend" — a good term but one which can be—and has been—misunderstood in lectures. *Mentor:* "experienced and trusted adviser" (OED).

2. condition — this continues the overall theme of the book, where the quest for enlightenment is presented through a quasi-causal analogy. Having shown the prime cause for striving for enlightenment and the basis, i.e. life-form where that basis can be best activated, this chapter shows the circumstances or conditions that must be present for the activation to work. A simple and classical illustration of these fundamental elements of a cause-based evolution is that of a flower: the prime cause being the seed, the basis being fertile soil and the conditions being light, heat, water, fertiliser etc.

1.   Justification

The necessity of being supported by good mentors is justified in three ways — scripturally, logically and through analogy.

1A   SCRIPTURAL JUSTIFICATION

In the *prajñâpâramitâ samcayagâthâ*[1] it says:

"Good disciples devoted to their teachers should always be guided by wise and skilful mentors. Why? Because that is how their (own) qualities of skill and wisdom will emerge."

In the *astasâhasrikâ-prajñâpâramitâ*[2] it says:

"Thus bodhisattva-mahasattvas[3] who wish to awaken—genuinely and totally—to peerless, utterly pure and perfect enlightenment[4] should from the very outset seek out, relate to and serve good mentors."

1B   LOGICAL JUSTIFICATION

It has been reasoned: "...given that you wish to attain omniscience [subject], you need to enter into relation with good mentors [predicate] because by yourself you know neither how to accrue spiritual wealth nor how to dispel obscurations [reason]." The

---

1. a shorter version of the prajñâpâramitâ.

2. 8,000 verse version of prajñâpâramitâ.

3. **bodhisattva-mahasattva** — see later chapters on the general meaning of bodhisattva. The bodhisattva-mahasattvas are bodhisattvas who have attained stable authentic realisation of voidness (see chapters 18 & 19 on the stages and levels of the path).

4. **peerless, utterly-pure, perfect enlightenment** — here, the term enlightenment (which reads more like "awakened plenitude" in Tibetan, to render the two main meanings of the Skt root *bodh*) is qualified by a string of adjectives. There is reason for this. The term enlightenment (Tib. *byan.chub* Skt. *bodhi*) and the verb to achieve enlightenment (Tib. *'tshang.rgya.ba* Skt. *bodh*) are used in Northern Buddhist scriptures to describe various states, achieved from the time of the attainment of unreverting true realisation of voidness onwards (1st of the 10 profound bodhisattva levels). When we read that enlightenment is "perfect enlightenment" — or "peerless" or "totally-pure" enlightenment or, as here, all three — we know with certainty that reference is being made to a buddha's enlightenment, the ultimate attainment.

buddhas of the three times[1] are an example substantiating this assertion. The pratyekabuddhas are an example of the contrary.

The above is explained as follows: in order for us to achieve perfect buddhahood it will be necessary to accrue all the spiritual wealths[2], summarised in terms of goodness and primordial awareness[3], and their accrual depends upon one's mentor. Furthermore, it will be necessary to get rid of all the obscurations, summarised in terms of the *defilements* and the *cognitive obscuration*. Their removal is also dependent upon one's mentor.

1C JUSTIFICATION BY ANALOGY

The good mentor is like a guide when travelling an unknown path, like an escort when in a dangerous land and like a ferryman when crossing a mighty river.

~ explanation of the first example: the guide ~

If one travels in unfamiliar lands without a guide, there is the danger either of taking a wrong direction or else of making a long or a short detour. If, on the other hand, one is accompanied by a guide there are none of these dangers and one can attain the destination without a single step having been wasted.

---

1. **three times** — past, present and future.

2. **accrue the spiritual wealths** (Tib. *tsogs.bsags*) — sometimes translated literally as "gather the accumulations". The two main aspects of this wealth are wisdom and compassion, the latter being synonymous with virtue (as the first five pâramitâ—see Ch. 11).

3. **primordial awareness** (Tib. *ye.śes* Skt. *jñāna*) A whole set of Sanskrit words are based around the syllable jñâ, which means, approximately, "awareness". Tibetan was faithful to this, creating an equivalent set of terms around the syllable śes. English translations up until now have generally not sought to maintain this consistency and have tried to hit the closest Western term to the individual meaning of each Tibetan or Sanskrit term. In a still clumsy attempt to maintain the consistency, the following translations are proposed:

Sanskrit	Tibetan	English
jñâ *na*	*ye.* śes	primordial awareness
pra jñâ	śes. *rab*	supreme awareness
sam jñâ	*'dus.* śes	ideating awareness = perception
vi jñâ *na*	r *nam.* śes	specific awareness = consciousness
jñâ *na*	śes. *pa*	awareness

Likewise, when one has set out on the path to peerless enlightenment and is heading for the state of perfect enlightenment, if one does not have a good mahayana mentor, there is the danger of mistakenly taking an aberrant[1] path or, even if one does not stray that far, of making the greater śrāvaka detour or of making the lesser detour of the pratyekabuddha.

When accompanied by the good mentor, who is like a guide, there is no longer the danger of taking a completely wrong path, or of a large or small detour, and one will reach the citadel of omniscience. Thus it says in Śrīsambhava's biography:

"Leading one along the path which reaches the other shore, the good mentor is like a guide."

~ explanation of the second example: the escort ~

In frightening places there are harmful things such as bandits, thieves, wild animals etc. Going to such places without an escort, one fears for one's possessions, physical safety and even life itself. When, however, one is accompanied by a powerful escort one can pass through without mishap.

Likewise, once on the path to enlightenment, accruing the spiritual wealths and heading for the citadel of omniscience, if one does not have a good mentor to act as an escort, there is a risk of the wealth of virtue being stolen by that host of thieves—ideas and mental defilements within and negative forces and misleading influences without. One even runs the risk of having one's life in the happier realms cut short. Therefore, it is said:

"As soon as that gang of robbers and thieves, the defilements,

---

1. **aberrant** — a loose translation of the Tibetan term *mu.stegs.pa*, itself the translation of the Sanskrit *tirthika*, sometimes questionably translated in English as *heretic*.The way this term is sometimes explained by some authoritative Tibetan lamas is complimentary, rather than derogatory: it refers to people who are spiritual, well-intentioned and seeking the truth, but who have taken up a philosophical stance which just misses the natural truth—of non-ego. The term can convey a meaning close to "thresholders", "heterodox" or "those on the rungs of the ladder to truth" — it applies to good people whose understanding is a little deficient. This having been said, it is true that it is popularly used by Tibetans more in the sense of "heretic".

finds the opportunity, it will steal one's virtue and even put an end to one's life in the higher states[1]."

If one remains unseparated from the good mentor, who is like an escort, one's wealth of virtue will not be lost, one's existence as a being in the higher realms will not be cut short and one will attain the citadel of omniscience. Thus it says in Śrisambhava's biography:

"All the merit of a bodhisattva is protected by the good mentor."

One also reads, in Upasika Acala's biography,

"Good mentors are like an escort since they assure our safe passage to the state of omniscience."

~ explanation of the third example: the ferryman ~

When crossing a mighty river in a boat, one may be aboard the vessel but if there is no ferryman one cannot reach the other shore and the boat may sink or be swept away by the currents. With a ferryman and through his striving, one *shall* reach the other shore.

Likewise, when one tries to traverse the ocean of samsara without the ferryman-like good mentor, one may well be aboard the ship of dharma yet one sinks into samsâra or is carried off by its currents. Thus, it is said,

"When there is no oarsman, the vessel will not reach the other shore. All qualities may be perfect yet, without a teacher, existence will be endless."

When one is supported by the ferryman-like good mentor one will attain nirvâna, the dry land of the further shore of samsâra. Therefore, it says in the *gandhavyûhasûtra*:

"Because the good mentor delivers us from the ocean of samsâra he is like a ferryman."

---

1. **higher states** — the three states, within the context of the six domains of existence, of relative happiness, i.e. the divine, semi-divine and human states.

Thus one really needs to be sustained by good mentors, who are like guides, escorts and ferrymen.

2. The different kinds of good mentor

There are four different categories: the good mentor as

- a specific individual[1],
- a bodhisattva established in the sublime states[2],
- a nirmanakâya[3] of a buddha and
- a sambhogakâya[4] aspect of a buddha.

These correspond to one's own situation: since one is totally unable to relate to buddhas or bodhisattvas when one is a beginner in dharma, one must relate to a good mentor in the form of a specific individual.[5] When one has purified most of the action-related obscurations (karma), one is able to relate to a good mentor who is a bodhisattva in the sublime states. From the greater level of the stage of accumulation[6] onwards one can adhere to a good mentor in the form of a nirmânakâya of a buddha and once one has reached the sublime states one is able to relate to a good mentor in the form of a sambhogakâya of a buddha.

---

1. **specific individual** (Tib. *so.so'i.skye.bo*) — a term used interchangeably with "immature being" to denote all beings who have not yet achieved the first of the profound levels of bodhisattva understanding, i.e. constant, authentic realisation of voidness.

2. **sublime states** — the ten major stages of a bodhisattva's evolution through realisation of voidness: see later chapter on the levels and phases.

3. **nirmanakâya** (Skt. = Tib. *sprul.sku*) — see later (fifth main) chapter. These are forms of the enlightened mind that can be experienced by "specific individuals" (see above).

4. **sambhogakâya** (Tib. *lons.spyod.rdzogs.pa'i.sku*) — see later (fifth main) chapter. These are aspects of the enlightened mind only perceivable by the pure minds of bodhisattvas in the sublime states (see note 2 above).

5. This means that the valid teachers to whom we turn <u>appear to us</u> as specific individuals. What lies behind this appearance could be anything from a genuine specific individual to an emanation of the Buddha. See paragraph which follows.

6. **greater level of the phase of accumulation** — see chapters 19 and 20 on the phases and the paths. This is the third of the three levels of the first of the five phases of the path to enlightenment. It is chiefly concerned with strongly establishing wholesomeness in one's being through the stability that comes from concentration meditation.

Which of these four types is kindest to us? At the outset, when we are still in the dark pit of action and defilement, were we to (try to) relate to good mentors of the three latter types we would not even be capable of seeing their faces: it is only due to our path being illuminated by the lamp held aloft by mentors who are specific individuals that we eventually will come to encounter them. Therefore mentors in the form of specific individuals are the kindest.

3. The specific characteristics of each of the four kinds of good mentor

Buddhas embody the highest and most complete form of purification because they have eliminated both sorts of obscuration[1]. They also embody the highest, most complete, form of primordial awareness because they possess the two knowledges.[2]

Good mentors as *bodhisattvas in the sublime states* will have which-ever degree of purification and primordial awareness is appropriate to their particular level, from the first to the tenth. Of particular import are bodhisattvas in the eighth to tenth levels for they have ten powers enabling them to nurture others: powers related to life, mind, requisites, action (karma), birth, aspiration, prayers, miracles, primordial awareness and dharma.

Power over life is the ability to stay in a world as long as wished, **power over mind** is the ability to enter stably into profound absorption[3], just as is wished,

---

1. the **defilement-obscuration** and **cognitive obscuration**   The latter is a mistaken, dualistic conception of reality. The former are the deluded mental states that this mistake nurtures—attachment and clinging, anger and rejection, ignorance and confusion etc.

2. **two knowledges** — knowledge of the true nature of everything, just as it is ("how-it-isness"), and of the myriad ways this is present in the relative ("manyness"). See Ch. 20.

3. **profound absorption** (Tib. *ting.nge.'dzin,* Skt *samādhi)* – the peaceful and well-settled state of mind, unperturbed by mental grossness, that results from concentration meditation. There are various stages of profound absorption, each characterised by the mental elements still needing to be removed and by the nature of the concentration itself. The basic journey through these stages is described in the Theravadin system through the *jhana* (Pali = Skt. *dhyāna).* As here we are discussing 8th-10th level bodhisattvas then we must also keep in mind the vastness of bodhisattva experience and the presence of understanding of both phenomenological voidness and personal voidness (non-ego).

power over requisites is the ability to shower an immeasurable rain of precious objects on beings,

power over action is the ability to re-program (results of) action (karma)[1]—in terms of dimension[2], state[3], type of existence and mode of birth[4]— so that they are experienced in other (more useful) ways,

power over birth is the ability to take birth in the sense dimension yet always to maintain profound meditative absorption and not experience any form of degeneration, remaining completely unsullied by the evils of that state,

power to fulfil aspiration is the ability to transform the elements—earth, water etc.— into one another as wished,

power of prayer is the ability to pray and make prayers in a way that will most properly accomplish the well-being of oneself and others; also the power to make prayers come true,

power over miracles is the ability to demonstrate countless miracles and supernormal feats in order to kindle aspiration in beings,

power of primordial awareness is knowledge that encompasses the ultimate meaning, in the very best possible way, of dharma, of meanings, of terminology, of the true sense of words and of

---

1. **action** — this term has a wide meaning in Buddhism, since it spans time to comprise the results that the actor will inevitably have to experience due to what he or she has done, as well as the initial act itself, i.e. it spans both cause and effect, treating the whole not as two but as one. This is easily understood if one considers the planting and growth of a seed. From the moment of the seed's existence onwards, it is really one long story of growth. From the farmer's point of view there is a causal phase (planting the seed) and a resultant phase (a plant appearing) — which to him appear more like two separate things, each isolated in time, the one dependent upon the other.

2. **dimension** — the three dimensions of existence are the **sense dimension** (comprising the six realms: gods, demi-gods, humans, animals, spirits and hell-beings), the **form dimension** (meditation-based) and the **formless dimension** (formless meditation based).

3. **state** — nine states of existence: the sense dimension, four aspects of the form dimension and four aspects of the formless dimension.

4. **modes of birth** — there are four: spontaneous, from an egg, from a womb and from heat and moisture.

bodhisattva prowess[1] and

power of dharma is the ability to teach beings that which is suited to them, in just the right amount. This is achieved by presenting all the different nouns, terms and characters of dharma, in the various sutra[2] and other teachings, in such a way that their sole speech is understood by each individual in his or her own language and in a totally satisfying way that makes sense to his or her own mentality.

Good mentors as *specific individuals* have as their characteristics qualities severally described as eightfold, fourfold or twofold.

Eightfold qualities   In the *bodhisattvabhūmi* it says, "...concerning the above, if one has eight things then one should be known as a bodhisattva who is completely qualified as a good mentor. What are the eight? They are:

1. to have a bodhisattva's right conduct,
2. to have studied the bodhisattva scriptures thoroughly,
3. to have realisation[3],
4. to be kind and loving to one's followers,
5. to be fearless,
6. to be forbearing,
7. to be of untiring mind and
8. to know how to use words."

Fourfold qualities   In the *mahâyâna-sûtrâlankâra* it says:

"Broad-based, eliminators of doubt, worthy of recollecting and teaching the two natures — such are the very best bodhisattva

---

1. A few pages would be needed to explain this sentence. Through primordial wisdom, one understands the very nature of things (dharma), the significance of each thing (meanings), how the significance is expressed through language (terminology), how that language is best expressed to individuals (words) and how to persist skilfully until it is understood (prowess).

2. **sutra** — a word that generally encompasses the popular teachings given by the Buddha, as opposed to the hermetic tantra teachings. When used more technically, it refers to one of the three collections (tripitaka) into which his teachings are classed, the other two being vinaya and abhidharma.

3. **realisation** (Tib. *rtogs.pa*) — a term used to denote useful, stable understanding and maturity, in contrast to mere glimpses of experience (Tib. *nyams*), which come and go.

teachers," meaning that:

1. their teaching is very *broad-based* because they have studied many things,
2. they can *remove* others' *doubts* because they themselves have superb discerning awareness,
3. their speech is *worthy of recollection* because their actions are those of holy beings and
4. *they teach the two natures*, i.e. the characteristics of the completely defiled and the utterly pure.

Twofold qualities   In the *bodhisattvacaryâvatâra* it says:

"The consistently good mentors are those skilled in the meaning of mahâyâna who would never give up the noble bodhisattva discipline even to save their lives."

1. They are skilled in the meanings of mahâyâna and
2. they have maintained their bodhisattva commitments.

4.   How to relate skilfully to good mentors

Once one has come into contact with such good mentors there are three ways of being supported by them:

A. by showing respect and rendering service,
B. by cultivating the relevant reverence and devotion and
C. by one's own practice and earnestness.

4A   RESPECT & SERVICE

The first of these two, showing respect, is accomplished by prostrating, rising quickly[1], bowing, circumambulating, speaking at the appropriate time with a loving mind, looking at them again and again with an insatiable mind etc. This was exemplified by the way that "Good Wealth", a powerful merchant's son, related to his mentor. It says in the *gandavyûhasûtra:*

"Gaze insatiably at your good mentor. Why? Good mentors are rarely seen, rarely manifest and seldom met with."

---

1. when they approach or enter the room or temple

The second, how to relate to one's good mentors by serving them, is accomplished by attending to their needs, i.e. by providing the sort of food, clothes, bedding, seating, medicines when they are unwell, funds etc. that accord with the Buddhist teaching. This is to be done without heed for one's own life or physical well-being, as exemplified by the realised being[1] "Ever-Crying". In Srisambhava's biography we read:

"A buddha's enlightenment is attained by serving good mentors."

2. REVERENCE & DEVOTION

Being convinced that one's mentor is a buddha, one takes whatever he says to be instruction and never transgresses it, all the time cultivating reverence, devotion and joyous trust. This was exemplified by the way Mahâpandita Naropa related to his mentor. It says, in the "Mother of the Victors" (prajnâpâramitâ[2]):

"You should earnestly cultivate reverence for good mentors, follow them and have joyous trust."

Besides this, one should give up negative thoughts about the personal conduct of one's mentors, which is in fact their skilful technique[3] at work, and instead cultivate the noblest devotion for it. This was exemplified in the biography of King Anala.

3. PRACTICE & EARNESTNESS

One trains in three areas of practice: studying dharma under one's mentors' guidance, contemplating its significance and making it an experienced reality. One should do these with earnestness

---

1. **realised being** (Tib. *'phags.pa*, Skt. *arya*) — those who have shaken off karmic rebirth and who have constant, authentic realisation of the void nature of experience; in mahâyâna this means the bodhisattvas of the ten profound levels.

2. *ekâksarîmâtâ-nâma-sarvatathâgata-prajnâ-pâramitâ*

3. **skilful technique** (Tib. *thabs.mkhas*, Skt. *upâya*) — bodhisattvas' particular ways of teaching based upon their insight into people and situations. These sometimes make the bodhisattva mentor act in a way which seems unorthodox, if that is what is necessary to bring home a point, e.g. they may appear to be angry with their disciple's bad conduct in order to make that person realise just how wrong, harmful or inappropriate their actions are.

and, of all things, it is this which will be most appreciated by the mentor. Thus the *mahâyâna-sûtrâlankâra* says:

"Relating to teachers by actually practising very properly what they have taught, is what pleases them most."

When one's mentors are satisfied one will attain buddhahood: it says in Srisambhava's biography:

"If one satisfies one's mentors one will attain the enlightenment of all the buddhas."

As far as requesting dharma teachings from one's good mentors is concerned, there are three phases: preparation, the actual instruction and the conclusion. The preparation is to have the bodhisattva attitude—bodhicitta—when requesting the teachings. During the actual instruction one should consider oneself to be like someone ill, the dharma to be like a medicine, the mentor to be like one's physician and the earnest practice of dharma to be the best and quickest way to recovery. The conclusion is to avoid three mistakes: being like an upturned container, a leaky container or a poisoned container.

5.   The benefits of being supported by good mentors

It also says, in Srisambhava's biography:

"My good child! A bodhisattva who is most properly nurtured by a good mentor will not fall into the lower states. A bodhisattva who is totally protected by a good mentor will not be swayed by corrupting friends. A bodhisattva who is perfectly trained by a good mentor will not quit the bodhisattva way. A bodhisattva who is most excellently sustained will completely transcend the activities of ordinary individuals."

The prajñâpâramitâ further says:

"A bodhisattva mahâsattva who is most properly nurtured will swiftly attain peerless, totally pure and perfect enlightenment."

PART FOUR:
THE MEANS

THE GOOD MENTORS'
INSTRUCTION

We possess the *essential nature* of enlightenment. Further, since samsâra is beginningless, we must also have obtained, from time to time, the *basis*—a precious human existence—in which we met the *condition*, the good mentor. What was it that prevented us from becoming buddhas? It was the harmful mistake of falling under the sway of four hindrances that prevented us and those like us attaining buddhahood.

Four impediments that prevent attainment of buddhahood

1. attachment to the experiences of this life,
2. attachment to worldly well-being,
3. attachment to the well-being of peace and
4. ignorance of the means by which buddhahood is achieved.

What can eliminate these four impediments? They are eliminated by heeding the instruction of good mentors and by putting those instructions into practice. What does the good mentors' advice comprise? The answer is given by the synopsis:

"All the good mentors' instruction can be summarised as four topics: meditation on impermanence, meditation on samsâra's faults and on actions and their consequences, meditation on love and compassion, and the teachings concerning the cultivation of bodhicitta."

i.e. the good mentors' instruction comprises:

1.   advice on how to meditate on impermanence,
2.   advice on how to meditate both on the shortcomings of samsâra and on actions and their consequences,
3.   advice on how to cultivate love and compassion and
4.   advice on cultivating a most enlightened mind (bodhicitta).

These will act as remedies in the following way:

<u>practice of:</u>	<u>serves as remedy to</u>:
meditation on impermanence	attachment to the experiences of this life
meditation on samsâra's shortcomings	attachment to worldly well-being
meditation on love & compassion	attachment to the well-being of peace
teaching on how to cultivate supreme enlightenment	ignorance of how to attain buddhahood

These cover all teachings—from taking refuge[1] through to the meaning of the two types of no-self[2] or from the five stages of the

---

1. **refuge**— to "take refuge" is to become a Buddhist. See ch.8.

2. **two types of no-self** — the ultimate insubstantiality (voidness) of the relatively meaningful concepts of personality (1) and objective reality (2).

path and the ten levels[1] down through all the teachings on bodhicitta. Some of these topics form the basis for bodhicitta, some are its objective, some are the rituals connected with bodhicitta development, some are advice pertinent to bodhicitta, some concern its qualities and benefits and some represent its results. There is no mahâyâna topic that is not included in the bodhicitta teachings. All those forms of instruction stem from the good mentor: they are dependent upon the good mentor. Thus the *gandavyûhasûtra* says:

> "The good mentor is the very source of all the teachings of virtue."
> "Omniscience is dependent upon the instruction given by good mentors."

---

1. **five stages and ten levels** — see later chapters (18 & 19).

Chapter Four:

Meditation on Impermanence:

the remedy for attachment to the experiences of this life

In general, every composite[1] thing is impermanent. Therefore the Buddha taught, "Bhikkhus! All composites are impermanent." How exactly are they impermanent? What is accumulated will eventually dwindle, what is built up will eventually decompose, what meets will eventually part and what lives will eventually die. Quoting the *udânavarga:*

> "The end of all accumulation is dispersal,
> the end of construction is disintegration,
> the end of meeting is parting and
> the end of life is death."

How to meditate on this is explained through the synopsis:

"Meditation on impermanence is completely summed up by three things: its categories, the meditation techniques and the benefits of having thus meditated."

---

1. **composite** — created through causes and conditions.

1.   Categories

There are two: the impermanence of the world (the outer vessel) and the impermanence of conscious beings (the inner essence).

The first of these, the impermanence of the world, the outer vessel, has two subcategories: gross impermanence and subtle impermanence.

The second, the impermanence of conscious beings, the inner essence, also has two subcategories: the impermanence of others and the impermanence of oneself.

2.   The Techniques for Meditating on These

2A   THE IMPERMANENCE OF THE WORLD, THE ENVIRONMENT
2A.1 The overall impermanence of the environment

There exists nothing, from the wind maṅdala[1] below up to the fourth level of concentrative stability[2] above, that will not change, that is permanent by its very nature or that has solidity. At one time everything below the first level of concentrative stability[3] is destroyed by fire. At one time everything below the second level of concentrative stability is destroyed by water. At one time everything below the third level of concentrative stability is destroyed by wind. During those times, when there is destruction by fire not even ashes are left, just as when oil is consumed by a flame. When there is destruction by water, not even sediment is left, just as when salt dissolves into water. When there is destruction by wind, nothing remains, just as when powder is blown away. Thus it says, in the *abhidharmakośa:*

> "There will be seven (destructions) by water (each preceded by) seven fires. Then there will be seven (destructions) by fire (alone). Then finally there will be destruction by wind."

---

1. **wind mandala** — primal movement as basic element of existence. In one old Indian world picture, this becomes the lowest basis for the universe.

2. This is the highest heaven in the dimension of form.

3. **levels of concentrative stability** (*dhyâna*) — see later chapter on meditative stability.

The fourth state of concentrative stability will not be destroyed by fire, water or air: the conscious beings in that state are subject to death and transmigration and so it is auto-destructive. Thus it says:

"The celestial abodes of the impermanent arise and disintegrate along with the conscious beings who inhabit them."

Also, the destruction, at some time, of this universe by fire is foretold in the *vīradatta-grhapatipariprcchāsūtra:*

"After one æon, this world, the nature of which is space, will become space: even the mountains will be completely burnt and destroyed."

2A.2   The subtler impermanence of the environment

This concerns impermanence in terms of the changing of the four seasons, the rising and setting of the sun and moon and moment-to-moment change. Let us consider the first of these.

Due to the powerful influence of the coming of *spring*, the world, our environment, changes as follows: the ground becomes soft, ruddy in colour and the trees, grasses and plants bud. However, this is but the manifestation of a transitory period. Due to the powerful influence of the coming of *summer*, the ground becomes predominantly blue-green and leaves and branches grow on the trees, grasses and plants. This too is but the manifestation of a transitory period. Due to the powerful influence of the coming of *autumn*, the ground becomes hard and predominantly yellow and the trees, grasses and plants bear fruit. This too is but the manifestation of a transitory period. Due to the powerful influence of the coming of *winter*, the ground becomes frozen and whitish and the trees, grasses and plants are dried up and brittle. This too is but the manifestation of a transitory period.

Now let us consider *impermanence in terms of the rising and setting of the sun and moon.* The power of day breaking makes the world, our environment, become light and bright. The power of night falling makes it disappear into darkness. These are also signs of impermanence

Finally, let us consider *impermanence in terms of moment-by-moment change*. The world, the environment, as it is in one small instant of time does not remain into the next instant of time. It gives the impression of being the same yet in fact another similar thing has taken its place. Cascading water is an example of this.

2B THE IMPERMANENCE OF THE INNER ESSENCE, CONSCIOUS BEINGS

2B.1 The impermanence of others

All conscious beings in the three dimensions of existence are impermanent: as it says in the *lalitavistara:*

"The three realms are impermanent, like autumn clouds."

2B.2 One's own impermanence

"I too am powerless when it comes to remaining (in this life), and must go (on to another)." The way to understand this is twofold: by examining one's own existence and by applying (to oneself observations) about others' existences.

~ examination of one's own existence ~

The way to meditate on the first of these is as follows: meditate on *death*, on the *specific characteristics of death*, on the *exhaustion of life* and on *separation*.

Meditation on death means to contemplate the idea, "I will not stay long in this world and will soon be moving into the next."

Meditation on the specific characteristics of death involves contemplating the following ideas, "This life-force of mine will be used up, the respiration will stop and this body will take on the appearance of a corpse, while this mind will be obliged to wander off to another life."

Meditation on the exhaustion of life is to contemplate the ideas, "Since a year ago, a year has passed and my life is now precisely that much shorter. Since a month ago, a month has passed and my life is now precisely that much shorter. From yesterday until today, a day has gone by and my life is now precisely that much shorter. A moment has just gone by and my life is precisely that much shorter." It says in the *bodhisattvacaryâvatâra:*

> "Without ever stopping for even a day or a night, this life is constantly on the wane. As what is left diminishes and disappears, how could the likes of me not die?"

Meditation on separation is to contemplate the ideas, "The friends and relatives, wealth and possessions, physique and so forth, that I have at present and value so much, will not always accompany me. Soon will we be parted." As it says, in the *bodhisattvacaryâvatâra:*

> "By my not knowing that I would have to leave everything behind and depart..." etc.

ninefold way of meditating on death

The ninefold technique is centred around contemplation of three ideas: *I certainly will die, the time of death is uncertain* and *nothing whatsoever can accompany me when I die.*

♦ *I certainly will die*—for three reasons: there was no one previously who did not die, the body is a composite phenomenon and life is consumed from moment to moment.

1/9   It is certain I will die because no one in the past did not die

The great master Aśvaghosa has said:

> "Did you ever witness, hear about or even put into question the existence of a being on earth or in the upper realms who, having been born, will never die?"

Therefore even rishis[1] endowed with supernormal abilities and unfathomable clear cognition[2] cannot find a place to go to escape death and find immortality. They will all die — not to mention the

---

1. **rishi** — the Tibetan *drang.song* means "those who are straightforward", implying honesty, ethics and absence of hypocrisy.

2. **clear cognition** — five, sometimes six, forms are given in abhidharma: clairvoyance, clairaudience, knowledge of others' minds, knowledge of former states and miraculous powers.

likes of us! It is said:

"Even were great rishis endowed with five types of clear cognition to travel far through space, they could not find an immortals' realm, no matter what sphere of experience they attained."

Besides that, even realised beings such as pratyekabuddhas and mahâśrâvakas — the arhats — had to leave their bodies in the end. What then for the likes of us! Thus it says, in the *udânavarga:*

"When even the pratyekabuddhas and the Buddha's śrâvakas have to give up their bodies, there is no point even mentioning the lot of ordinary folk."

Besides this, if even the totally-purified, utterly-perfect, emanation of the Buddha, the nirmânakâya, adorned with the marks[1] and tokens[2] of a super-being, the very nature of which was like a vajra[3], had to leave behind his body: then so much the more is it true of ordinary folk like us. The great master Aśvaghosa said:

"If even the buddhas' bodies—vajra bodies adorned with the special marks and tokens—are impermanent, then no need even to mention the 'banana tree'[4] bodies of other beings."

2/9   It is certain I will die, because my body is something composite

Any composite whatsoever is impermanent and every composite is destructible by nature. The *udânavarga* says:

"Alas, all composites are impermanent, subject to arisal and decay."

---

1. **marks** — the special characteristics of a buddha's body, each the sign of an aspect of his perfection and of his having brought to perfection certain qualities, while on the path to enlightenment. 32 major marks, such as the head-mound, are given in the scriptures — see mahayanottaratantrasastra ("Changeless Nature").

2. **tokens** — see note above, on **marks**. These are the 80 etc. signs of a super-being, other than the 32 just referred to.

3. **vajra** — this fabled weapon of Indra, itself indestructible, was able to destroy anything.

4. i.e. hollow like a banana tree, having no core or essence.

Hence, since this body is not non-composite but composite then it is impermanent and so it is certain that I will die.

3/9   *It is certain that I will die, because life is consumed from moment to moment*

Life gets closer and closer to death with the passing of each instant. If this is not obvious, let us examine examples that bear some similarity with it—those of an arrow shot by a strong archer, of a torrent cascading over a steep cliff and of a prisoner being led to the place of execution where he will soon die.

The first example is that of *an arrow shot by a strong archer*. Not remaining even for an instant at any one place in space, it speeds swiftly to its target. Life too never stands still, even for an instant, but heads swiftly towards death. As is said:

"An arrow loosed from a bowstring by a mighty archer never hovers but speeds to its target; human life is like that too."

The second example is that of a *torrent cascading over a steep cliff*. It tumbles down without pausing even for an instant. Likewise it is extremely obvious that human life is unable to pause. This is stated in the *mahāsannipātaratnaketudhāraṇī*, where it says:

"Friends, this life passes quickly, as swiftly as turbulent water over a waterfall. The immature, unaware of this and living unskilfully, proudly intoxicate themselves with sensorial pleasures."

Furthermore, it says in the *udānavarga:*

"Like the current of a mighty river, it flows on, without ever turning back."

The third example is that of *a prisoner being led to the place of execution,* whose every step brings him closer to death. We are just like that. In the Noble Tree Sûtra, it says:

"Just like a prisoner being led to the place of execution, whose every step brings him closer to death."

The *udānavarga* also says:

"Just as those on their way to execution draw closer to their death with every step they take, so is the life force of humans."

• *The time of death is uncertain*—for three reasons: life span is uncertain, the body has no one vital essence and there are many causes of death.

4/9   *The time of death is uncertain because lifespan is uncertain*

Although the lifespan is certain for some other human beings, in some other places in the cosmos, the lifespan of ordinary people in this world is uncertain. In the *abhidharmakośa* it says:

"Here it is uncertain — ten years at the end and inestimable at the beginning[1]."

Just how uncertain it is, is explained in the *udānavarga:*

"Some will die in the womb, some when they are born, some when they can only crawl, some when they can run, some when aged, some when young and some in the prime of life. Eventually they all go."

5/9   *The time of death is uncertain because the body has no vital core*

This body has no single, solid enduring, essence—only its 36 impure substances. Thus the *bodhisattvacaryāvatāra* says:

"Using the scalpel of discerning awareness, dissect the body mentally, starting with the skin and going through the flesh and bones. Having dissected the bones and got to the marrow, examining carefully, ask yourself, "What is there that could be its essence?" This is what we ought to look into."

---

1. According to some teachings, the beings at the beginning of our cosmic age were so subtle and refined that they had no bodies, no need to eat etc. and could live for incalculable periods. Becoming grosser, their bodies and worlds became more and more solid and polluted, eventually reaching our present condition. Things will reach, sometime in the future, a low point with a 10 year life expectancy, before things turn for the better.

6/9 The time of death is uncertain because there are many causes of death

There is nothing that could not become a cause of death for oneself or someone else. It says, in the *suhrllekha*:

"There are many things which harm life. As it is more unstable than an air bubble in water, it is a wonder that in-breaths turn into out-breaths and that one wakes up from sleep."

• *Nothing can accompany one, once dead*–for three reasons: wealth and objects cannot accompany one, friends and relatives are unable to accompany one and one's own body cannot accompany one.

7/9   Wealth and objects cannot accompany one after death

As it says in the *bodhisattvacaryavatara*:

"Although one may have encountered and obtained many things and perhaps enjoyed them for a long time, one has to go naked and empty-handed, as though robbed by thieves."

Besides the fact that wealth and possessions cannot accompany one at death, they are harmful in this life and the next. They spoil this life by being the cause of suffering i.e. one gets into disputes over them, has to protect them and becomes their slave. The maturation of these (samsaric) actions clouds future lives, taking one to the lower states.

8/9   Friends and relatives cannot accompany one at death

As it says in the *bodhisattvacaryavatara*:

"When the time comes to die, children will not be a refuge, nor father nor mother nor friends nor loved ones. There will be no one who can be your refuge."

Besides the fact that relatives and friends cannot accompany one at death, they harm both this life and the next. They harm this life through the anguish brought about by (people's) fear for each others' health and life. Maturation of these fears (and the actions they provoke) spoils future lives by taking one to the lower realms.

9/9   One's own body cannot accompany one at death

One can be accompanied by neither the *physical qualities* nor *the body itself.*

i. As far as the *physical qualities* are concerned, no strong or courageous person can turn death away, no swift athlete can outrun it and no eloquent speaker or negotiator can dissuade it: it would be like trying to prevent or delay the sun from setting behind a mountain — no one can.

ii. Nor can the *physical substance* of the body accompany one. It says, in the *bodhisattvacaryâvatâra:*

"Your body, which you have clothed and fed at the expense of great hardship, will be unable to help you: it will be eaten by jackals or birds or burnt by fire or rot in water or be buried in a grave."

One's own body, besides not being able to accompany one—as explained above—also spoils both this life and the next. It spoils this life, causing great suffering when it cannot bear sickness, heat, cold, hunger or thirst or when there is fear of being killed, bound or beaten. Not only this, it also drags one into the lower states in future lives by the liabilities it is creating now.[1]

~ observing what happens to others and applying it to oneself ~

This second area of contemplation means applying to oneself what happens to other people—whose deaths have been *seen, heard about* or *recollected*—and meditating accordingly.

In the case of other people one has *seen* die: this is to think of those closely related to oneself, who used to be strong—of healthy complexion, feeling happy and never giving a thought to death—but who were then stricken by fatal illness. Their bodily strength waned, they could not even sit up, their complexion lost its lustre and became pallid and dry and they suffered distress. There was no way to cure the pain or lessen the emotional

---

1. i.e. due to these sufferings, one may act (react) in a way which produces bad rebirth later.

burden. Medicines and examinations ceased being of help and even religious ceremonies and special prayers could not make them better. They knew that they would die and that nothing could be done to prevent it. Surrounded by their remaining friends, they ate their last meal and spoke their last words. Considering these images, one contemplates, thinking, "I too am of this nature. I shall also be subject to this. I too have these characteristics and have not transcended this particular phenomenon."

From the time the breath stopped, the person's body was no longer considered fit to remain even a day in that place, even though previously it had been the beloved home from which he or she could not bear to be parted. Once the corpse had been laid on a bier, bound up and tied, it was lifted up and carried out of the house. At that moment some embraced it and clung to it, some wept and wailed, some fainted and were overcome with grief. Yet others remarked, "This corpse is but (matter like) earth and rock; such behaviour is small-minded!" Contemplating such scenes as a corpse makes its one-way journey over the threshold, think, "I too am of this nature..."

Then, contemplating the corpse once it has been deposited in the cemetery where it is ripped apart by jackals and dogs, decomposed by insects and where skeletons are already disintegrating, think, "I too am like this..."

The way to apply to oneself the instances of other peoples' deaths that one *hears* about is the following: whenever people say, "Such and such a person has died" or "There is a corpse in such and such a place," one thinks, as above, "I too am like that..."

The way to apply to oneself the instances of other peoples' deaths that one *recollects* is the following: one thinks about all the people—some elderly, some young and some lifelong friends—that have died in one's area, one's town or one's own house. Bearing their deaths in mind, one thinks, as above, that "I too am like this..." and reflects how, before not too long, one will also go that way. It is said in the sûtra:

"Since no one knows which will come first—tomorrow or the next life—it makes sense to strive for what has meaning in the next life and not to put a lot of effort into what is just for tomorrow."

3. The benefits of meditating on impermanence

By understanding that all composite things are impermanent one will counter strong craving for this life. Besides, this will plant the seed of trust, reinforce one's diligence and act as a cause for realising the sameness of all things, through quickly eliminating attraction and rejection.

This concludes the fourth chapter, concerning impermanence, of this Gems of Dharma, Jewels of Freedom

Chapter Five:

Meditation on the Shortcomings of Samsâra

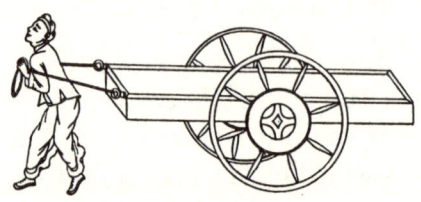

— the first remedy for attachment to existence in general—

"What does it matter if there is impermanence and death? Will I not have to be reborn anyway? In the next life I may possibly experience the very best that the human or divine condition has to offer and that is fine by me!" To think like this is to be attached to the pleasure of existence. The remedy for this is systematic contemplation of the shortcomings of samsâra. The synopsis is:

"The shortcomings of samsâra are covered by three topics: the sufferings inherent to the composite, the sufferings due to change and suffering manifest as suffering."

These three sufferings can be explained *through examples*:

‣ the suffering inherent to the composite[1] is like unripe rice,
‣ the suffering of change is like rice broth mixed with poison and
‣ manifest suffering is like the stomach inflammation due to eating the (poisoned) rice.

---

1. **composite**—means created by and continuing to exist through causes and conditions. A perceived object—such as another human or a chair—appears to be one lasting thing, yet it is in fact multiple and changing. The image present in the mind, as one perceives the object, is a temporary reality highly dependent upon the <u>conditions</u> of the moment. It manifests as it does due to specific <u>causes</u>, some of them to do with the object and some to do with oneself. According to Buddhism, we perceive ourselves and the world, in the subjective way we each do, as a consequence of all that happened to our mind in the past. Composite perception, through ignorance, is the second of the 12 Links of Interdependence (see chapter 16). By its very nature, i.e. because it is rooted in ignorance of ultimate truth and because it clings to delusions, composite samsaric perception is riddled with suffering.

The three sufferings can also be explained *in terms of their character*:

▸ suffering inherent to the composite has an indifferent feeling
▸ the suffering of change (is based on) feelings of pleasure and
▸ suffering as actual suffering feels unpleasant.

The three sufferings can also be explained *in terms of their essential characteristics:*

1. The suffering inherent to the composite

One is a sufferer just through the fact of having taken on (this life composed of) the aggregates[1] to which suffering is inherent. "Ordinary Individuals"[2] do not feel this suffering inherent to the composite and can be compared to people stricken by a raging fever, who at the time are insensitive to a minor physical ailment, such as an itchy ear. Stream-entrants[3] and the other three types of liberated being *can* perceive the suffering inherent to the composite. They could be compared to someone almost cured of a fever and hence quite sensitive to minor physical ailments and pains. A small hair put on the palm of the hand causes neither discomfort nor pain but should the same hair get into the eye it will provoke great irritation and unpleasantness. In a similar way, ordinary individuals are insensitive to the suffering inherent to the composite whereas realised beings are greatly pained by it. Thus it says, in the commentary to the *abhidharmakośa:*

> "Just one hair, gone from the palm of the hand into the eye, generates discomfort and suffering: the immature, like the palm of the hand, do not understand the suffering inherent to the composite whereas realised beings, who are like the eye, do see the suffering inherent to the composite."

---

1. **aggregates** (Tib. *phung.po*, Skt. *skandha*) – a Buddhist way of defining and subdividing perceived realities, in terms of five main domains of existence—form, feeling, perception, mental activity and consciousness. The aggregates are taught as being the complex result of past actions. Their name actually means "heaps" or "conglomerates"—because each of the five areas is not one thing but myriads of impermanent things of that type.

2. **ordinary individual**—anyone who has not yet attained stable realisation of voidness.

3. **stream-entrant**—the first of four stages of achievement in the Buddhist path: a stage where conviction in the Four Truths is like a strong current that will carry one along.

2. Suffering due to Change

It is called "suffering due to change" because all the pleasures of samsâra, whatever they may be, will eventually change into suffering. Therefore the *mahâkarunâpundarîkasûtra* states:

"The divine realms are a cause for the occurrence of suffering. The human realms are also a cause for suffering."

Hence, in time, even those who attain the status of the greatest of human monarchs—a *cakravartin*—will change and then find themselves in a state of suffering. It says, in the *suhrllekha:*

"Even one who has become a cakravartin will, in the course of time, become a servant."

Furthermore, even one who achieved the form and experience-realm of Indra, Lord of the Gods, will eventually fall from that state—first dying, then transmigrating. It is said:

"Even having become he who is worthy of offerings—Indra—one will eventually fall back to an earthly condition, through the power of action (karma)."

Besides, even the likes of Brahmâ, King of the Gods, who have transcended sensual desire and attained the felicity of evenly resting in stabilised concentration, are (also) beings who will eventually fall. It is said:

"From the desireless well-being of Brahmâhood, he will have to put up with the unceasing suffering of being firewood for the 'worst agony' (hell)."

3. Suffering as Manifest Suffering

On top of the sufferings that one experiences through having taken on a life composed of the "aggregates which attract misery", there are also important and manifest sufferings, which are to be understood through two principal categories: the sufferings of the lower states of existence and the sufferings of the higher states of existence.

3.1 THE SUFFERINGS OF THE LOWER STATES OF EXISTENCE

There are three lower states: the hells, the deprived spirit realms and the animal kingdom. They are each to be understood through four points:

1. the subcategories of each,
2. their location,
3. the sorts of sufferings beings in those states experience and
4. the sort of lifespans they have.

3.1A   The Hells[1]

subcategories: There are eight hot hells, eight cold hells, occasional hells and peripheral hells—making 18 types in all.

Hot Hells

location: Where are these hot hells? They are situated beneath this world (Jambudvîpa), for there are many who go from here to there. Lowest live those who inhabit the *worst agony* hell. Above them, working upwards, are the *extremely hot, hot, great wailing, wailing, gathering & crushing, black line* and *reviving* hells, respectively. Therefore the *abhidharmakośa* says:

"20,000 [?] beneath here is the "worst agony" with seven other hells above it."

sufferings endured there: The reason for their names and a general explanation will be given:

---

1. **Hells** The classic Buddhist teachings on hells—and even the word *hell* itself—seem to pose a problem for many Buddhist teachers. Anxious to avoid resemblance with *hellfire and damnation* approaches in some forms of religion, and perhaps wary of frightening off their audience, they can easily fall into the trap of diluting or interpreting the Buddha's teaching in terms of their own projections. Hell, like any other station of existence, is a state of mind. For those in such a state of mind—and those who can perceive them—there is a location and certain local conditions, just as humans and animals experience their locations and localised conditions, generated by their states of mind. To deny the possibility of mind experiencing the hell agonies described in this section is simply immature wishful thinking. One only has to think of nightmares or visit psychiatric hospitals to appreciate how far a *human* mind can fall in its anguish—let alone a mind let loose among the hallucinations generated by its own inner fears and neuroses, after death.

The first is the *reviving hell* where people bind and impale each other and hack each other to death. Then a cold wind blows to revive them. This continues relentlessly throughout their stay there.

In the *black line* hell, a black line is traced on the body, which is then sawn with blazing saws and chopped with flaming red-hot axes. As it says:

"Some are cut up with saws: others chopped up by unbearably sharp axes."

In the *gathering and crushing* hell, beings are gathered between mountains and also crushed and squeezed in iron presses. In the first instance, mountains in the form of sheep heads ram together, crushing the beings between them. The hills then draw apart and a cold wind arises and restores the people to their former condition. They are crushed and restored time after time. The *śisyalekha* says:

"Two terrifying mountains, like rams with long horns, crush all the bodies gathered between them and grind them to powder" etc.

Some are squeezed between iron presses, their blood squirting out like four rivers. It says:

"Some are ground like sesame seeds and others milled to dust like fine flour."

Beings in the *wailing* hell scream with terror as they are burnt.

Beings in the *great wailing* hell scream even more loudly.

In the *hot* hell beings are tortured by fire etc: boiling metal poured into their mouths burns their insides and they are transpierced by one-pointed, spiked staves from the anus through to the top of the head.

In the *very hot* hell they undergo even worse tortures. Without skin, they are burnt by molten metal being poured down their throats; so much that fire comes out of the bodily orifices. Then they too are pierced, by tridents which go through the two soles of the feet and the anus, up to the top of the head and the shoulders. It says:

> "Similarly some are forced to drink a blazing liquid of molten metal while others are impaled on blazing iron stakes bearing many spikes."

The *worst agony* hell is a blazing iron building, 20,000 *paktsé*[1] in height and breadth, within which there are copper and iron cauldrons, several *paktsé* wide, into which are poured molten bronze and iron, kept boiling by unbearable fires coming from the four directions. It says:

> "Some are cast head first into iron cauldrons and boiled up like rice soup."

It is so named[2] because the suffering there is unremitting.

lifespan: "In the first six, starting with the reviving hell, a day and night is equivalent to the life of the sense-dimension gods and so their lives are calculable working from the lifespans of the sense-dimension gods." The lifespan of the class of the Four Great King gods is equivalent to a day and night in the reviving hell. Thirty days make a month and twelve months make a year. As reviving hell beings live 500 of their own years, this makes their lifespan 612 x 10^{10} human years.

If, in a similar way, we calculate the black line hell lifespan according to that of the gods of the "33rd", since beings can live there for up to 1,000 years, then this makes their lifespan the equivalent of 1,299 x 10^{10} human years.

Comparing the gathering and crushing hell with the "Aggressionless" god realm then, since beings can be there for 2,000 hell years, this makes their lifespan the equivalent of 10,068 x 10^{10} human years.

Comparing the wailing hell with the "Joyful" god realm: beings can live there for 4,000 hell years—the equivalent of 84,542 x 10^{10}

---

1. **paktsé** — an ancient linear measure, equivalent to 768,000 finger widths ≅ 15 km.

2. The actual name of the worst agony hell is *"no suffering"* (is worse than that).

human years.

Comparing the great wailing hell with the "Happy to Emanate" gods: the beings can live there for 8,000 hell years—the equivalent of 663,552 x 10^{10} human years.

Comparing the hot hell with the "Other Emanation" gods: the beings can live there for 16,000 hell years—the equivalent of 5,108,416 x 10^{10} human years.

Those in the very hot hell can stay there for half of an intermediate cosmic aeon and those in the worst agony hell for a whole intermediate cosmic aeon. As it says:

"In the very hot—a half—and in the worst agony—a whole—intermediate cosmic aeon."

The Neighbouring Hells

These are situated in the four cardinal points around the eight hells mentioned above. The first of these is the *glowing coals* hell, where there are knee-deep glowing coals. As the beings there take steps—in order to escape—their flesh, skin and blood are completely burnt off when they put their feet down, yet restored as they lift them up again. That is the first additional hell.

In front of that is the *impure swamp of putrefaction* hell, infested by white worms with black heads. With their sharp, pointed beaks, they dig into beings' flesh, right to the bone. This is the second additional hell.

In front of that is the *great razor highway* hell, where beings are molested by a forest of sword-like leaves, terrifying large black dogs, iron trees with slicing leaves and branches and ravens with iron beaks. This is the third additional hell.

In front of that is the *"Most Extreme" river, full of boiling lye* in which the beings there are cooked. They are prevented from leaving the river by guardians bearing weapons, who stand along the banks. This is the fourth additional hell. It says, about these,

"Besides the eight there are sixteen others, in the four cardinal points from them: the *glowing coals*, a *swamp of putrefaction*, the *razor highway* etc. and the *river*."

One may wonder whether the guardians of the hells—those with the appearance of humans or the ravens with the iron beaks—are sentient beings or not. The Vaibhâsikas hold them to be sentient beings whereas the Sautrântikas say they are not. The explanation given by the Yogâcâras and the patriarchal transmission of Marpa and Mila is that these types of experience are in fact manifestations of beings' own minds; experiences generated by the evils they themselves have committed. This is borne out in the *bodhisattvacaryâvatâra:*

> "The beings there and their hellish weapons: who could have created them for that purpose? Who made the burning iron ground and from what are the fires generated? The Great Sage has said that these and all other similar things are due to the existence of an unwholesome mind."

The Eight Cold Hells

These are the

1. cold sore hell,
2. burst cold sore hell,
3. chattering teeth hell,
4. sneezing hell,
5. *alas* hell,
6. hell where frostbitten skin cracks in *utpal* flower shapes,
7. hell where the cracks are like a lotus and the
8. hell where the cracks are like a giant lotus. It is said,

"There are eight cold hells—the *cold sore* hell and the others."

location: They are beneath this Jambudvîpa, alongside the hot hells.

sufferings experienced: This is a general outline of their sufferings, which also accounts for their nomenclature. In the first two hells the cold is so unbearable that the beings have cold sores or (in the second) festering cold sores. The next three are named after the sounds and cries that one hears the beings there make, due to the unbearable cold. The latter three derive their names from the bodily changes that take place there: in the sixth the skin turns blue with cold and cracks open in five or six-fold cracks, looking like an utpal flower, in the seventh it has turned from blue to red and the cracks have ten or more lips, looking like a lotus, and in the last the skin is violently inflamed and split into a hundred or more flaps, like an open giant lotus.

duration: The Transcendent, Victorious Accomplished One has given an example of the duration of these hells:

> "O bhiksu, to take an example, if a storehouse holding eighty bushels of sesame seeds, like those of this land Maghada, were to be filled with such seeds and one grain were to be removed from it once every hundred years, after a certain period all eighty bushels of that Maghada sesame would eventually be emptied from that store. I could not tell you which of the two—that period of time or the lifespan of those in the cold sore hell—would be the longer. Bhiksu! The lifespan in the open cold sore hell is twenty times that of the cold sore hell........Bhiksu! The lifespan in the great open lotus hell is twenty times that in the open lotus hell."

Teacher Vasubhandu taught this in a summarised form:

> "The lifespan in the cold sore hell (approximates to) the time it would take to empty a store of sesame seeds by taking just one seed out every hundred years. The lifespan in the others is increased by a factor of twenty."

Thus if the lifespan in the cold sore hell is the time it would take to empty such a full sesame store, that of the open cold sore hell is 20 times longer, that of the chattering teeth hell 400 times longer, that of the sneezing hell 8,000 times longer, that of the alas hell 160,000 times longer, that of the utpal-like wound hell 3,200,000 times longer, that of the lotus-like wounds 64,000,000 times longer and that of the great lotus type wounds 1,280,000,000 times longer.

The Occasional Hells

These are created by either an individual or two people or many people's actions (karma). They have many different forms but no definite location: some beings live in rivers, some in the hills and some in desolate areas or other places. Some such beings are subterraneans. Some are in the human realm, such as those seen by the Realised Being Maudgalyâyanipûtra. Likewise some are in destitute places, like those seen by Sangharaksita. The lifespans are not fixed. This concludes the explanation of hell beings' sufferings.

3.1B Deprived Spirits

categories: There is the king of the deprived spirits—Yama, Lord of Ghosts—and there are his emissaries.

location: Yama, ruler of the deprived spirits, lives some 500 paktsé beneath this Jambudvîpa. His emissaries have no fixed location, living in deserts and the like. There are three types of the latter:

- those who have an external eating or drinking impediment,
- those who have an internal impediment and
- those with a general eating or drinking impediment.

sufferings endured: Some deprived spirits have supernatural powers and experience almost god-like splendours. However, *those with an external eating or drinking impediment* see food and drink as blood, sometimes being unable to eat or drink it because they are prevented from so doing by others. *Those with an internal impediment* are not prevented from ingesting by others but are unable to do so on account of their own condition. It is said:

> "Some have a mouth the size of a needle but a belly the size of a mountain. Anguished with hunger, those who have the strength to look for food cannot find a morsel even among rubbish."

Among those with an eating and drinking impediment there are two types: *fire-garlands* and *filth-eaters*. The first are burnt (internally) by fire as soon as they ingest food or drink. The second eat faeces, drink urine and cut off their own flesh to eat. This was seen in a wilderness by one known as *gro.bzhin.skes.rna.pa.bye.ba.ri.* (Tib.)

lifespan: A month of human time is the equivalent of a day and night of deprived spirit time. Their lifespan—500 of their years—can be computed from this day-to-month comparison. It is said: "Deprived spirits live to 500: a day being a month."

3.1C Animals

categories: there are four main types: many-legged ones, quadrupeds, bipeds and legless.

habitat: the worlds they mainly experience are water, the plains or the forests. Their principal habitat, however, is the oceans.

sufferings experienced: these are the sufferings:

1.   of enslavement,
2.   of being slaughtered and cut up and
3.   of being eaten by one another.

The first applies to animals exploited by humans. It says:

"Powerless, they are beaten, kicked, whipped and goaded: enslaved."

The second type applies to wild animals and the like. It says:

"There are those slaughtered for their pearls, wool, bones, blood, flesh or hides."

The third type mainly concerns those living in the great oceans:

"They eat whatever is before their faces."

lifespan: Animals' lifespan is not fixed. The longest living can live for up to an intermediate cosmic aeon. It says:

"The lifespan of animals is a cosmic aeon, at best."

This concludes the section on the sufferings of the lower states.

3.2 THE SUFFERING OF THE HIGHER STATES OF EXISTENCE

There are three domains: the sufferings of humans, the sufferings of the demi-gods and the sufferings of the gods.

3.2A.   Humans

Humans have eight principal sufferings. It says in the *garbhāvakrāntisūtra:*

> "Likewise birth is suffering, ageing is suffering, sickness is suffering, death is suffering, to be separated from what one likes is suffering, to encounter what one dislikes is suffering, striving after and obtaining what one wants is suffering and also the difficulty involved in maintaining what one has is suffering."

The first of these is the **suffering of birth,** which also serves as the root of all the others. Although four modes of birth are taught, most (humans) are born from a womb. On account of this, there are various sufferings, occuring from the period starting at the *becoming* intermediate state[1] up until actual residence in the womb. In general, intermediate-state beings have certain supernatural abilities—they are able to fly through space and see remote birth states through a sort of divine vision. This eventually gives way to four types of delusions created by the force of former actions, such as the stirring of a mighty wind, a heavy fall of rain, a darkening of the sky and the frightening clamour of great crowds.

Then, according to the quality of one's karma, one of the following notions, presented in descending order of purity, may occur. One thinks,

"I'm entering a celestial palace" or
"I'm going to the top of a many storeyed building" or
"I'm approaching a throne" or
"I'm entering a thatched hut" or
"I'm going into a house made of leaves" or
"I'm slipping in between blades of grass" or
"I'm entering a forest" or
"I'm going through a hole in a wall" or
"I'm slipping in between straws."

---

1. **"becoming" intermediate state** (Tib. *srid.pa'i.bar.do*) — the time immediately preceding entry into a new existence (usually conception) when the general between-life hallucinations give way to certain images indicative of possible rebirth.

Then, seeing (future) parents in sexual embrace from afar, they make towards them. Beings who have gathered a great store of merit and who will have a high rebirth see the celestial palace, the many storeyed building and so forth, and head for them. Those who have gathered a middling store of merit and will have a middling rebirth see a grass-thatched hut etc. and head towards that. Those who have gathered no merit and who will have a bad rebirth see the hole in the wall etc. and head towards that. Having reached there, one who is to be born a boy will feel attraction for the mother and aversion towards the father, whereas one who is to be born a girl will feel attraction for the father and aversion towards the mother. With these feelings of attraction and aversion, the awareness of the intermediate state becomes fused with the impure secretions of the parents.

From that moment on, it is said that one will spend 38 weeks in the womb. Some spend eight months, some nine and some ten, it is also said. Some spend an indefinite period and there are even some who spend up to sixty years in the womb.

During the *first week* in the mother's womb, it is just like being cooked and fried in a hot cooking pot, as consciousness (newly) combined with the physical constituents causes the experience of unbearable suffering. This (stage of the embryo), called *the ovoid*, is in form like rice broth or yoghurt curd.

In the *second week* in the mother's womb, the prâna[1] known as the *all-touching* stirs. Its contact with the mother's womb makes the four elements become manifest. This (stage of the embryo), called *the oblong*, is like curds or churned butter in appearance.

In the *third week* in the mother's womb, the prâna known as *the activator* stirs the womb making the four elements really manifest; this (stage of the embryo), known as *the lump*, looks like an iron

---

1. **prâna** (Tib. *rlung*) The Sanskrit term prâna is being used here as no equivalent term or notion exists in the West. Literally, these are the winds or energies which depend upon mind for their own nature, location and characteristics and which, in turn, govern the way in which our own material existence, as well as that of the universe, appears to the mind. Along with the channels (*nâdî*) and centres (*cakra*) through which they operate and points of intensity (*bindu*), these make up the subtle body which is the command structure of material existence and the subject of much attention in Buddhist yogins' meditation.

spoon or an ant.

Likewise, in the *seventh week* spent in the mother's womb, there arises the prâna known as *the twister*. The effect of its contact with the womb causes formation of the two arms and two legs. The suffering that occurs during this period feels as though one strong person were pulling out one's limbs while another was using a rolling pin to spread one out.

Likewise, in the *eleventh week* spent in the mother's womb, the *orifice maker* prâna arises. The effect of its contact on the womb is to cause the nine bodily orifices to appear. The suffering at that time is like that of a fresh wound being probed by a finger.

Furthermore, when the mother eats irregularly or eats predominantly cold food, one suffers as if one had been thrown naked onto ice. Very hot, sour or spicy foods will likewise create pain. If the mother overeats, the pain is like that of being crushed between rocks. If she undereats, one suffers too—feeling as if one had been sent spinning through space. When she moves quickly, jumps, turns around sharply or suddenly bends her body, one is pained as though one had fallen over a precipice. At times of violent intercourse, one suffers as though being beaten by thorny sticks.

In the *thirty seventh* week one realises that one is in a womb, thinking of it as a dirty, foul-smelling, pitch-black prison. Unable to tolerate it any longer, the thought of leaving it occurs. In the *thirty-eighth* week, the prâna called *flower gatherer* stirs the mother's womb, turning the foetus around towards the gateway of birth. The suffering at that time is like that of being tortured on iron racks.

Thus, during the pregnancy, while developing from being a one-week embryo to a fully-developed foetus, one is boiled and stirred around in the womb, as in a hot or even scalding pot, one is affected and shoved around by the 28 different prâna and one is nurtured and developed by nutrients coming from the mother's blood etc. Therefore it says, in the *garbhavakrantisûtra:*

"From the one-week embryo—the ovoid—a flesh bubble arises and from this occurs the 'oblong', the second-week embryo. This grows more solid, giving rise to the head and four limbs and, once the bones are well formed and connected, the body becomes complete. The cause of all this happening is action (karma)."

Then arises the *face-down* prâna, which turns the head downwards. The body leaves the womb, arms outstretched, experiencing pains that feel as though it were being pulled through an iron press. Some are stillborn. Sometimes both mother and child die through childbirth.

At the time of birth itself, when the child has its first contact with surfaces, it suffers as though thrown onto a bed of thorns. A little later (when it is wiped) it feels as though its skin had been peeled off and its body rubbed against a wall.

Throughout one's stay (in the womb), it is as uncomfortable, as confined, as dark and impure as that (described above). Were one even to offer a really tough person three measures of gold, in return for putting up with being in that impure filthy hole for just three days, who could manage it? The suffering of being in the womb is worse than that. Therefore it is said, in the *sisyalekha:*

> "Stifled by unbearable smells and impurities, totally confined in utter darkness, staying in a womb is like being in hell, as one has to put up with great suffering, the body totally constricted."

Once convinced of this, think, "Who could possibly go even one more time into a womb."

Although the **sufferings of ageing** are also immeasurable, they can be summarised as tenfold: sufferings caused by marked changes in one's physique, hair, skin, complexion, abilities and faculties, prestige, quality of life, good health, mental capacity and sufferings caused by reaching life's end when one's time is up.

1. marked physical change—the body which was previously strong and robust, holding itself erect, will change, becoming bent, twisted and having to support itself with a stick.

2. marked change in one's hair—hair, formerly jet-black, changes to become white or else one becomes bald.

3.   marked epidermal change—the skin, once as fine and smooth as Benares cotton or Chinese silk, becomes coarse, lined and heavily wrinkled, looking like braided copper bangles.

4.   marked changes of complexion—the complexion, once filled with brightness and lustre, like a freshly-opened lotus, fades, becoming bluish or greyish like an old withered flower.

5.   marked changes in ability and faculties—the enthusiasm and ability that one previously had will change, as a decline in physical strength prevents one from undertaking difficult tasks and a mental decline takes away any enthusiasm for doing things. The senses become blunt and cannot perceive their objects or else have a confused perception of them.

6.   marked changes in prestige—whereas formerly one was praised and respected, one now wanes in people's esteem and becomes an object of inferiors' scorn. Even strangers take an automatic dislike to one's company and one becomes the object of children's tricks and young relatives' shame.

7.   marked change in quality of life—there is a deterioration in the (pleasure given by) possessions, food and drink. The body cannot feel properly warm nor the mouth find nice taste in anything. One fancies what is not available and it is difficult to get others to provide for one and feed one.

8.   marked change of health—once stricken by the greatest of illnesses—old age itself—one suffers, for it brings on all the other diseases.

9.   marked change in mental ability —becoming senile and confused, one forgets almost immediately what one has just said or done.

10.   when one's time is up, life's end is reached—one is short of breath and starts wheezing. As all the component elements of the body have worn out, death is at hand.

The *lalitavistara* says of all this: "Old age turns a pleasant physique into an unpleasant one. Old age steals one's prestige and damages one's abilities and strength. Old age steals happiness and increases suffering. Old age is the maker of death and the robber of beauty."

Although the **sufferings of sickness** are also incalculable, they can be summed up as sevenfold—i.e. the sufferings of:

- being struck down by a powerful disease,
- painful physical examinations,
- having to take strong medicine,
- being prevented from eating and drinking what one enjoys,
- having to follow the doctor's orders,
- sickness diminishing one's wealth and
- fearing death.

The *lalitavistara* says of this:

> "Tormented by being prey to and actually falling victim to the sufferings of hundreds of maladies, they are like human ghosts."

The **sufferings of death** are also countless. It says of them, in the *râjâvavâdaka:*

> "Great King! When, like this, one has been tormented on the torture spike of death, one is no longer so arrogant—one is without protectors, allies or friend. Stricken by disease, the mouth is thirsty, one's face changes, the limbs give way, one is unable to work, filthies one's body with saliva, snot, urine and disgusting vomit and wheezes noisily. The doctors abandon hope, one sleeps on one's bed for the last time, sinks into the stream of samsâra and becomes frightened of Yama's emissaries. The breathing stops, the mouth and nostrils gape. One leaves this world behind and heads for the next. It is the great departure, the entrance into deepest darkness, the fall over the greatest precipice and being swept away by the mighty ocean. Gusted away by the wind of karma, one goes to the place of no settling, unable to take even one tiny fraction of one's possessions. Though one cries out, 'Oh, mother; oh father, oh my children!' there is at that time, great king, no other protector, no other refuge, no other ally, than dharma."

There is also the **suffering of being separated from loved ones**. When loved ones—father, mother, children and friends—die, there is immeasurable suffering in the form of misery, grief, weeping, wailing and so forth.

The **suffering of encountering the unwanted** is the distress due to the quarrelling that occurs when meeting hated enemies. There are many such sufferings—argument, physical violence etc.

The **last two types of suffering** (the strife of obtaining things and the difficulty of maintaining them) are self-evident.

3.2B Demi-gods

Besides having suffering akin to that of the gods, the demi-gods also suffer from pride, jealousy, fighting and quarrelling. It says:

"The demi-gods endure great mental torment because they are, by their very nature, resentful of the gods' splendour and enjoyments."

3.2C Gods

Sense-dimension gods suffer through having to fight off the demi-gods, through feeling unsatiated—on account of their endless desire—and through losing their confidence. They also suffer due to their limbs being mutilated and parts of their bodies being severed, due to being killed or expelled, and finally they suffer death, going to another existence and loss of divine status. It is said:

"When death comes, divine child, five signs will appear: clothes start to smell bad, flower garlands wither, the two armpits start to sweat, foul smells arise from the body and dissatisfaction with one's divine seat arises."

Gods of the form and formless dimensions do not have the above-mentioned sufferings. However, since they die, transmigrate and do not have the power to remain in their state, they suffer in consequence through having to take birth in a lower place.

Likewise, once the good karma of humans or gods of any level is exhausted, they have to fall into states of suffering. Therefore the whole condition of samsâra, the very nature of which is suffering, is like that of a house ablaze. To quote the *garbhâvakrântisûtra*:

"Alas and woe! Because this ocean of ongoing existence is ablaze, completely flaming, really burning, totally blazing, not even a few remain undefeated by it. What is this raging inferno? It is the fire of aggression, passion and stupidity, the fire of birth, ageing and death, the fire of sorrow, lamentation, distress and unrest. As these fires are constantly raging and blazing, no one escapes them."

Thus, knowing the shortcomings of samsâra will turn the mind away from the pleasures of existence. To quote the *pitâputrasamâ-gamanasûtra:*

"When someone sees the shortcomings of samsâra, there will arise true weariness for it, and fear of the prison of its three dimensions will stimulate a diligent abandoning of it."

The great teacher Nâgârjuna has also said, in a similar vein:

"Since samsâra is like that, then birth as a god, a human, a hell-being, a deprived spirit or an animal is in no way a good birth—know them to be vessels filled with many harms."

This was the fifth chapter, explaining the sufferings of samsâra, from this Gems of Dharma, Jewels of Freedom.

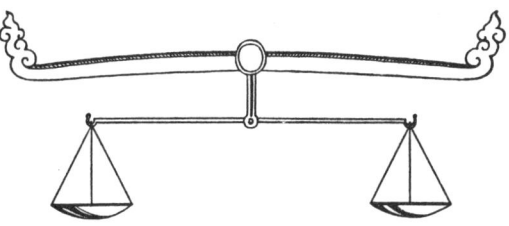

Chapter Six:

Meditation on Karma, Cause & Effect

the second remedy to attachment to existence in general

Someone wondering what causes the above-mentioned sufferings should realise that they arise from tainted[1] activity[2]—karma. The *karmaśatakasūtra* says of this:

"Actions, themselves of various kinds, have created beings in all their variety."

---

1. **tainted**   This term is different from many other derogatory terms which qualify action—"bad", "unvirtuous", "unwholesome" etc. Whereas they all refer solely to unvirtuous action, "tainted" applies also to virtuous, non-virtuous and meditation activity. It means that they are still "tainted" by ignorance and its consequences—dualism, triplicity, ego-delusion etc.—and so therefore will create a worldly result—happy, suffering etc. according to the nature of the act. **Untainted** action transcends triplicity (i.e. is without concept of subject, action and object) and is not included in the karma teachings since it does not belong to worldly cause and effect.

2. **activity**   A choice had to be made between using the now well-known Sanskrit form *karma* and this, its English meaning. There are good arguments for using each of them. Karma often appears in a fuller form in the Tibetan, as *las.rgyu.'bras*, which means "action, (in terms of both) cause and effect". This highlights the Buddhist concept of action, in which not only the initial action itself, but also its longer term consequences, are considered together to be one action, one karma. It is very easy for an observer to think of causes and their consequences as two separate things rather than as one ongoing process. When, for instance, one sees the seeds being sown in the field in autumn, it is one thing. The green shoots of spring look like another thing, a consequence. In reality, there has been an unbroken continuum of events. Likewise, our actions in one life and their consequences in another may seem quite distinct, yet there has been one continuum.

In the *mahākaruṇāpuṇḍarīkasūtra* it says:

"The worlds have been made by actions; their manifestation is due to actions. Sentient beings have been created by actions; have their cause in actions and owe their differences to actions."

The *abhidharmakośa* says: "The various worlds were generated by actions."

If you wonder what exactly action is, know that it falls into two areas: mental activity and activity due to intention. The *abhidharmasamuccaya* says of this:

"What is action? It is mental activity (itself) and mentally-motivated action."

In the *abhidharmakośa* it says:

"Action is intention and what is done because of that."

Furthermore, in the *mūlamadhyamakākārikā* it says:

"The Supremely-Truthful One has said that action is mental activity and what is done because of thought."

One may wonder what these two actually are:

1. *mental* activity—the actions of mind.
2. whatever *physical* and *verbal* activity has been intended by mind, i.e. whatever mental activity gives rise to.

The *abhidharmakośa* says:

"Intention is mental activity: what it generates is physical and verbal activity."

The following synopsis outlines such actions and the results they generate:

Actions and their results are summed up through six points: categories, characteristics, determination of one's lot, apportioning, great evolving from small, and ineluctability.

1. Categories

These are to be known as three:

1. unvirtuous action, cause and result,
2. virtuous action, cause and result, and
3. unwavering concentration as activity, cause and result.

2.   Characteristics

2A UNVIRTUOUS ACTION, CAUSE & EFFECT

Although, generally speaking, there are many sorts of unvirtuous action, they can be summarised as the **ten non-virtues.** Three are physical: killing etc. Four are verbal: lying etc. Three are mental: greed etc. Each of these is itself treated through three points: their categories, their results and some particular instances (worst possible case).

2A.1 Killing

This has three *categories:*

- ▸ killing through desire and attachment,
- ▸ killing through anger and aversion and
- ▸ killing through stupidity.

The first of these is killing for the sake of meat, hides and so forth or for sport or financial gain or in order to safeguard oneself or one's loved ones.
The second is killing those to whom one feels averse on account of grudges or competition and the like.
The third is done in order to make offerings.

The *results* of killing are also threefold: the *fully-developed* result, the result *corresponding to the cause* and the *resulting influence:*

The fully-developed result is rebirth as a hell-being. The result corresponding to the cause is that even if one is reborn human one will have a short life and many sicknesses. The resulting influence is to be reborn in an ill-fated and unattractive land. The *particular instance* or worst case among all the forms of killing, the most sinful[1] one, is that of killing an Arhat who is also one's father.

2A.2 Stealing   The three categories are:

- stealing by force,
- stealing by stealth and
- stealing through cheating or fraudulence.

The first of these is to rob using unnecessary violence.
The second is to steal unnoticed, by burgling houses etc.
The third is to cheat by corrupt weights and measures.

Of the three types of result, the fully-developed result is to be reborn as a deprived spirit. The result corresponding to the cause is that even if one is reborn as a human, one will experience material impoverishment[2]. The resulting influence is to be reborn in a place where there is much frost and hail. The worst case of stealing, the greatest sin, is to take wealth belonging to one's guru or the three precious refuges.

2A.3 Sexual misconduct[3] There are three categories (involving sexual activity with another person):

- precluded by family relationship,
- precluded by their commitment to someone else and
- precluded by religious concerns.

The first of these is intercourse with one's mother, sister etc.

---

1. **sin** After much hesitation, we have decided to risk using this word here to translate the Tibetan *sdig.pa*. Many people detest the term, for it carries many connotations linked with other religious conditioning. However, in this context of being one of the darkest actions one could possibly do, with unimaginably ghastly consequences, substitute terms fail to carry the raw punch of the idea conveyed by the Tibetan. In terms of its impact, the word "sin" is a close translation, also in the sense of *transgressing natural law* (OED).

2. This could be read straightforwardly as being poor, or more meaningfully as feeling dissatisfied with what one has, even if it is a lot.

3. Tib: *'dod.pas.logs.par.gyems.pa* meaning something like "wrong sexual activity, rooted in lust." A term like "unskilful sexuality" may have been more appealing to a modern reader but would be too far from the power of language conveyed by the Tibetan words.

The second is intercourse with someone married (committed) to another person or belonging to a king[1] and

The third covers all situations of sexual relationship with an appropriate partner but which are considered inappropriate by Buddhist convention. In this, there are five areas of inadmissable intercourse—determined by organs, place, time, degree or manner. The first, inappropriate organs, means oral or anal intercourse. An inappropriate place is in the proximity of a guru, temple, stupa or a large gathering. Inappropriate times are those when lay precepts[2] are being observed, during pregnancy, while the mother is breastfeeding or during daylight hours[3]. An inappropriate degree is five or more times consecutively. Inadmissible forms of intercourse are the likes of rape[4] and anal or oral intercourse with a person of the same sex or an hermaphrodite.

Of the three types of result, the fully-developed result is to be reborn as a deprived spirit. The corresponding result is that even if one is reborn human, one's partner will be like a hateful enemy and the resulting influence is to be reborn in a very dusty land. The worst case is the great sin of having intercourse with one's own mother who also happens to be an *arhani*.

---

1. one of a harem.

2. usually when the five or eight temporary precepts are being observed often for one day. Gampopa specifically mentions the eight *gso. byong* precepts: not killing, stealing, lying, taking intoxicants, committing sexual misconduct, eating after lunch, dressing ostentatiously or participating in song and dance.

3. the main problem being being visible.

4. i.e. against the other's will.

2A.4 Lying is of three types: lies that are one's undoing, big lies and trivial lies.

The first concerns "false guruhood"; pretence about achievement[1]. The second are lies designed to benefit oneself or harm others. The third concerns lies that are neither beneficial nor harmful.

Of the three types of result, the fully-developed result is to be reborn as an animal. The corresponding result is that even should one be reborn human, one will be derided by others. The resulting influence is to have bad breath. The worst sin is to have slandered the tathâgatha and then lied to one's guru.

2A.5 Alienating speech is of three types—vehement, insinuated and via third parties.

The first of these separates friends by direct slander.
The second separates them through insinuations.
The third separates friends through rumour.

Of the three types of result, the fully-developed result is to be reborn in hell. The corresponding result is that, even if one is reborn human, one will be separated from one's friends. The resulting influence is to be born in a place where the terrain is erratic and dangerous. The worst instance among such alienating speech is the great sin of causing dissent among the sangha.

2A.6 Wounding speech is of three types: direct, insinuated and via third parties.

The first is to tell someone openly of their faults and weaknesses.
The second means to say nasty things relevant to someone in a half-disguised manner mingled with jest.
The third is to reveal someone's faults or weaknesses to their friends and others.

Of the three types of result, the fully-developed result is to be

---

1. literally "lama's lies"—saying or implying that one has special powers (siddhi) or that one has achieved advanced spiritual levels (see later chapters).

reborn in hell. The corresponding result is that, even if one is reborn a human, one will hear disturbing sounds and words. The resulting influence is to be reborn in a hot and arid place where there is much evil[1]. The worst instance of wounding speech is to speak woundingly to one's father, mother or to a realised being[2].

2A.7 Useless speech is of three types: deluded useless speech, useless worldly chatter and true but useless speech.

The first concerns the formulæ and recitations of mistaken beliefs.
The second concerns silly talk, jokes and so on.
The third concerns attempts to explain dharma to those lacking respect or the appropriate frame of mind.

Of the three types of result, the fully-developed result is to be reborn an animal. The corresponding result is that, even should one be reborn human, one's words will carry no weight. The resulting influence is to be reborn in a place where the seasons are completely erratic. The worst instance, the most sinful type of useless speech, is that which distracts those who are practising dharma.

2A.8 Greed is of three types:

- greed concerning one's own possessions,
- greed concerning other people's possessions and
- greed which belongs to neither of these categories.

The first is a grasping attachment to one's own family status, physical appearance, qualities, wealth and possessions thinking, "There is no one quite like me."
The second is to covet the good things others possess. One thinks, "If only this were mine."
The third involves coveting things which belong neither to oneself

---

1. the Tibetan here could be read as "much evil" or "many scorpions".

2. **realised being** (Tib: *'phags.pa* Skt: *arya*) — one who has achieved stable, unreverting perception of voidness and truth.

nor to others, such as precious substances buried in the earth etc., thinking, "If only I could take possession of that."

Of the three types of result of greed, the fully-developed result is to be reborn as a deprived spirit. The corresponding result is that even if one is reborn human, greed will dominate one's mind. The resulting influence is to be born in a place where the quality of food[1] is poor. Of all sorts of greed, the greatest sin is to wish to steal the possessions of those who have truly renounced the world.

2A.9 Malevolence is of three types: due to hatred, jealousy or resentment.

The first is to harbour, because of hatred, the idea of killing[2] another, as in times of war.
The second is to harbour, through competitiveness and the like, the idea of killing or harming another through fear of being surpassed.
The third is to harbour, through long-standing resentment, the idea of killing or hurting someone who has previously wronged one etc.

Of the three types of result of malevolence, the fully-developed result is rebirth in hell. The corresponding result is that even if one is reborn human, hatred will dominate one's mind. The resulting influence is to be reborn in a place where the food is bitter and coarse. Of all types of malevolence, the worst instance, the greatest sin, is to plan to commit one of the *acts bearing immediate consequence*.[3]

2A.10 Aberrant belief is of three types:

- ▸ aberrant beliefs about actions and their consequences,
- ▸ aberrant beliefs about the truth(s) and
- ▸ aberrant beliefs about the precious refuges.

---

1. literally the quality of grains is poor.

2. and, as with the first bad action (killing), by extension the idea of harming others.

3. literally act "without interval" or "irreprievable act". They are so called because their karmic consequence occurs immediately upon death, without one first passing through the intermediate state (bar.do). Often five such acts are cited: parricide, matricide, injuring a buddha, killing an arhat and causing schism in the sangha while the Buddha is alive.

The first is not to believe that actions, virtuous or non-virtuous, generate their specific consequences of happiness or suffering.
The second is to consider that the Truth of Cessation will not be achieved by one who practises the Truth of the Path.[1]
The third is to deprecate the three precious Refuges, believing them to be untrue.

Of the three types of result of aberrant belief, the fully-developed result is to be reborn an animal. The corresponding result is that even if one is reborn human, stupidity and confusion will dominate one's mind. The resulting influence is to be reborn in a place where there are no harvests[2] at all. The worst instance, the greatest sin among aberrant belief, is to have been afflicted by the "thorn-like" disbelief[3].

The above was a general explanation of the fully-developed results of such actions. Three kinds of fully-developed result can be distinguished according to whether the action is considered:

1. in terms of the defilement[4] present,
2. in terms of its frequency or
3. in terms of its object.

▸ 1. If the actions were done through anger/hatred, one is more likely to be reborn in hell. If they were done through passion/attachment one is more likely to be reborn as a deprived

---

1. The **Truth of Cessation** concerns the definite ceasing of suffering, due to a way of action, the **Truth of the Path**, which removes its causes. These are the latter two of the Four Noble Truths (see p 23), the fundamental doctrine of Buddhism. In this text, the Four Truths are not discussed as a distinct topic. Teachings on the **Truth of Suffering** are covered by Ch. 5, on suffering. Teachings on the **Truth of Origination** of Suffering are those given in this chapter and in Ch. 16 (meditation), in the section on interdependence.

2. literally "no fruits".

3. disbelief in karma, past and future lives etc.

4. **defilement** (Skt· *klesa* Tib: *nyon.mongs*) The term *klesa* has been translated variously as: conflicting emotions, poisons, cankers, pollution, affliction, affective negativity etc.

spirit. If they were done through ignorance/stupidity one is more likely to be reborn as an animal. Thus the *ratnâvalî* says:

> "Through passion, one will become a deprived spirit, through anger one will be hurtled into hell and through confusion one becomes an animal."

▸ 2. Innumerable unvirtuous acts lead to rebirth in hell. A great deal of unvirtuous acts lead to rebirth as a deprived spirit. A few such bad actions lead to rebirth as an animal.

▸ 3. If the unvirtuous act is committed against a special[1] person, one may be reborn in hell. If committed against a medium being, one may be reborn a deprived spirit and if against a lesser being, one may be reborn an animal.

The above was an explanation of non-meritorious actions (cause and consequence). To quote the *ratnâvalî*:

> "Clinging, anger, ignorance and the actions that they give rise to are non-virtue. Through non-virtue there (arise) all the sufferings and hence all the lower states of existence."

---

1. the three precious Refuges, one's guru, one's parents, the sick or needy etc.

2B VIRTUOUS ACTION (CAUSE AND CONSEQUENCE)

2B.1 The actions. The ten virtuous actions are to give up the unvirtuous ones and, moreover, to engage in the corresponding (counterpart) actions, namely:

- to protect the lives of others,
- to give lavishly,
- to maintain sexual purity,
- to speak the truth straightforwardly,
- to dispel unfriendliness and bring harmony,
- to speak peacefully, appeasingly and in a way that is pleasant for others,
- to speak in a way that is meaningful,
- to reduce desires and be content with what one has,
- to cultivate loving kindness and so forth and
- to penetrate the highest meaning.

2B.2 These actions have threefold consequence

The fully-developed result is to gain rebirth in the human or divine planes of the sense dimension. The corresponding result will be that, having abandoned harming others and having protected life, one will gain longevity—and so forth for the other virtues. The resulting influence is that by giving up killing one will be reborn in a very prosperous and powerful place—and so forth, corresponding to the virtue concerned.

This was an explanation of good action (cause and consequence). The *ratnâvalî* says:

"Virtue is what is generated by being unattached, without anger and without ignorance and from virtue (arise) all the higher states of existence and happiness in all lifetimes."

2C UNWAVERING (CONCENTRATION[1]) AS ACTION (CAUSE AND CONSEQUENCE)

Through having cultivated, by meditation, the cause—the dhyâna[2] (stabilised absorption) of controlled evenness[3]—one will attain, as a result, rebirth in such absorption. Of these, the dhyâna of controlled evenness (consists of) the eight approaching concentrations[4], the eight actual absorptions and the special absorption. The consequence, the rebirth absorptions, consists of the seventeen classes of form-dimension god and the gods (absorbed in) the four types of formless operational field[5]. The general condition for these specific cause-and-effect situations to happen is the practice of the ten virtues.

One launches the **1st dhyâna** by meditatively cultivating its

---

1. Tib: *mi.gyo.bai.las*—literally unwavering action, immobility action.

2. Skt: *dhyâna* Tib: *bsam.gtan*. The Sanskrit term has been kept here for want of a fully suitable English one. Further, there is a difference is emphasis between the Sanskrit and Tibetan terms. Dhyâna (and especially jhâna, its Pali equivalent) means "absorption". The Tibetans rendered this as *bsam.gtan*—which suggests something closer to "stabilised thinking", "stabilised mind". The literal meaning is common—a state free from distraction or vacillation wherein the attention is perfectly fixed on, absorbed into, its object. But what this *really* means in practice varies enormously according to the meditation system followed.

3. Skt: *samâpatti* Tib: *snoms.'jug* The Sanskrit has a meaning close to "possessor of peace" and the Pali describes this word as having a sense of attainment: "achiever of peace". There are eight of these achievement stages, one in each dhyâna (see later in chapter), nine if one includes total extinction. The Tibetan translation means "entered into evenness": the obstacles to a certain stage of absorption having been overcome, one enjoys the balanced absorption of that state, which becomes in its turn the beginning stage for something more subtle.

4. Skt: *sâmantaka-samâdhi* seems to correspond to Pali *upacâra-samâdhi* Tib: *nyer.bsdog*s—concentration approaching but not yet attaining the absorption sought. This intermediary stage follows the preparatory concentration (Pali: *parikarma-samâdhi* Tib: *'phen.byed* literally launching concentration) and makes possible the absorption achieved stage (Pali: *appanâ samâdhi* Tib: *dngos.gzhi*) which later in the text is also referred to as "perfecting absorption", showing that this achievement is relative and just part of a larger process of mental refinement.

5. Skt: *âyatana* Tib: *skye.mched* The "bases" or "sources" upon which mental processes depend. These are mainly 12: the five physical sense faculties and the mental faculty and their six objects (visibles, audibles etc.) Also known as "sense doorways". Here we have specific cases of the fields of experience in which the mental faculty operates.

obstacle-removing stage, the approaching concentration which clears away inability. This leads to the actual 1st perfecting dhyâna, which is a profound absorption[1] accompanied by concept, analysis, joy and physical well-being. Through cultivating this, one will be reborn among the gods of the brahmâ realms. By then cultivating the special aspect of this dhyâna, one will be reborn in the mahâbrahmâ heaven.

One launches the **2nd dhyâna** by meditatively cultivating its obstacle-removing stage, the approaching concentration. This leads to the actual 2nd perfecting dhyâna, a profound absorption accompanied by joy and physical well-being but from which concept and analysis have been left aside. By cultivating this, one will be reborn among the gods of the 2nd dhyâna, in the "small light" heavens and so forth.

It is likewise for the launching meditations of the **3rd and 4th dhyâna**.

By cultivating the actual profound absorption of the 3rd perfecting dhyâna, in which there is physical well-being but mental joy is left aside, one will be reborn among the 3rd dhyâna gods of the "lesser virtue" heavens and so forth.

By cultivating the actual profound absorption of the 4th perfecting dhyâna, in which concept, analysis, joy and physical well-being have all been left aside, one will be reborn among the 4th dhyâna gods of the "cloudless" heavens and so forth.

It is by meditatively cultivating the operational field of **"limitless space"** that one then transcends the four dhyâna. This gives rise to rebirth as a god of the limitless space operational field.

It is by meditatively cultivating the operational field of **"limitless consciousness"** that this is in turn transcended. This gives rise to rebirth as a god of the limitless consciousness operational field.

It is by meditatively cultivating the operational field of **"nothing whatsoever"** that this is in turn transcended. This gives rise to rebirth as a god of the nothing whatsoever operational field.

It is by meditatively cultivating the operational field of **"neither cognition nor absence of cognition"** that this is in turn

---

1. Skt: *samâdhi*   Tib: *ting.nge.'dzin*

transcended. This gives rise to rebirth as a god of the neither cognition nor absence of cognition operational field.

What exactly is meant by this phrase "...that this is in turn transcended"? It is because the (next stage of meditation) starts off in the previous/lower mind condition and moves towards another condition which is (relatively) freer from desire and attachment.

Are the "limitless space operational field" and so forth so called because limitless space etc. are actually focussed upon (during meditation)? No. The first three are called *limitless space* etc. because the mind is anchored by evoking these terms, through repeating "limitless space" etc. during preparatory practice, i.e. during the approaching profound absorption. Later, when the approaching stage is over, there is no such mind anchoring. The last of the four is so called because of its inferior cognition. Although there is barely any lucid cognition one cannot say that there is absolutely none at all.

All the eight actual absorptions are concentrated, virtuous mind. They are given here as the teaching on unwavering concentration as action (cause and consequence). The *ratnavali* says:

"It is through dhyâna, the infinite[1], the formless, that the happiness of the brahmâ (realms) etc. is experienced."

Thus it is the three kinds of tainted action[2] that give rise to the substance of samsâra.

3. Actions make one's own lot

The consequences of actions that one has oneself done will be experienced by oneself: they come to maturity in the aggregates of the one who did them and in no one else. In the *abhidharma-samuccaya* it is said:

---

1. the 4 infinite contemplations *(brahmâvihâra)*

2. virtuous, unvirtuous and unwavering, as just described in the chapter. One needs to distinguish between these three—which give rise to samsâra with its respective joys, sufferings and god realms—and untainted action, which is devoid of notion of self. See note on **tainted**, p. 72.

"What does it mean, 'action makes one's own lot'? Because one experiences the full maturation of actions done by oneself and since that shares nothing in common with others, it is called 'one's own'."

Were this not the case, then karma (action) could dwindle or become exhausted or one might encounter evil consequences from acts not committed by oneself. This is why the sûtra say:

"The deeds committed by Devadatta will not come to maturity in the earth or in water etc. They will come to maturity solely in his very own aggregates and operational fields. In those of whom else could they possibly come to maturity?"

4.   Actions strictly determine experiences

One will infallibly experience happiness and suffering as the respective consequences of one's virtuous or sinful actions. By having established[1] virtuous action, one experiences happiness as a result. By having established unvirtuous action, one will experience suffering as a result. The *abhidharmasamuccaya* says of this:

"How will one's experience be determined? One is subject to the fully-developed result of one's actions, experiencing shares which correspond specifically to the virtuous or unvirtuous actions that one has done."

The *dran.pa.nyer.bszag.chung.ba* says:

"Through virtue one obtains happiness. Through non-virtue suffering occurs. This is why virtuous and non-virtuous actions and their consequences have been clearly taught."

---

1. **established karma** means an action that meets with all the requirements for being able to produce a result. The factors that need to come together—such as intention to do, satisfaction with, the action etc.—are sometimes listed as six. Once these factors come together, the action establishes an imprint in the mind that will ineluctably lead to a result, one day, unless purification takes place. The term *bsags*, translated here as "established," is more currently translated literally as "gathered".

And in the *surataparipṛcchāsūtra*:

"From the seeds of pungent plants will develop pungent fruits: from sweet seeds, sweet plants. Wise and skilful people should take this as an example and know the full consequence of sin to be like the bitter and the full consequence of pure action to be like the sweet."

5.   Great results can be created by a small cause

In terms of sinful action, this means that it is even possible, as has been taught, that a single moment (of bad action) can cause an age of hell to be experienced. As is said in the *bodhicaryāvatara*:

"The Sage has said that whoever generates a malevolent intention against such a one, the benefactor, the bodhisattva, will stay in hell for as many ages as there were moments of bad mind."

It is also said that one will experience suffering for 500 existences for each outburst of bad speech, and so forth. The *udānavarga* says:

"Even though one may have done a small bad action, in a future existence it can create much fear and a lot of damage: it is as though a poison had got into one's system."

It is also the case that even a small virtuous act can induce great consequence. The *udānavarga* says:

"Even the doing of a small wholesome act can produce great happiness in future existences and have great consequences: it is like grains that produce most abundant harvests."

6.   Karma never just fades away

Except for cases where an action has been properly remedied, it will not be lost or become any the weaker even though the karmic result of that action may not ripen for endless[1] ages. Although one may have enjoyed a state of ease for a considerable

---

1. **endless** this is not to be taken literally. "Endless" means 10^{60}.

time, whenever the relevant circumstances are encountered and whatever they may be, the result will be induced.

If one is convinced of the link between actions and their consequences, as explained above, and one fears samsâra's sufferings, then, as it is said:

> "One who turns his or her back on worldly pleasure, turns away from harmful action and strives solely for their own peace—such is the middle type of person leading a meaningful life[1]."

The "middling" person, who cultivates such an approach would be the likes of the seven girls of King Krai.Ka Thus it is said in the *karmaśatakasûtra:*

> "The actions of physical beings are not lost or weakened even (should they lie dormant) for a hundred ages. Once they have been established, whenever the appropriate time comes, their result will occur."

In the *dren.pa.nyer.bzhag.chung.ba* it says:

"Fire may become cold,
the wind may be caught by a lasso,
sun and moon may fall down,
but the consequence of karma is infallible."

This concludes the sixth chapter, concerning action, as cause and consequence, of this Gems of Dharma, Jewels of Freedom.

---

1. "leading a meaningful life" has been chosen to translate the Skt: *purusa* here.

Chapter Seven:

Loving Kindness and Compassion

the remedy to clinging to the well-being of mere peace

"Clinging to the well-being of mere peace[1]" signifies the *lower capacity[2]* attitude wherein the longing to transcend suffering[3] is focussed on oneself alone. This precludes the cherishing of others and hence there is little development of altruism. As it is said: "When one's own welfare takes priority, by thinking, *In order to really benefit myself I must drop all the various things needed to be done to help others*, then self interest has taken control."

When loving kindness and compassion become part of one, there is so much care for other conscious beings that one could not bear to liberate oneself alone. Therefore there is a need to cultivate loving kindness and compassion. Master Manjuśrîkîrti has said:

"A *mahâyâna* follower should not be without loving kindness and compassion for even a single moment" and

"It is not anger and hatred but loving kindness and compassion that vouchsafe the welfare of others."

---

1. The Tibetan *zhi.ba* means "peace." It is translated as "mere peace" in this section of the book, since it is used by Gampopa to denote the relatively compassionless peace that results from developing only concentration meditation.

2. **hinayana**: "lesser capacity" often translated as "lesser vehicle". The terms implies the ability to carry a burden. In this case the burden is oneself since one's commitment is to bring only oneself to liberation, not everyone (as is the case in the mahayana, the "greater capacity").

3. i.e. attain nirvâna

THE DEVELOPMENT OF LOVING KINDNESS

The first of these two topics is loving kindness. The synopsis for this section is:

"Limitless loving kindness is well summarised by six topics: its categories, its frame of reference, the form it takes, the means for cultivating it, its measure and its qualities."

1. Categories

There are three:

1. loving kindness with sentient beings as its frame of reference,
2. loving kindness with the nature of things as frame of reference,
3. loving kindness without frame of reference.

It says of these, in the *akshayamatipariprcchāsūtra*:

"Loving kindness focussed upon sentient beings is that of *bodhisattvas*[1] first cultivating *bodhicitta*.[2] Loving kindness focussed upon the nature of things is that of the *bodhisattva* well established in practice and loving kindness without any frame of reference is that of *bodhisattvas* who have attained the ability to 'forbear'[3] the uncreated'."

2. Frame of reference

This present work will only explain loving kindness with all sentient beings as its frame of reference, i.e. loving kindness as benevolence.

---

1. bodhisattva: *Bodhi* is enlightenment—the ultimate achievement for oneself and that which helps others more than anything else can—and *sattva* means someone with a courageous mind. A *bodhisattva* is someone who has the determination and courage to work towards enlightenment so as to be of real use to other beings.

2. bodhicitta: Behind this small word lies a mountain of explanations. *Bodhi* is the word for enlightenment and *citta* is the word for mind. *Bodhicitta* can refer to the enlightened mind and also to the mind working towards enlightenment. The chapters that follow are all about bodhicitta.

3. This refers to bodhisattvas who have reached the 3rd level of the second of the five major stages of the path to enlightenment: see later chapter on levels and paths.

3.   The form it takes

It is an attitude wherein one longs for (all sentient beings) to encounter happiness.

4.   The way to cultivate loving kindness

Remembering kindness is the root of love. Thus one considers the kindness of sentient beings. In this context, the one who has been kindest of all to us in this life is our own mother. In what way? She has been kind by generating our body, kind through undergoing hardships, kind by nurturing our life-force and kind in teaching us the ways of the world. The *astasâhasrikâ-prajnâ-pâramitâ* says:

"Why is this? This mother gave birth to us, she underwent hardships, she gave us our lives and taught us all about the world."

The kindness of creating our body

This body of ours did not start out fully grown in size, its flesh fully-developed and with a healthy complexion. It developed inside the mother through the different embryonic and foetal stages, being gradually created and nourished by vital fluids coming from her very own flesh and blood. It grew thanks to the nourishment coming from the food she ate. It came into being by her having to put up with all sorts of embarrassment, sickness and sufferings. Furthermore, generally speaking, it was she who helped make this body, which started out a tiny infant, into (its present) bulk as big as a yak.

The kindness of undergoing hardships

At first we did not come here clothed, finely adorned, with money in our pocket and with provision to travel. When we came into this unknown place, where we knew no one at all, we had nothing whatsoever — our only wealth was our howling mouth and empty stomach. Our mother gave us food so that we would not go hungry, drink to keep us from thirst, clothes to fend off the cold and wealth to keep us from poverty. It was not as though she just gave us things no longer of use to herself: she herself went without food, without drink and without new clothes.

Furthermore, not only did she sacrifice her happiness as far as this existence is concerned, she also deprived herself of using her assets (as offerings) to provide for her own prosperity in future lives. In brief, without regard to her own happiness, in both this life and the next, she devoted herself to rearing and caring for her child.

Nor was it the case that she obtained what was needed easily and pleasurably; to provide for her child she was obliged to sin, to suffer and to toil. She sinned by having to resort to fishing, killing animals and so on in order to care for us. She suffered because what she gave her child was the fruit of trading, labouring in the fields and so forth, wearing the late evening or early morning frost for her boots, the stars as a hat, riding the horse of her calves, beaten by the whip of the long grass, her legs exposed to the bites of dogs and her face exposed to the looks of men.

She also treated this stranger who has become her child with more love than her own father, mother or lama, even though she knew not who this being was or what it would become. She looked at her child with loving eyes, gave her gentle warmth, cradled him in her arms and talked with sweet words saying, "My joy, ah my sunshine, my treasure, coochi coochi, aren't you mummy's joy" and so forth.

The kindness of nurturing our life

It is not as though we were born as we are now, knowing how to feed ourselves and endowed with the necessary ability to accomplish difficult tasks. When we were helpless, useless little worms, unable to think, our mother did not discard us but did an inconceivable quantity of things in order to nurture our existence. She took us on her lap, protected us from fire and water, held us away from dangerous precipices, removed all harmful things and prayed for us. At those times when she feared for our life or health, she resorted to divinations, astrology, exorcisms, recitations of texts, special ceremonies and so on.

The kindness of teaching us the ways of the world

At first we were not the clever, experienced, strong-minded people we are now. Apart from being able to bawl out to other members of the family and flap our limbs about, we were quite ignorant. When we did not know how to feed ourselves, it was she who taught us how to eat. When we knew not how to dress ourselves, it was she who taught us. When we did not know how to walk, it was she who taught us. When we could not even speak, it was she who taught us, repeating "Mama, dada" and so on. Having taught us various crafts and skills, she helped us to become a balanced being, strengthening our weaker points and introducing us to the unfamiliar.

Furthermore, apart from being our mother in this life she has also been our mother in previous lives, an uncountable number of times, due to the unending round of existences that has been going on since beginningless time. The Beginningless Time Sutra says:

"Were one person to place a little juniper berry for every piece of earth, stone, plant or forest that there is in the world and a second person to count them, there would eventually come a time when the count would be completed. Were one, however, to try to count the number of times that one being has been our mother, it would be impossible."

The *suhrllekha* says:

"If one reduced the earth to little balls, the size of juniper berries, their number would be smaller than the number of times any one being has been our mother."

One contemplates, in the way described above, each and every kindness shown by one's mother in former existences. Considering all that, our mother's kindness towards us is seen as being totally immeasurable. Bearing this carefully in mind, one cultivates the most sincere and wholesome attitude towards her—a state of mind that longs for her to be happy.

Besides this, all sentient beings have been our mothers and have all shown us the same kindnesses as were enumerated above. Just how many sentient beings are there? As far as space stretches, there are sentient beings. The *bhadracaryâpranidhânamahârâja paribandha* says:

"Whatever the furthest end of space may be, that is the extent of sentient beings' existence."

Therefore one must cultivate a sincere, strong mind that longs to benefit and bring happiness to all beings throughout space. When that has arisen, it is true loving kindness. The *mahâyâna-sûtrâlankâra* says:

"A *bodhisattva* acts towards sentient beings as though they were his only child, with a loving kindness so great that it comes from the very marrow of his bones. In such a way, he wishes to constantly benefit them."

Great loving kindness is benevolence so strong that it brings tears to the eyes and makes the hairs of the body stand on end. *Limitless loving kindness* occurs when one no longer discriminates between beings.

5.   The gauge of accomplishment

One has achieved loving kindness when one's sole wish is for others to be happy and one's mind is (hence) freed from wishing for one's own happiness.

6.   The benefits

The benefits of cultivating loving kindness are immeasurable. The *chandrapradîpasûtra* says:

"However many limitless offerings one makes to the Supreme Being, even filling a hexillion buddhafields, their merit will not equal the benefit coming from a benevolent mind."

The goodness generated by even an instant's practice of loving kindness are countless. The *ratnâvalî* says:

"The merit of giving, three times a day, every day, 300 meals fit for a king, cannot even begin to compare with that created by one tiny instant of loving kindness."

Until buddhahood is achieved, this practice will bear eight benefits. These are described in the *ratnâvalî:*

"One will be loved (1) and protected (2) by gods and humans. One's mind will be happy (3) and will encounter happy circumstances (4). Unharmed by poisons (5) and weapons (6), one will accomplish one's aims effortlessly (7) and be reborn in the *brahma* realms (8). Until such time as liberation is achieved, these eight benefits will be derived from loving kindness."

The practice of loving kindness also affords one excellent protection. This is illustrated in the story of Brahmadatta. It also affords excellent protection for others, as illustrated by the example of King Maitrîbala.

Once loving kindness has been attained, it will not be difficult to cultivate compassion.

THE DEVELOPMENT OF COMPASSION

The synopsis for this sub-chapter is:

"Limitless compassion is well summarised by six topics: its categories, its frame of reference, the form it takes, the means for cultivating it, its measure and its qualities."

1. Categories

There are three:

1. compassion with sentient beings as its frame of reference,
2. compassion with the nature of things as frame of reference,
3. compassion without a frame of reference.

▸ The first kind is compassion which arises through understanding the sufferings of beings in the lower states of existence.
▸ The second kind occurs when there is familiarity with the meaning of the Four Noble Truths and knowledge of the two domains of causality[1]: these counteract belief in permanent, concrete realities. Compassion arises through considering how other beings are unaware of cause and effect and take reality as concrete and lasting.
▸ The third kind occurs when one's own meditative penetration has brought realisation of the voidness of all phenomena. Extraordinary compassion then arises towards (other) sentient beings, who still believe in reality. As it says,

> "When, through the stable penetrative power of meditation, a bodhisattva's (practice) is perfected, special compassion arises towards those in the grip of the demon of belief in reality."

Of these three, we will only discuss here how to develop the first.

2. Frame of reference

This first type of compassion has all sentient beings as its frame of reference.

1.. i.e. the causes which create samsâra as a result and the causes which bring nirvâna as a result.

3.   The form it takes

It takes the form of an attitude wherein one longs for (all sentient beings) to become free from suffering.

4.   The way to cultivate compassion

Compassion is cultivated through reflections based upon one's own mother. Thus one imagines one's own mother right there, before one, being cut up by some people and beaten, boiled or burnt by others. Or perhaps her body is completely frozen with cold, to a point where it is covered with cold sores, blistered and cracked open. If this were the case, would one not feel compassion for her? Since it is a definite fact that those beings suffering in *hell* have also been our mothers and that they are currently enduring such sufferings, how can compassion not arise towards them too? One cultivates actual compassion by contemplating in this way and wishing those beings to be free from suffering and its causes.

Equally, were one's own mother to be there before one, tormented by hunger and thirst, afflicted by disease and pain, full of fear, utterly terrified and completely disheartened, would one not feel very much compassion for her? It is certain that those *deprived spirits* who suffer torments like these have all been our own mothers. How can one not feel compassion? Contemplate this and wish them to be freed from their sufferings.

Equally, were one's own mother to be here before one, old and withered by age, and yet nevertheless other people made her labour as a defenceless slave, beat her hard, killed or chopped her up alive, would one not feel great compassion? It is certain that beings born as *animals* are subject to these sufferings and they were formerly our very own mothers. How can one not feel compassion? Contemplate this and wish them to be free from suffering.

Equally, were one's own mother to be here before one, blind, standing near the edge of a precipice a thousand miles deep, unaware of her danger and without anyone who could lead her away or cry out "Be careful of the abyss!" and then she started heading towards the edge, would one not feel very great compassion? It is certain that *gods, demi-gods and humans* are all three standing at the edge of the abyss which is the lower states of suffering. Unaware of causality, they do not know that (to avoid falling) they must give up unwholesome action and practise virtue. As they do not benefit from the support of a good mentor, they fall into and experience the three lower realms. Since it is so hard to get out of those states, how can one not feel great compassion for them, for they too were formerly one's very own mother? One contemplates compassion thus and wishes them all to be free of suffering.

5. The gauge of accomplishment

Compassion has been achieved when one has cast off the shackles of cherishing oneself more than others and when there is a real, rather than merely verbal, longing that all beings may be liberated from suffering.

6. The benefits

The benefits of this practice are immeasurable. The "Text Discussing Avalokiteśvara Realisation" says,

"If there were one thing that could be placed in the palm of one's hand (to represent) all the buddhas' qualities, what would it be? Great compassion!"

The *dharmasangītisūtra* says,

"O Accomplished, Victorious, Transcendent One! It is like this: wherever the precious wheel of the universal monarch goes, it is automatically accompanied by all his attendant hosts.
O Buddha! Wherever the great compassion of the *bodhisattva* goes, all the enlightened qualities accompany it."

Also, it says in the *tathāgatācintyaguhyanirdesha,*

"O Master of the Secret Teaching (Vajrapani)! The all-knowing primordial essence-wisdom is rooted in compassion."

As taught above, through loving kindness one wishes for the happiness of all beings and through compassion one wishes them all to be free from suffering. When this is the case, one can no longer find contentment in striving for the happiness of peace for oneself alone[1]. Since one is happy to achieve buddhahood for the sake of all beings, this constitutes the remedy to clinging to the well-being of mere peace.

Once loving kindness and compassion have arisen, one will cherish others more than oneself. It is said that one who has understood suffering in his own being and strongly wishes for others' sufferings to end, is an excellent being. Among those who have become such "excellent beings" were Brahmin "Great Generosity" and so forth.

This concludes the seventh chapter, concerning love and compassion, of this Gems of Dharma, Jewels of Freedom.

---

1. the nirvana attained by śrāvaka and pratyekabuddha.

HOW TO DEVELOP PERFECT BODHICITTA

the remedy to ignorance of the means for becoming enlightened[1]

As a remedy to not knowing the means needed for achieving enlightenment, there now follow various teachings on how to develop *bodhicitta*[2]: the mind set on supreme enlightenment. The synopsis for this section is:

"The development of supreme bodhicitta is covered through 12 topics: basis, nature, different types, aim, cause, source from which the vow is taken, ceremony, benefits, failings, causes for breaking, methods of restoration and instructions."

I. Beings who constitute a suitable basis for the cultivation of bodhictta

These are those who:

1. possess a mahâyâna potential,
2. have taken refuge in the Three Most Precious Refuges,
3. keep one of the seven classes of *individual liberation*[3] vow and
4. have developed the aspiration for enlightenment.

---

1. This is a very important heading, launching the next 150 pages of text. However, in terms of the book's structure, it is neither one of the six main parts nor one of the 21 chapters.

2. bodhicitta: for want of a satisfactory English translation of this term, the Sanskrit has been kept. Henceforward, it will not be italicised in the text. The problems (in finding an equivalent) stem from the many senses of the root bodh and citta and from the fact that, as explained above, this term applies to both the mind striving for enlightenment and the mind which rests in enlightenment: meaning that simple translations such as "enlightened attitude" or "awakening mind" are always inadequate and partial.

3. **self-liberating**: Skt. *pratimokśa*

Whereas to have taken refuge in the Three Precious Refuges is the minimum requirement for one's life becoming a suitable basis for **aspiration bodhicitta,** the above four conditions make one's life a proper basis for also cultivating **practice bodhicitta.** Why is this? It is explained in the *bodhisattvabhûmi* that aspiration must precede actual practice and it is explained in the *bodhipathapradîpa* that one needs to have taken refuge in order to develop aspiration. Furthermore, the latter text also states that one needs one of the individual liberation commitments as a foundation for practice bodhicitta and the *abhidharmakośa* says that refuge is the basis upon which the individual liberation vows are taken. Lastly, the *bodhisattvabhûmi* says that bodhicitta development cannot even occur in those who do not have the mahâyâna potential. Thus a combination of all these various factors must be present.

1.1 The first point, the need for mahâyâna potential, has been explained above in the cause/buddha nature chapter.

1.2 The second point concerns the need to have taken refuge.

Chapter Eight:
Taking Refuge

Should one seek refuge in powerful worldly deities, such as Brahma, Vishnu, Shiva etc. or in local forces such as gods or nâga that inhabit mountains, rocks, lakes, ancient trees and so forth? These are not true refuges because none of them has the power to be a refuge. A sûtra says of this,

"People of the world seek protection from the gods of the mountains and forests, from shrines and offering groves and from sacred trees but these refuges are not true refuges."

Should one then perhaps seek refuge in one's parents, friends, relatives and so forth — those beings who care for and are willing to help one? In fact, these cannot be a refuge either. It says, in the *manjushrîvikrîditasûtra*:

"Parents are not your refuge; neither are loved ones or relatives. They abandon you to go wherever they please."

Why are none of these able to provide refuge? Because in order to be a refuge, they must be without fear of samsâra and be liberated from its sufferings. None of the above have transcended fear and they are still subject to suffering. Other than **buddhas**, no one is definitively liberated from suffering. Other than **dharma**, there is no way to achieve buddhahood. Other than the **sangha**, there are none who can help us practise dharma. Hence one should take refuge in those three. It is said:

"Today, take your refuge in the Buddha, in the dharma and in the supreme community, the sangha, for it is they who make the fearful dispel their fears and it is they who provide protection for the unprotected."

Since they do possess the ability to protect, do not let yourself be devoured by doubt, wondering, "Can they really protect us once we have taken refuge in them?" The *mahâparinirvânasûtra* says:

> "One who has taken refuge in the Three Precious Refuges will attain fearlessness."

The synopsis explaining refuge in those three is:

"Taking refuge is summarised through nine topics: categories, basis, source, duration, motivation, ceremony, function, instruction and benefits."

1.   Categories

There are two different kinds of refuge: general and particular.

2.   Basis[1]

There are two types of individual who form a basis for taking refuge:
1.   those who constitute the *common basis;* individuals who fear samsâra's sufferings and who conceive of the Three Precious Refuges as deities and
2.   those constituting the *particular basis*; individuals of mahâyâna potential who have a fairly pure human or divine existence.

3.   Source

There are also two sources of refuge:

1. THE COMMON SOURCE: The *most precious buddha* is the Victorious[2] Accomplished Transcendent One, Awakened Plenitude[3], who has the most excellent purity, primordial wisdom and greatness of nature. The *most precious dharma* has two aspects, namely the *dharma*

---

1. **basis**: refers to a person globally, in terms of their whole life, their overall state of mind. Sometimes this word is almost interchangeable with "existence".

2. **Victorious Accomplished Transcendent** This translates the single Sanskrit word *bhâgavan*, (Tib. *bcom.ldan.'das*), which conveys all these three meanings. It is a very respectful epithet for the Buddha.

3. **Awakened Plenitude** This is a literal rendering of the Tibetan *sangs.rgyas*, the two syllables of which render two of the senses of the Sanskrit root *bodh.* from which we have the word "Buddha".

of teachings, comprising the twelve branches of (the Buddha's) supreme speech, and the *dharma as realisation,* comprising the truths of the cessation and the path. The *most precious sangha* is also twofold: the sangha composed of worldly individuals—a gathering of four or more bhiksu who have properly maintained their vows—and the most excellent sangha—the eight types of being belonging to the four stages of result[1].

2. THE PARTICULAR SOURCE: This is explained as:

a. the source actually present,
b. the source that is direct realisation and
c. the ultimate source.

2a. The source actually present is the Buddha, as an image of the tathâgata, the dharma as mahâyâna scriptures and the sangha as the bodhisattva sangha.

2b. The source in terms of direct realisation The *Buddha* is the one possessing the nature of the three kâya, the *dharma* is the sublime dharma of peace and nirvâna and the *sangha* are bodhisattvas established in the levels of sublime realisation.

2c. The ultimate source In terms of the ultimate essence only the Buddha is the source of refuge. About this the *mahâyanottaratantrashâstra* says:

"In terms of the ultimate, the refuge of beings is Buddha and Buddha alone."

Why is the Buddha capable of providing the (only) totally dependable source of refuge?

"Because the Sage possesses the **dharma**kâya and, in terms of the sangha, he is the ultimate **sangha**."

The Sages, free from generation and cessation, totally pure and without desire, are the highest refuge because they possess the dharmakâya and because they are the ultimate achievement of the

---

1. The four groups are: stream entrant, once-returner, non-returner and arhat. These each have two subsections: those who achieve the state and those who fully enjoy its fruition.

sangha of the three yâna, having attained the dharmakâya, the ultimate conclusion of total purity. Then are the dharma and the sangha lasting refuges or not? The *uttaratantra* says:

"The two aspects of dharma and the most excellent sangha are not the supreme lasting refuge."

Why are they not a lasting source of refuge? Of the two types of dharma, the *dharma as teachings* is a collection of terms and an assembly of letters, and as such is something to be abandoned once it has served its purpose, like a vehicle once the journey is done. So it is not a lasting refuge. As for the two aspects of *dharma as realisation*, the truth of the path is not a refuge because it is by its very nature unreliable, being impermanent on account of being a composite creation. The truth of cessation is not a lasting refuge because, as it is held to be by the śrâvakas, it is a non-existence, the end of a continuum, like the extinction of a flame. As for the *sangha*, they themselves take refuge in the Buddha through fear of samsâra and cannot constitute a supreme and lasting refuge because of having that fear. The *uttaratantra* says:

"Because of having to be abandoned, because of being an unreliable phenomenon, because of being non-existent and because of being afraid, the two aspects of dharma and the most excellent sangha are not a supreme and lasting refuge."

Thus Master Asanga said:

"The inexhaustible refuge, the permanent refuge, the eternal refuge, the most elevated refuge is one and one only. What is that? It is the Tathagâta, the Arhat, the totally and utterly perfect Buddha."

Well then, does this not contradict what has been said above about the three refuges? The latter originated as a skilful method for guiding those training as Buddhists. The Great Liberation Sûtra says:

"In brief, the refuge is one but, in terms of method, is three."

As skilful method, how are these three refuges presented? The *uttaratantra:*

"The three refuges are presented as *teacher, teaching* and *those training*[1], in terms of the three yâna, activities and aspirations."

Thus the refuges are presented in terms of three qualities, three yânas, three modes of action and three types of aspiration:

1.   To emphasise the *quality* of the teacher and for followers of the bodhisattva *yâna* and those who *aspire* to focus their *actions* principally upon the Buddha, the refuge is the Buddha: "I take refuge in the Buddha, the most sublime of humans."

2.   To emphasise the qualities of the teachings and for followers of the pratyekabuddha yâna and those aspiring to act in a way that focusses principally on dharma, the refuge is the dharma: "I take refuge in the dharma, the most sublime of all that transcends desire and attachment."

3.   To emphasise the qualities of the trainees and for followers of the śrâvaka yâna and those who aspire to act in a way principally focussed on the sangha, the refuge is the sangha: "I take refuge in the sangha, the most sublime of communities."

Thus the above three points present the three refuges in terms of six types of person[2]. The Victorious Accomplished Transcendent One has taught that these are mere conventional realities, designed to help beings progress gradually through their respective courses of training.

4.   Duration

There are two. The common[3] duration is to take refuge from that time onwards for as long as one lives. The particular duration is to

---

1. **"those training"**: an interesting definition of the sangha. It shows that even the highest of bodhisattvas are still on the way to total perfection and purity. They are analysed through the first four of the five stages of the "path". The fifth stage, Buddhahood, is that of "no more training".

2. **six types of person**: those of the three yâna and those whose acts are directed towards the Buddha, dharma or sangha.

3. **common** in the sense of shared, i.e. common to all Buddhists.

take refuge from that time onwards, up until one reaches the essence, enlightenment.

5.   Motivation

There are two. The common motivation is to think that one cannot bear oneself to suffer. The particular motivation is to think that one cannot bear others to suffer.

6.   Ceremony

There are two: the common and the particular.

6A   COMMON CEREMONY

First the refuge-seeker requests refuge from the teacher. Then the teacher either makes offerings to the Three Precious Refuges as a prelude to the ceremony, or else, when there are no representations present, visualises them in space and makes mental homage and offerings. Then the refuge-seeker repeats the following, three times, after the teacher, with utmost sincerity:

> "All Buddhas and bodhisattvas, please heed me I pray. Master, please heed me, I pray. I, ... by name, take my refuge from now until I reach the essence, enlightenment, in the Buddha, the most sublime of all humans, in the dharma, the most sublime of all that transcends desire, and in the sangha, the most sublime of communities."

6B   PARTICULAR CEREMONY

This is in three parts: a preparation, the actual ceremony and a conclusion.

Preparation

Having offered a mandala, together with flowers, to an appropriate preceptor, one requests him to confer refuge. Provided that the supplicant be a suitable person and one with mahâyâna potential, the preceptor will accept the request and on the first evening set up representations of the Three Precious Refuges, arrange the offerings and explain both the benefits of taking refuge and the shortcomings of not doing so.

The Actual Ceremony

This takes place on the second evening. First one cultivates the notion that the (symbols of refuge) set up before one are the real presence of the most precious (refuges) and then pays homage and makes prostration (to them). Then one repeats the following words three times, after the preceptor:

"All Buddhas and bodhisattvas, please heed me, I pray. Master, please heed me, I pray. I, ... by name, from this moment on until the enlightened essence is reached, take my refuge in the Buddhas, the Victorious Accomplished Transcendent Ones who are the most sublime beings on two legs. I take refuge in the dharmas which are peace and nirvana, the most sublime of all that is free from desire and attachment. I take refuge in the sangha of realised bodhisattvas who are beyond turning back, the most sublime of communities."

Then, inviting the sources (of refuge) in terms of direct realisation and imagining them to be really present, one pays homage and makes offerings, thinking, "Whatever I do, please think of me." Following this, one repeats the refuge prayer, as above.

Then, in terms of the one-and-only essence as a source of refuge, one pays homage, makes offerings and takes refuge in a way in which the three spheres[1] are totally pure: since, from the very beginning, all phenomena have been without self and without any truly-existing nature, one must envisage the Buddha, dharma and sangha as also being thus. This is the inexhaustible refuge, the permanent refuge, the eternal refuge. Thus the *anavataptanâgarâja-pariprcchâsûtra* says:

"What is it to have taken refuge with a mind free from pollution (of belief in reality)? By knowing all phenomena not (truly[2]) to

---

1. **three spheres** These are subject, object and interaction between these two.

2. **truly exist:** Things normally exist merely dependently and impermanently. They *depend* on other relative phenomena for the *temporary* nature of existence they exhibit. This is relative existence. For something to exist truly in its own right, the characteristics of its existence should not have to depend on other phenomena and it would have to be lasting.

exist, by not envisaging them as being form, as possessing characteristics or as being something but as being totally pure "awakened plenitude" (*Buddha*) one has taken refuge in the Buddha. By envisaging all phenomena as consequent on dharmadhâtu, one has taken refuge in the dharma. By not envisaging the composite and the unfabricated as two separate things, one has taken refuge in the sangha."

Conclusion

On the third evening, there is the concluding ceremony, during which one makes thanksgiving offerings to the most precious (sources of refuge).

7.   Function

It says, in the *mahâyânasûtrâlankâra:*

"It is the highest refuge because it protects one from all sorts of harm, from the lower states, from ineffective courses of action, from the *perishable and composite*[1] and from inferior ways."

The common refuge protects one from all harms, from falling into the lower states, from ineffective courses of action and from the *perishable and composite* philosophical views. The particular refuge protects one from the lower paths as well as all of those.

8.   The instructions

There are nine: three common instructions, three particular instructions and three specific instructions.

8A   THREE COMMON[2] INSTRUCTIONS

One should at all times strive to makes offerings to the three precious refuges, at least offering the first mouthful of one's food

---

1. "perishable and composite" (Tib: *'jig.tshogs*) A literal translation of the term used to describe all the various types of philosophy/attitude based on a notion of self. The are four basic ways of ideating self in terms of any of the five aggregates, making 20 main types of view possible.

2. i.e. common to all three refuges.

when eating. One should never abandon the three precious refuges even should this cost one's life or involve personal loss. One should develop the habit of repeatedly calling to mind the qualities of the three jewels and taking refuge in them.

8B THREE PARTICULAR[1] INSTRUCTIONS

Having taken refuge in the Buddhas, one need no longer seek refuge from any other deity[2]. The *mahâparinirvânasûtra* says:
"The best of all lovers of virtue are those who have taken refuge in the Buddhas. They will never go soliciting refuge from any other divinities."

Having taken refuge in the dharma, one should no longer do any harm to sentient beings. A sûtra says:
"Having taken refuge in the noble dharma, one is far removed from a mentality of harm and violence."

Having taken refuge in the sangha, one should not put one's trust in the misguided[3]. The sûtras say:
"Those who have taken refuge in the sangha will not side with the misguided."

8C THREE SPECIFIC[4] INSTRUCTIONS

One should show respect for images of the tathâgata, whatever they may be, from a small image moulded in clay upwards,

---

1. **particular** i.e. one for each particular refuge.

2. **deity/divinity** It is not correct to refer to the Buddha as a "divinity". Gods (devas) are samsaric beings. Buddha is neither samsaric nor a being. The word is used here very broadly and could be translated as, "not take refuge in deities or other religious entities".

3. **misguided** Tib. *mu.stegs.pa* Skt. *tirthika* This general term refers to people whose religious or philosophical beliefs and practices are based upon delusion. If we assume that buddhism is, as it claims to be, the exposition of universal truth, then this means, by definition, all non-Buddhists. Some translators use terms such as "heretics" to translate this word. However, it has a positive rather than negative connotation, inasmuch as it indicates spiritual commitment that is slightly misfounded, with the implication that this is better than no commitment at all. The specific teachings of other religions that coincide with Buddhist ones—universal love, generosity etc.—fall outwith the definition of this term. See note p. 30.

4. i.e. one for each refuge specifically.

because they represent the real most precious Buddha. One should show respect for the volumes and collected works of scripture, from a mere letter of text upwards, because they represent the most precious dharma. One should show respect for Buddhist garb, from a simple patch of yellow cloth upwards, because it represents the most precious sangha.

9.   The Benefits

There are eight (principal) benefits which come from taking refuge:

1.   one becomes a Buddhist[1],
2.   it is the basis for all the commitments[2],
3.   all the evils one has formerly committed will be consumed[3]
4.   one will not be affected by hindrances created by humans or non-humans,
5.   one will achieve all one's material aims,
6.   one will become endowed with great merit, the cause for
7.   one not falling into the lower states and
8.   one becoming truly and perfectly enlightened.

The first point, in this overall section on the persons who constitute a **basis** for bodhicitta, was the necessity for mahâyâna potential. The second point was the need to have taken **refuge**, explained above. The third point is the need to have taken one of the "individual liberation" (pratimokśa) **commitments**.

1.3   Vows of Individual Liberation

There are four main types but, in terms of the individuals who take them, these make eight. Of these, if one discounts the

---

1. the text actually says something which reads literally as "one of awakened plenitude, an 'inner'". Buddhists are within the truth whereas others stray beyond it and are "outsiders".

2. other Buddhist commitments such as precepts, bodhisattva vow, vajrayana vows etc.

3. not necessarily immediately but in time, as a logical consequence of what the refuge process is setting up.

upavasatha [Tib. bsnyen.gnas] short-term partial fasting commitment, there are seven types. Whichever one of these seven is appropriate is adopted. The seven classes of individual liberation commitment are:

bhikṣu	[Tib. Gélong[1]]	full male ordination
bhikṣunî	[Tib.Gélongma]	full female ordination
śiksamâna	[Tib. Gélopma]	female ordination[2]
śramanera	[Tib Gétsul]	male novice
śramanerikâ	[Tib. Gétsulma]	female novice
upâsaka	[Tib. Gényen]	layman's precepts
upâsikâ	[Tib. Gényenma]	laywoman's precepts.

The *bodhisattvabhûmi* says of these:

"The seven categories of those who have most properly adopted the precepts of individual liberation are these: those (observing) the right conduct of the bhikṣu, the bhikṣunî, the śiksamâna, the śramanera, the śramanerikâ, the upâsaka and the upâsikâ. According to their content, these precepts are those of laypersons or renunciates, as appropriate."

Someone doubting the need for being committed to individual liberation precepts in order to be able actually to practise bodhicitta, should develop understanding of the necessity of keeping those precepts as a basis (for bodhicitta) in three ways: by **simile**, by **scriptural authority** and by **reason**.

1. By simile

The place to which one invites a great universal monarch to come and stay should not be filled with impurity such as dung and rubbish. It should be an excellent and good dwelling place, spotlessly clean and decorated with many fine adornments made

---

1. The way the Tibetan sounds is given here.. The actual word, and those which follow immediately below are respectively: *dge.slong,   dge.slong.ma,   dge.slob.ma,   dge.tsul, dge.tsul.ma,   dge.bsnyen* and *dge.bsnyen.maē*

2. There is no male equivalent of this set of precepts. As the bhikkhuni tradition was lost in Tibet, this was an alternative ordination held by Tibetan nuns.

of precious substances and so on—a pleasing place. Likewise, when one is cultivating the great monarch bodhicitta and hoping for it to remain, the "place" where it can abide is not in an individual who is not committed to avoiding wrong physical, verbal and mental action; not in one who is tarnished by the stains of evil. It is to be invited to reside in someone without the stains of physical, verbal and mental evil; one whose physical existence is properly adorned with the right conduct of commitment.

2.   By scriptural authority

It says, in the bodhicitta section of the *mahâyâna-sûtrâlankâra*, "Its basis is extensive commitment."   The upavasatha (see above) commitment is one of limited extent, as it only lasts for a day and a night. Unlike this, the (other) seven classes of precept are commitments of great extent and this is why those seven are taught as constituting the foundation for bodhicitta. Further, the *bodhipathapradîpa* states:

"Those who have the lasting commitment of the seven classes of self-liberation precepts as their other vows, are suitable for the bodhisattva vow: not so others."

This is explained as meaning that one needs to have whichever one of those seven types is appropriate.

3.   By logical necessity

Through the self-liberation precepts, one abandons harm to others, along with its basis. Through the bodhisattva vow, one is benefitting others. There is no way in which one can benefit others without first renouncing harming them. However, according to some people the self-liberation vows are not necessarily a prerequisite for giving rise to the bodhisattva vow because hermaphrodites, eunuchs, gods and so on who are *unable* to take the self-liberation precepts *are able* to give rise to bodhicitta. Some also assert that the self-liberation precepts cannot be a prerequisite because they expire at death, whereas the bodhicitta does not. If one wonders about these points, one should understand that the self-liberation precepts fall into three categories, determined by the attitude in which they are taken:

a. when these vows are taken because of a motivation to reach happiness in the three dimensions of existence they are called the *right conduct of vested interest,*

b. when they are taken with the wish of ridding oneself of suffering forever they are known as the *right conduct of srâvaka renunciation* and

c. when they are taken because one wishes to achieve great enlightenment they are called the *right conduct of the bodhisattva vow.*

The first two of the above cannot be taken by hermaphrodites, eunuchs, gods etc. They finish at death and cannot be restored if damaged and so are not the foundation for the bodhisattva vow. The *right conduct of the bodhisattva vow* can be taken by hermaphrodites, eunuchs, gods and so on, is not lost at death and can be restored if damaged. For these reasons it is the prerequisite for both taking and keeping the bodhisattva vow. Thus it says in the commentary to the *mahâyânasûtrâlankâra:*

"What is the foundation of that mentality? The vow of bodhisattva right conduct is its foundation."

Therefore pratimokśa is needed as a basis for giving rise (to bodhicitta) but not necessarily required as a continuous basis for maintaining bodhicitta.

"This is a similar case to the dhyâna bond being a necessary basis for giving rise to the 'untainted bond' but not necessarily required for the latter's continuance."[1]

There is no need to take the bodhisattva self-liberation precepts through a special ceremony. If they have already been taken as part of śrâvaka training, they will still be extant when one's mind

---

1. At first, one needs to discipline oneself somewhat in order for concentration meditation to produce its results. Vows designed to reduce attachments play an important role in this (see meditation chapter). Eventually a natural disgust with attachment arises through profound meditative absorption and this is the basis for a naturally developing purity. Once that purity is stabilised, it automatically precludes attachment and the more artificial anti-attachment means are no longer needed.

has the special inspiration (of bodhicitta) and will (automatically) become the bodhisattva's self-liberation commitment, since the lesser motivation will have been abandoned but not the spirit of renouncing wrong.

Thus we have seen that someone who has mahâyâna potential, who has taken refuge in the three most precious refuges and who has taken whichever is appropriate of the seven classes of self-liberation vow is suitable for giving rise to bodhicitta.

This concludes the eighth chapter, concerning refuge and taking precepts, of this Gems of Dharma, Jewels of Freedom.

Chapter Nine:

The Proper Adoption of Bodhicitta

II The Essential Nature of Bodhicitta Development

It is clearly defined in the *abhisamayâlankâra:* "Developing bodhicitta means longing for true, perfect enlightenment in order to benefit others."

III The Different Types of Supreme Bodhicitta

These are described in three ways; by simile, according to what demarcates levels and according to characteristic.

IIIA SIMILE

How bodhicitta can be typified from that of an individual, through to that of a Buddha, was taught by the noble one, Maitreya, in the *abhisamayâlankâra:*

> "These are the 22 examples: earth, gold, the moon, fire, a treasure, a jewel mine, an ocean, a vajra, a mountain, medicine, a spiritual mentor, a wish-fulfilling gem, the sun, music, a king, a treasury, a great highway, a steed, an inexhaustible spring, a harp, a great river and a cloud."

These twenty-two similes cover the main thrust of bodhicitta from (initial) aspiration through to (final) dharmakâya: they will be presented in terms of the five phases of the path.

---

1. When bodhicitta is endowed with **aspiration,** it is like **earth,** being the very stuff which forms the foundation for all good qualities.
2. When bodhicitta is endowed with **commitment,** it is like **gold:** it will not change until enlightenment is achieved.

3.   When bodhicitta is endowed with **profound commitment,** it is like a **waxing moon**: every virtuous quality will increase.

The above three constitute the beginners' stage, i.e. the lower, middle and higher sections of the phase of accumulation[1].

4.   When bodhicitta is endowed with **integration,** it is like **fire,** burning as its fuel the blockages to the three sorts of omniscience[2].

The above represents the stage of junction.

5.   When bodhicitta is endowed with the **pâramitâ of generosity,** it is like a **great treasure** bringing satisfaction to all beings.

6.   When bodhicitta is endowed with **the pâramitâ of right conduct,** it is like a **jewel mine,** providing the ground for precious qualities.

7.   When bodhicitta is endowed with **the pâramitâ of forbearance,** it is like a **great ocean,** untroubled by whatever unwanted thing falls into it.

8.   When bodhicitta is endowed with **the pâramitâ of diligence,** it is like a **vajra,** strong through being unbreakable.

9.   When bodhicitta is endowed with **the pâramitâ of concentration meditation,** it is like the **king of mountains,** unshaken by distractions due to mind's objects of attention.

10.   When bodhicitta is endowed with **the pâramitâ of prajnâ,** it is like **medicine,** calming the sicknesses which are the defilement and knowledge obscurations.

11.   When bodhicitta is endowed with **the pâramitâ of skilful means,** it is like a **spiritual mentor,** never relenting from bringing benefit to beings, no matter what the circumstances.

12.   When bodhicitta is endowed with **the pâramitâ of prayer,** it

1. the five stages of the "path" to enlightenment are those of accumulation, integration, insight, cultivation and the ultimate stage—Buddhahood. These are explained in detail in chapter 18.

2. total knowledge of the basis—the non-existence of individual self, total knowledge of the path—knowing all paths and phenomena as unborn—and total knowledge of everything.

is like a **wish-fulfilling gem**, achieving whatever result one wishes.
13. When bodhicitta is endowed with **the pâramitâ of powers**, it is like the **sun**, bringing disciples to full maturity.
14. When bodhicitta is endowed with **the pâramitâ of jnâna**, it is like the **melody of dharma**, giving disciples dharma teachings which inspire them.

The ten points mentioned above are grouped according to the ten bodhisattva levels, from the first, "Joy Supreme", to the tenth, in due order. These cover the stage of insight (1st-7th levels, points 5-11) and the stage of cultivation (8th-10th levels, points 12-14).

15. When bodhicitta is endowed with **clear awareness**, it benefits others like a **powerful king**, because its power is unimpeded.
16. When bodhicitta is endowed with **goodness and jnâna**, it is like a **treasury**, becoming a storehouse of many accumulations.
17. When bodhicitta is endowed with **the factors conducive to enlightenment**, it is like a **great highway**, as one treads the way that all the noble ones have trodden.
18. When bodhicitta is endowed with **great compassion and deeper insight**, it is like a **steed**, travelling directly to its goal without straying into either samsâra or nirvâna as mere peace.
19. When bodhicitta is endowed with **dharâni and prowess**[1], it is like a **reservoir**; everything learnt through study or otherwise will be retained and not wasted.

The above five points constitute the special bodhisattva path[2].

---

1. **dharâni** and **prowess** (Tib: *gzungs* and *spobs*) For a more detailed explanation of these see the *mkhas.'jug* of Mipam Rinpoché. Dharâni means "retention" and is somewhat like mantra: it starts with sounds being invested with associated meanings which trigger memory and ends up as the power of mantra. Prowess is accumulated skill, making great tasks possible.

2. these are special qualities possessed by bodhisattvas in the 8th-10th levels, known as the "pure" levels.

20. When bodhicitta is endowed with the **"beautiful garden of dharma"**, it is like **listening to a fascinating musical instrument**, its sound being melodiously uplifting to disciples intent on liberation.

21. When bodhicitta is endowed with **"the one and only way"**, it is like the **current of a great river**, never diverted from its purpose of benefitting others.

22. When bodhicitta is endowed with the **dharmakâya**, it is like a **raincloud**, because the benefitting of beings depends upon it, through its demonstrating (deeds) such as residing in Tusita etc.[1]

These last three points refer to the stage of Buddhahood. Thus the 22 similes cover everything from the beginners' level through to that of Buddhahood.

IIIB   IN TERMS OF WHAT DEMARCATES LEVELS

This categorisation is fourfold:

- ► bodhicitta endowed with aspiration,
- ► bodhicitta endowed with profound commitment,
- ► bodhicitta in its full maturity and
- ► bodhicitta with obscurations eliminated.

The first of the above corresponds to the levels of practice motivated by aspiration; the second applies to the first seven (mahâbodhisattva) levels; the third to the eighth through to tenth levels and the fourth to the level of Buddhahood.

Thus the *mahâyânasûtrâlankâra* says:

"Bodhicitta in its various levels is held to be accompanied by aspiration, pure profound commitment, full maturity and elimination of all obscurations."

---

1. referred to here are the 12 deeds of the nirmanakâya, which form the basis for all the teachings.

IIIC IN TERMS OF ESSENTIAL CHARACTERISTICS

This is twofold: **ultimate bodhicitta** and **artificial bodhicitta.**[1]
As the *sandhinirmocanasûtra* says: "There are two aspects to
bodhicitta: ultimate bodhicitta and quite artificial bodhicitta."

What is **ultimate bodhicitta?** It is voidness with compassion as
its essence, clear and unwavering, free from speculative extremes.
Therefore the *mahâyânasûtrâlankâra* says:

> "Of those, ultimate bodhicitta transcends the world, is without
> any speculative extreme, is extremely clear, has the ultimate
> meaning as its object, is unpolluted and is unwavering, as bright
> as a steady flame when there is no breeze."

And what would be **bodhicitta that is artificial** (relative
bodhicitta)? Quoting the same sûtra:

> "Artificial bodhicitta is the commitment, through compassion, to
> lead all sentient beings out of samsâra."

Of the two forms of bodhicitta mentioned above, ultimate
meaning bodhicitta is that of those who have attained (realised) the
universal essence (dharmatâ). Artificial bodhicitta is something
adopted, in the proper way, and which arises via token meanings.[2]
(The former) is well explained in the *mahâyânasûtrâlankâra.*

> "At what stage is there ultimate bodhicitta?—from the first
> mahâbodhisattva level 'Supremely Joyous' onwards."

The commentary to the *mahâyânasûtrâlankâra* says:

> "This ultimate meaning bodhicitta is that of those of the first
> level, Joy Supreme."

---

1. These two terms are now very commonly called **ultimate bodhicitta** and **relative
bodhicitta**. A fairly literal translation has been kept here to show the strength of the term
used in Tibetan for relative bodhicitta—*kun.rdzob*—which means "quite artificial" or "a total
fake".

2. The two forms of bodhicitta are contrasted here. Whereas ultimate bodhicitta is naturally
present, artificial bodhicitta is adopted. Ultimate bodhicitta is non-conceptual voidness full
of natural meaning, whereas artificial b. relies upon conceptual conventions as meanings.

In terms of categories, artificial bodhicitta has two aspects: **aspiration bodhicitta** and **application bodhicitta**. Thus the *bodhicaryâvatâra* says:

"That (type of) bodhicitta, in brief, should be known as (being) of two kinds—aspiring to enlightenment and actually applying oneself to enlightenment."

There are many different explanations of the particularities of these two aspects of relative bodhicitta—aspiration and application. According to Master Śantideva, of the tradition stemming from Arya Manjuśri through Master Nagârjuna, *aspiration* is like a wish to go and comprises in reality all the intentions which long to attain perfect Buddhahood, whereas *application* is like the actual going and is in reality the practical application of all that will achieve Buddhahood. Thus the *bodhicaryâvatâra* says:

"Just as one knows the difference between wanting to go and actually going, so the sage should distinguish between these two respectively."

According to Great Dharmakîrti, of the lineage stemming from Arya Maitreya through Master Asanga, *aspiration* is to take a promise committing oneself to the result, thinking, "For the benefit of all sentient beings I will attain perfect Buddhahood," whereas *application* is to take a promise committing oneself to the cause, thinking, "I will train in the six pâramitâ, as the cause of Buddhahood." In line with this interpretation, the *abhidharmasamuccaya* says:

"Bodhicitta development is of two types: unextraordinary and extraordinarily excellent. Of these, the unextraordinary one means thinking, *Oh, if only I could become totally enlightened in insurpassable, totally pure and perfect Buddhahood.* The extraordinarily excellent one means thinking, *May I totally perfect the paramitâ of generosity* ... and so forth through to the paramitâ of supreme awareness."

IV   The Focus of Bodhicitta

Its focus encompasses enlightenment and the benefit of beings.

The *bodhisattvabhūmi* says of this

"Hence bodhicitta is that which is focussed upon enlightenment and that which is focussed upon sentient beings."

Of these two, *bodhicitta focussed upon enlightenment* is that which is focussed upon striving for mahâyâna primordial awareness. In the chapter on developing bodhicitta, in the *mahâyâna-sûtrâlankâra*, it says:

"...likewise that which is focussed upon its primordial awareness."

That which is *focussed on sentient beings* does not mean focussed on just one, two or several beings: wherever there is space, there is conscious life and wherever there are sentient beings, there is action *(karma)* and defilement *(kleśa)*. Wherever the latter pervade, suffering pervades also and bodhicitta is developed in order to remove those beings' sufferings. Thus the *bhadracaryâpranidhâna* says:

"Whatever the limits of space may be, such are the limits of sentient beings. Such are the limits of action and defilements and, furthermore, such are the limits of my aspirations."

V   The Causes for Bodhicitta Development

The *dasadharmakasûtra* says:

"That mind will arise on account of four causes: insight into the benefits and qualities of such a mentality, faith in the tathâgata, seeing the sufferings of sentient beings and proper encouragement from one's dharma mentors."

Further, the *bodhisattvabhūmi* says:

"What are the four causes of that?

1. The first cause for the arising of the bodhisattva mind is that of the very best potential.
2. The second cause for the arising of the bodhisattva mind is to be properly supported by the Buddhas, bodhisattvas and by dharma mentors.
3. The third cause for the arising of the bodhisattva mind is

compassion for sentient beings.

4.   The fourth cause for the arising of the bodhisattva mind is fearlessness in the face of samsâra's suffering and the sufferings of undergoing hardships, even though these may be long enduring, manifold, difficult to cope with and without respite."

It is said in the *mahâyânasûtrâlankâra* that there are separate causes for the generation of two aspects of bodhicitta:

▸   that which is the cause for generating bodhicitta as *something most properly received and occurring through token meanings* and
▸   that which is the cause for generating *ultimate* bodhicitta.

Of these, the former is explained as something *taught by others* and occurring due to both *enduring* and *non-enduring* causes, through *the power of dharma support, the power of the prime cause, the power of the root, the power of learning* and through *being habituated to virtue.*

This "generation of bodhicitta which is *taught by others*" is artificial bodhicitta, also known as "that which is most properly received and which occurs through token meanings", since it is a state of mind received thanks to the intelligent awareness of others. The *power of dharma support* is that which occurs through the presence of dharma teachers. The *power of the prime cause* is that which arises through the ability of potential (Buddha nature).

The *power of the roots* of virtue[1] is that which occurs through activation of that potential. The *power of learning* is that which occurs through dharma terminology and explanations of its meanings. *Being habituated to virtue* refers to that which occurs through whatever has been consistently studied, directly understood, firmly adhered to etc. in this life. Of the above, that which occurs in the presence of dharma teachers is non-enduring and that which occurs through

---

1.   **roots of virtue.** The specific result created by ordinary action depends upon many momentary factors, such as the action itself, the motivation of the moment etc. The action, good or bad, <u>generates result potential only while it is being enacted</u>. Certain enduring states of mind however, and in particular those created by dedicated commitment such as vows and precepts, are <u>constantly generating results</u> until such time as the commitment ceases, <u>whether one is actually doing something or not</u>. These latter are called "roots" of virtue because, like a root, they constantly support growth and fruition

the power of the prime cause and the other powers is enduring.

Concerning the causes for ultimate meaning bodhicitta occurring, it is said that:

"It is held to be ultimate because it occurs through a primordial awareness of phenomena that is non-conceptual; this through having well pleased the perfect Buddhas because one has supremely established accumulations of wholesomeness and primordial awareness."

This ultimate bodhicitta is generated through the particular qualities of scriptural authority, achievement in practice and realisation.

VI   The Source from which one Adopts the Bodhisattva Mind

There are two ways (of taking the bodhisattva commitment): one involving a preceptor and one without a preceptor. If it poses no obstacle to life or one's practice of purity, one should go to a preceptor, when there is one, and take the commitment personally, even if that person is far away. The characteristic qualities of such teachers are:

▸ to be skilled in the ritual ceremony for administering the vow,
▸ to have received the vow themselves and to have kept it unimpaired,
▸ to be able to make one understand the meaning of the ritual's physical gestures and words and
▸ to be those who nurture their disciples, with love and without involvement in materialism.

Thus it says, in the *bodhipathapradīpa:*

"Take the commitment from a good guru, one with the very best characteristics: a good lama should be known as someone skilled in the ceremony for taking the vow, who has himself kept whatever the vow entails and who gives the vow patiently and compassionately."

The *bodhisattvabhūmi* says:

> "Those who, through having practised the bodhisattva prayer, are in accord with dharma, have taken the vow, are skilled, know how to communicate the meaning of the ritual words and know how to make the disciple understand..."

Even should such a lama reside close by but there be the possibility of some obstacle to life or purity occurring by going to him, then there is the "lama-less" (method). For this, one stands before an image of the tathâgata and recites sincerely three times the words of the aspiration or application bodhicitta vow, whichever is appropriate. Thereby one receives the aspiration or application vow. Thus, in the *bodhisattvabhūmi:*

> "Should it happen that there be no such individual with the requisite qualities, bodhisattvas go before an image of the tathâgata and most properly take the commitment of bodhisattva right conduct by themselves."

If one can find neither a preceptor nor a Buddha image, one recites the words of the aspiration or application bodhicitta vow three times in front of Buddhas and bodhisattvas that one meditates upon as being really present, assembled in space before one. Thus the *śikṣâsamuccaya* says:

> "Further, should there be no such mentor, one meditates that the Buddhas and bodhisattvas dwelling in the ten directions are really present. One obtains the vow by the strength of one's own mind's application."

VII   The Ceremony for Adopting Bodhicitta

Many ways and traditions of taking the bodhisattva vow have appeared, evolving from the specific styles of instruction of the lineages originating from the great learned gurus. Though there are many, the subject matter here concerns the two (main) traditions: **Dharma Master Santideva's tradition**, of the lineages passed down from Arya Manjusri to Master Nagârjuna, and **Dharma Master Dharmakirti's tradition** of the lineages passed down from Arya Maitreya to Master Asanga.

Master Santideva's Tradition

—of the lineage passed down from Arya Manjusri to Master Nagârjuna, has a ceremony in three stages: it consists of a preparation, the actual giving of the precepts and a conclusion.

THE PREPARATION

This is in six parts:

- making offerings,
- regret for past wrongs,
- appreciation of virtue,
- request to Buddhas to teach dharma,
- praying to the Buddhas not to abandon the world and
- dedication of roots of virtue

1. Offerings

These need to be understood in terms of both those to whom offerings are made and the offerings themselves. Those to whom one offers are the (three) most precious Refuges. Since it is explained that making offerings to them (creates) the same merit whether one is actually in their presence or not, one makes offering to those present and to those not actually present. Thus the *mahâyânasûtrâlankâra* says:

> "With a mind filled with faith one makes real and imaginary offerings, of robes and so forth, to the Buddhas, in order to complete the two accumulations."

As for the offerings (themselves) there are two types: surpassable and insurpassable offerings.

SURPASSABLE OFFERINGS—are also twofold: offerings of material goods and of realisation.

a. material offerings These entail offering prostrations, praise, material offerings neatly and properly set out in the right order and also things that belong to no one in particular. These can be actual things, of good quality, as well as creations of one's imagination and the offering of one's own body. Such offerings may be studied in detail in other works.

b. realisation as an offering   This entails offering mahâmûdra meditation of the sublime bodies[1] and the various dispositions that emerge from the profound absorptions of the bodhisattvas.

INSURPASSABLE OFFERINGS are twofold: those involving the idea of objective realities and those without such ideas.

a. objectified offerings—this is bodhicitta meditation, as is said:

> "The wise and skilful totally familiarise themselves with bodhicitta. This is the highest offering one can make to the Buddhas and their sons."

b. unobjectified offerings—meditation within egolessness, the supreme offering. Therefore it says, in the chapter on teachings requested by the young god Susthitamati:

> "Were one bodhisattva, desirous of enlightenment, to make offerings to the Buddha, the best of all humans, offering quantities of flowers, incense, food and drink equivalent in number to the grains of sand on the banks of the river Ganges, so doing for ten million cosmic ages, and were another such bodhisattva to offer his study of the teachings on the non-existence of ego, life and personality, along with the resulting achievement of being able to endure clear lucidity—it would be the latter bodhisattva who made the better offering."

It also says, in the "Lion's Roar Sûtra":

> "Not to create ideas or descriptions is to make offerings to the Tathâgata. To be without adopting or rejecting and to penetrate that which is non-dual is to make offerings to the Tathâgata.

---

1. **sublime bodies**—*lha'i.sku*. The various representations of wisdom-beings and facets of the enlightened mind are called *lha* in Tibetan. This term is often literally translated as "deity", a term avoided here as it could lead to confusion, especially in comparison with theistic tantra.

Friends! since the very character of the Tathâgatakâya is to be insubstantial, one does not make offerings by considering it to be substantial."

This concludes the section on making offerings.

2. Removing the Effects of Past Wrongs

Generally speaking good and evil depend upon the mind's motivation: mind is the master and body and speech are its servants. The *ratnâvalî* says:

"Since mind precedes all things, it is often said, *Mind is master*."

Hence when the mind is motivated by a defiled state—desire, anger etc.—one may commit the five irreprievable wrongs, the five like them or the ten bad actions or one may break vows or one's profound samaya commitments or perhaps incite others to do such things; even if one does not do these things personally, one may rejoice in the fact that others are perpetrating evils like them. All the preceding are what is meant by the terms *wrong* and *non-virtue*. Not only those (manifestly wrong actions) but even dharma activities such as study, contemplation or practice that are motivated by a mind under the sway of desire, anger and the defilements also become non-virtue. Thus the *ratnâvalî* says:

"Whatever is generated by the three factors—desire/attachment, anger/hatred and ignorance—is non-virtue. Through non-virtue there is suffering and likewise all that belongs to the lower states."

Further, the *bodhicaryâvatâra* says:

"From non-virtue will arise suffering. The correct thing to do, day and night and in every circumstance, is to contemplate one thing and one thing alone: "How can I attain definite release from this?"

This is the reason why every past wrong needs to be laid bare. Will facing up to one's wrongs actually purify them though? Most definitely! The *mahâparinirvânasûtra* says:

"Although one may have committed a wrong, a later regret will put things right, much in the same way as certain precious substances restore water's clarity or as the moon recovers her brilliance when emerging from clouds" and

"Hence it is by disclosure of wrong-doings, with regret and without dissimulation, that there will be purity."

In what way exactly should one expose one's own wrong-doings? By applying the four powers. Thus it says, in the Sûtra which Teaches the Four Qualities:

"Maitreya! If a bodhisattva mahâsattva has these four things, they will overcome evils that have been committed and established[1]. What are these four? They are these:

▸   the power of thorough application of true regret,
▸   the power of thorough application of remedy,
▸   the power of renouncing evil and
▸   the power of support."

1. THE POWER OF THOROUGH APPLICATION OF TOTAL REGRET

This is to disclose sincerely and with ardent regret, in the presence of the refuges, the wrongs one has done in the past. How can one stimulate regret? There are three ways:

a. giving rise to regret through considering pointlessness,
b. giving rise to regret through considering fear and
c. giving rise to regret through considering the urgent need for purification.

1a. regret through considering pointlessness

One reflects, "I have committed wrongs—sometimes in order to subdue my enemies, sometimes to protect my friends, sometimes for the sustenance of my own body and sometimes to accumulate

---

1. **established** — any action (karma) that one has done and that sows, in the continuum of one's being, a potential for future results is said to have been "established". This term is often translated as "gathered" but the actual mean is that of being lastingly established—implanted—in one.

material wealth. However, when the time comes to move on to another life, i.e. when I die, my enemies and friends, my country and my body and my wealth and possessions will not accompany me. Yet I *shall* be shadowed by the wrongs and obscurations created by my negative actions: no matter where I am reborn these will rise up as my executioners." This is why the *viradatta-grhapati-pariprcchâsûtra* says:

"Father, mother, brothers, sisters, spouse, servants, wealth and acquaintances cannot accompany someone who dies but their actions do go with them and trail after them." It also says: "When great suffering comes, children and spouse offer no refuge. One experiences the agony alone and they cannot share one's lot."

The *bodhicaryâvatâra* says:

"We must go leaving everything behind. Unconscious of this, we commit various wrongs for the sake of the ones we love and on account of those we dislike. However, those we like will cease to exist, those we dislike will cease to exist and even we ourselves will cease to exist: in such a way does everything come to the end of its existence."

Thus we have committed wrongs for the sake of those four: friends, enemies, our body and possessions. Those four will not be around us for very long, yet for them we have made wrongs which bring much trouble and little benefit. Contemplating the reality of this, great regret will arise.

Should one consider that even if wrong actions are of little benefit they will not really bring harm back upon oneself, one should contemplate the second point:

1b. Regret through reflection upon fear

Thinking, "The consequence of wrong is fear," one will feel regret. Wrong actions result in three main times of fear: fear prior to death, fear when actually dying and fear after death.

Prior to death, those who have committed wrongs will experience unbearable sufferings, feeling struck to their very marrow etc. It is said:

"As I lie on my bed, I may be surrounded by my friends and relatives but it is I and I alone who will experience the feelings of life coming to its end."

At the time of actual death, the result of wrong-doing is fear. (One experiences) the henchmen of the Lord of Death, black and horrible beings brandishing lassos, coming to place their lassos around one's neck so as to lead one off to hell. Later, others bearing sticks, swords and all sorts of weapons, torture and torment one in all sorts of ways:

"When grabbed by Yama's henchmen, what use relatives, what use friends? At that time merit alone provides shelter and merit have I none."

The *sisyalekha* says:

"Having locked time's noose around our necks, Yama's ferocious henchmen prod us with sticks and drag us along."

One who thinks, *I shan't be afraid of Yama's henchmen* should reflect as follows: "If, when the time comes for them to be taken to the place where their limbs will be hacked off, people become terror-stricken and dry-mouthed, with their eyes bulging and bloodshot and so forth, then what need to mention the unspeakable horror and reactions of one gripped by fear when the time of transformation (death) comes and they are seized by the totally terrifying emissaries of the Lord of Death, apparent as if in flesh and blood."

As a consequence of wrong-doing, there will also be fear **beyond death**. Once one has descended into the great hells, one experiences the unbearable sufferings of being boiled, burnt and so on and thus is quite terrified:

"Seeing hells depicted, hearing about them, remembering what one has heard about them, reading about them and seeing models of them makes one shudder with fear—then no need to mention how it will be when one actually experiences the unbearable fruition of one's acts and is reborn there."

Thus one will come to regret wrong-doing by understanding the terrible fear that results from it.

1c. Regret through realising the urgency (for purification)

If one thinks that it will probably suffice to rectify one's wrong-doings at some later time, one needs to realise that it will not suffice at all and that one needs to atone urgently. Why? Because there is a distinct possibility that death will come before one's wrongs have been purified. It says:

"I pray with extreme urgency for refuge, that there may be certainty of liberation from my wrongdoings, for death may well occur before these are purified."

If one thinks that somehow one will not die before misdeeds have been purified, then one should consider this: the Lord of Death will not bother in the least about how many misdeeds have or have not been purified—he will steal one's life away whenever the opportunity presents itself; the time of one's death is uncertain. Thus it says:

"It is wrong to feel so confident. My death will not wait for me to finish the things I have to do. As far as this ephemeral life is concerned, there is certainty for no one—sick or healthy."

Since those who do not realise the uncertainty of their life-span are quite likely to die without having cleared up their misdeeds, one should purify all wrongs as soon as possible. The risk is very real, so one should give rise to great regret (for the wrongs one has committed). When sincere regret has been stimulated by the three contemplations described above, one should admit misdeeds and ask for purification, before either the common or special sources[1].

"Thus the power of total repentance will purify misdeeds, just as a plea from someone who cannot afford to repay a debt to a rich man may persuade him to wipe out that debt."

---

1. The common sources could be the Three Precious Refuges. The special sources would be the likes of Vajrasattva in vajrayâna practice.

There was once a bad person known as "Finger Garland" (Angulîmâla). Even though he had committed grave misdeeds —killing 999 people—he managed to purify his errors and achieve the state of Arhat by practising this power of thorough application of total and utter regret:

"Once someone who previously did not care learns to care, they become beautified, like the moon breaking free from clouds—as was the case with Nanda, Angulîmâla, Ajâtashatru and Udayana."

2. THE POWER OF THE THOROUGH APPLICATION OF REMEDY

Virtuous actions are the remedy for misdeeds. They will consume impurities. Thus the *abhidharmasamuccaya* says:

"Actions with antidote power will prevent corresponding misdeeds from coming to unwholesome fruition, because their remedial ability transforms the consequence into something else."

It is said in the Treasury of the Tathâgatas that cultivating (awareness of) voidness purifies misdeeds. The Diamond Cutter says that misdeeds will be purified by reciting the profound scriptures. The *trisamayavyûharâja* and the *subâhupariprcchâtantra* says that misdeeds will be purified by reciting mantras. The *pushpakûta-nâmadhâranî* says that faults are purified by making offerings to the tathâgatas' stupas. It is also said, in the section on Buddha images, that making images of the tathâgata will purify misdeeds. Elsewhere it is said that listening to teachings, reading or writing out the scriptures and so forth—whichever one feels for most—will also purify wrong actions. The *vinayâgamotta-viśesâgama-prashnavrtti* says:

"Whosoever has committed evil action but then annihilates it through virtue, shines in this world like the sun or moon emerging from clouds."

One may wonder about this, thinking, "If engaging in virtue is the antidote for evil, then does one have to enact an equivalent quantity of good as one has done bad?   Not so. The *mahâparinirvânasûtra* tells us:

> "Even a single virtuous act overcomes many evils," and
> "Just as a small vajra can destroy a mountain or a little fire can
> burn down a forest or a minute amount of poison can kill
> beings, likewise a small good action can overcome a great
> wrong; it is highly efficient!"

The *survanaprabhâsottamasûtra* explains:

> "Someone may have committed unbearable evils for a thousand
> ages, yet should they make just one perfect confession, this will
> purify all their wrongs."

As is said, "Thus misdeeds will be purified by the power of
thoroughly applying remedies. It is, for example, like someone who
has fallen into a putrid swamp but who, once out of the swamp,
bathes and is annointed with perfumed oils."

There was once a nobleman's son called Udayana. Even though
he had killed his own mother, he managed, through this power of
thoroughly applying a remedy, to purify himself of his misdeeds,
to be reborn as a deva and obtain the dharma result of "stream-
entrant".

> "Once someone who previously did not care learns to care,
> they become beautified, like the moon breaking free from
> clouds—as was the case with Nanda, Angulîmâla, Ajâtashatru
> and Udayana."

3. THE POWER OF RENOUNCING EVIL

Fearful of the full consequences of one's actions, one will desist
from wrong action henceforth:

> "You, guides of humanity, please remove these evils I have
> committed. These misdeeds are bad indeed; I shall never do
> them again."

As is said, "The power of renouncing evil will purify misdeeds,
just as diverting a dangerous river removes the threat from a town."

Once there was a person called Nanda who harboured much desire for women. Even though he had committed wrongs, through practising this power of renouncing evil his faults were purified and he attained the state of being an Arhat.

"Once someone who previously did not care learns to care, they become beautified, like the moon breaking free from clouds—as was the case with Nanda, Angulîmâla, Ajâtashatru and Udayana."

4. THE POWER OF SUPPORT

This comes from taking refuge and developing bodhicitta. Seeking shelter in the three most precious Refuges will purify misdeeds. It says, in the *sûkarikâvadâna,*

"Those who have taken refuge in the Buddhas will not take birth in states of suffering. Having left their mortal bodies, they will obtain celestial ones."

The *mahâparinirvânasûtra* says:

"One who has sought refuge in the three most precious Refuges will attain fearlessness."

The development of bodhicitta will purify misdeeds. The *gandhavyûhasûtra* says:

"...will put an end to all unvirtuous actions, like burying them for good, and will burn up all evil, like the fire at the end of the aeon."

The *bodhicaryâvatâra* also tells us:

"The support of someone strong and fearless can free one from fear. Likewise, one who is so supported will be quickly liberated, even though they may have committed unbearable wrongs. How could those who care not rely on such support?"

Thus the power of support purifies faults. "The support of refuge could be compared to that of a strong person helping weak followers. The support of bodhicitta development could be compared to the neutralisation of a powerful poison by the appropriate mantra recitation."

There was once a prince called Ajâtashatru who had committed the great evil of parricide. Nevertheless he was purified through the power of support and became a bodhisattva.

"Once someone who previously did not care learns to care, they become beautified, like the moon breaking free from clouds—as was the case with Nanda, Angulîmâla, Ajâtashatru and Udayana."

Since each of the above four powers is capable of purifying misdeeds, no need to even mention how effective all four together will be as purifiers. In actual practice, those who do admit and repair their wrongs, in the ways explained above, experience signs of their purification in dreams. In the *cundhadhârant* it explains:

"Dreams of the following are signs of breaking free from fault: vomiting bad food or drinking milk or yoghourt or the like; seeing the sun and the moon; flying in the sky; seeing a blazing fire; seeing buffalo; seeing a dark powerful person or an assembly of monks or nuns; seeing a milk-producing tree; seeing elephants or mighty bulls; sitting on a mountain, a lion throne or the roof of a mansion; listening to dharma teachings etc."

This concludes the explanation on the disclosure of misdeeds.

3. Rejoicing in Virtue

One should cultivate a joyous appreciation of all the virtuous actions of sentient beings throughout the three times[1]. One contemplates, thinking:

"I rejoice in all the roots of virtue established by every one of the

---

1. [see Mipham's "Entering the Sages' Wisdom" Kagyü Samyé Ling]: chapter on time. Although the three times are commonly presented as past, present and future, quite what this means can be explained severally—in terms of linear time, the unfolding of karma etc.

limitless, inconceivable enlightened beings who appeared in the past, throughout the universe, from those of their first generating bodhicitta all the way through to their perfect enlightened plenitude, due to their amassing the two accumulations[1] and purifying the two obscurations[2]. I further rejoice in whatever roots of virtue were produced subsequent to their enlightenment, from the time that they turned the wheel of dharma[3] in order to bring to maturity those ready for instruction until the time they manifested leaving the world of suffering. I also rejoice in the roots of virtue generated by their teachings between their parinirvana[4] and the eventual disappearance of their teaching, as well as in the virtue produced by whatever bodhisattvas appear in the interim period before the manifestation the the following Buddha. I further rejoice in whatever roots of virtue were produced by accomplished pratyekabuddhas who appeared and likewise those of the śrâvakas that appeared. Further, I rejoice in the roots of virtue generated by ordinary individuals."

By contemplating joyfully in the above way, one cultivates appreciation. In a like fashion, one nurtures similar thoughts with respect to the virtuous actions being performed in the present moment and those that will be performed in the future. In each

---

1. virtue and wisdom

2. the **defilement obscuration**, i.e. the grosser impure mind activities of passion, aggression, ignorance and their offshoots, and the **cognitive obscuration**, the more subtle thought habits which give rise to the former and which obscure awareness of mind's true nature.

3. To **"turn the wheel of dharma"** means to teach the universal truths that constitute the Buddha's, and in fact all the Buddhas', teachings. The image of the wheel turning evokes a movement that is now as it always was and will be—truths to do with the nature and workings of mind itself rather than the changing social phenomena that are mind's imagery of the moment. For instance, the mind gets attached to acquiring objects: whether that object be a caveman's flint or a computer, the nature of attachment itself is the same and it is about attachment, rather than flints and computers, that Buddhism teaches. As long as there will be minds, its message will remain fresh and relevant.

4. **parinirvâna** — the relative demonstration—death from a human point of view—of leaving their human existence and entering the total peace of their spiritual accomplishment. It has to be relative because the actual condition of their mind is the eternal changeless nature, beyond birth and death, coming or going. See "Changeless Nature": Kagyü Samyé Ling.

instance one trains in cultivating joyous appreciation. As is said,

> "I rejoice in the Enlightenment of all the (Buddhas our) Protectors and also in the levels of (attainment achieved by the bodhisattvas,) the Victors' spiritual heirs.

4. Requesting that the Wheel of Dharma be Turned

In all the worlds of the ten directions[1] there are many Buddhas who have not taught the dharma. Addressing them in one's mind, one offers the request for the dharma to be taught: "With hands joined, I beseech the Buddhas throughout the directions. Please light the torch of dharma for all beings obscured in the darkness of suffering." Thus is it said[2].

5. Supplicating the Buddhas not to Pass Away from the Worlds in Suffering

At present there are Buddhas in the worlds of the ten directions who are on the point of entering their parinirvâna—in order to stimulate those who believe in permanence to abandon their misconceptions and to inspire those who are lazy to diligence. With these in mind, one supplicates them not to pass beyond their worlds in suffering:

> "I pray with joined hands to those Victorious Ones who are considering passing from their particular worlds in suffering that they do not leave all those beings in blindness but remain with

---

1. **Ten directions** simply means, in such a context, throughout space. The directions are N, S, E, W, NE, SE, SW, NW, the zenith and the nadir.

2. This, and the next topic, can seem a little strange to some people, who wonder why Buddhas need to be requested to give teachings and not to pass into nirvana. They feel that when and where to teach or to die should depend upon the Buddhas' wisdom and not upon ordinary people's requests. It jars a little with the idea of spontaneous buddha activity. The point is this: one performs these six preparatory contemplations in order to make one's own mind positive and appreciative and in order to overcome a weakness or lack of awareness. In these two instances one is developing one's own positive appreciation of the teaching and reminding oneself of the Buddhist ethic of non-proselytising (requesting the turning) and training in appreciating time spent in the presence of the wise (requesting not to pass away).

them for countless ages."

6. Dedication of the Roots of Virtue

One dedicates all these previous roots of virtue that they may remove the sufferings of all beings and that they may become the cause for their achieving happiness:

"May all such good actions and whatever virtue I have gathered clear away the sufferings of all beings."

This and the above concludes the explanation of the preparatory stage of the bodhisattva vow ceremony.

2. THE ACTUAL CEREMONY

According to the *siksasamuccaya*, when Arya Mañjuśrî was King Amba, he took the pratimoksa and bodhisattva commitments together, from Buddha "Melody of Thunder". His formula is used to make the actual commitment:

"For as long as this beginningless samsara endures, I will accomplish a limitless quantity of actions to benefit all other beings. Before the Buddha, protector of the world, I dedicate my mind to supreme enlightenment."

These words are to be repeated three times. Also, following the way the (bodhicitta commitment is expressed) in the *bodhicarya-avatâra*, one takes the commitment by saying:

"Just as the Sugatas[1] of the past cultivated their minds towards supreme enlightenment so will I also gradually progress through the bodhisattva training. Likewise, having taken the commitment to reach enlightenment in order to benefit sentient beings, I also will train stage by stage in the relevant disciplines."

---

1.   **sugata**: an epithet of the Buddha, litt. "those passed into happiness".

This is repeated three times. Should one wish to take the commitments of aspiration and practice separately, then one should recite the words relevant to the aspect one wishes to undertake. This concludes the actual ceremony.

3. The Conclusion of the Ceremony

One should make offerings of thanksgiving to the most precious Refuges and give rise to great joy and delight by considering the very great benefit (that has been accomplished).

"Once reasonable people have taken the bodhisattva commitment with complete and clear trust, their new dedication should be held in high esteem, like this, in order that it may increase subsequently."

This and more is said. This concludes the explanations on the preparation, actual ceremony and conclusion for taking the bodhisattva commitment according to the tradition of Acarya Santideva.

Master Dharmakirti's Tradition

This is the way of the lineages passed down from Arya Maitreya to Master Asanga. It is in two parts: commitment to the bodhisattva aspiration and commitment to bodhisattva practice.

the vow of bodhisattva aspiration

Giving Rise to the Vow of Aspiration is in three parts: the preparation, the actual ceremony and its conclusion.

1. PREPARATION

This is also in three parts: requesting the vow, establishing[1] the accumulations and taking the special form of refuge.

1A   THE REQUEST

The person wishing to dedicate him- or herself to enlightenment should go to a properly qualified preceptor/mentor and pay homage. The mentor gives some instruction, instils a revulsion for samsara in the person and helps the supplicant experience compassion, aspire to enlightenment and feel increasing respect and devotion for the three precious Refuges and the gurus. The following formula is then repeated after the preceptor:

"Teacher, consider me with kindness. In the same way as the Tathâgatas, the Liberated Ones, the Perfectly Gifted and Victorious Ones of the past first raised the essential longing for true and perfect enlightenment, and as likewise did the bodhisattvas who are now actually established in the bodhisattva levels, so also I .... by name, in the same way, pray you, the teacher, to awaken in me the essential force for insurpassable, true, perfect and great enlightenment."

1B ESTABLISHING THE ACCUMULATIONS

First, one should prostrate to the rare and precious guru. Then one presents the material offerings that one has prepared for the occasion and any amount of mentally-created offerings and so forth.

It is taught that the *getsul (sramanera)* vow is received from a khempo together with a teacher, the *gelong (bhikkhu)* vows are received from the sangha and the two aspects of bodhicitta commitment are attained through the accumulation of virtue.

It would be inappropriate for someone who is wealthy to make

---

1.   most books translate this phrase as "gathering the accumulations". The term *bsags.* does literally mean "to gather" but in the abhidharma explanation of this term, we find that it means the coming together of certain factors needed in order for an act [karma] to produce a long term result, thereby establishing a potential in the base consciousness.

meagre offerings; such a person should offer on a grand scale. There were certain extremely wealthy bodhisattvas in the past who made vast offerings. There were even some who, when they gave rise to bodhicitta, took the vow making offerings as extensive as ten million dharma libraries. The Good Age Sûtra tells us:

"When the tathâgata Drajin was a monarch of Jambudvip, he first gave rise to bodhicitta having made an offering of ten million dharma libraries to the tathâgata Dawai Tok."

However, it is quite sufficient for someone who is not rich to offer little. In the past, some poor bodhisattvas offered very simply; there were even some who gave rise to bodhicitta making an offering of a rustic candle made from blades of dried grass.

"At a time when the tathâgata Radiant Light was a city dweller, he first gave rise to bodhicitta having made offering of a grass 'candle' to the tathâgata Limitless."

One who possesses nothing at all need not even make physical offerings. It suffices to make three prostrations. In the past there were certain bodhisattvas who had nothing and who awakened their bodhicitta having joined their hands in homage three times.

"The tathâgata Yonten Trengden made homage to the tathâgata Jiden Shu by joining his hands three times in salutation when he first gave rise to bodhicitta."

1C THE SPECIAL REFUGE

This is to be taken as explained already in a previous chapter.

B. THE ACTUAL CEREMONY

The teacher should instruct the person taking the vow as follows. He explains, "Wherever there is space there are sentient beings. Wherever there are beings, there are defilements. Wherever there are defilements, there is bad karma and whenever there is bad karma, there will be suffering. All those beings beset by suffering are actually our parents; all parents who have been exceedingly kind to us. All those former fathers and mothers who previously were so good are presently plunged in this powerful ocean of samsara, enduring immeasurable sufferings. With no one to protect them and be their refuge, they undergo terrible hardships and great pain. Thinking, "Oh, if only they could find happiness; if only they could get free from suffering," rest your mind in loving kindness and compassion for a while."

"Now think, 'At present, I have no power to help these beings. Therefore, in order to be able to come to their aid, I will achieve "pure and perfect enlightenment"—the ending of all that is wrong, the perfection of every quality, the power to accomplish a great benefitting of all beings, however many they may be.' Rest your mind in these thoughts for a while."

After this, one repeats the following formula thrice, after the preceptor:

"All Buddhas and bodhisattvas throughout the ten directions, pray consider me. I, ... by name, do now, by the power of the roots of virtue that I gathered in former lives through the practice of generosity, right conduct and meditation, through the roots of virtue that I have encouraged others to establish and through those which I have joyfully appreciated, take the commitment to reach insurpassable, pure and perfect enlightenment, in the same way as in the past the Tathāgatas, the Victorious Ones, the Pure and Perfect Buddhas, the Perfectly Gifted and Liberated Victors first took the commitment to reach pure, perfect and great enlightenment and as also did those bodhisattvas of the bodhisattva levels. So now, like them, will I, ... by name, from this moment until I reach the essence of enlightenment, awaken the force of insurpassable, pure and perfect great enlightenment in order to rescue beings who are to be carried over to liberate those who are not free, to let those who are holding their breath release it and to take completely beyond suffering those who have not yet completely gone beyond it."

The vow is taken through repeating the above words, after the teacher. (The significance of the words is as follows:)

▸ *those who are to be carried over* are hell-beings, deprived spirits and animals, since they have yet to cross the ocean-like sufferings of samsara.

▸ *to rescue* them means to free them from the sufferings of the three lower states and establish them in the higher states so that they can continue in human or divine existences.

▸ *those who are not free* are the humans and gods, since they are not yet free from the ties of the defilements, which are like shackles.

▸ *to liberate* means to help get them free from the bondage of the defilements by setting them on the path of liberation so that they can attain liberation.

▸ *those who have not yet let their breath out* are the śrâvakas and the pratyekabuddhas, because they have not yet relaxed into the mahayana path.

▸ *those who have not yet gone completely beyond suffering* are the bodhisattvas, because they have yet to achieve the nirvana which is rooted neither in samsara nor peace.

▸ *in order to* is the commitment to achieve Buddhahood in order to be able to accomplish all the above aims.

C. THE CONCLUSION

Cultivate great joy and delight, thinking that a tremendous and useful thing has just been achieved, and recite prayers according to the preceptor's instructions[1].

One who has thus developed the initial commitment of bodhicitta is called a bodhisattva. A bodhisattva has the wish to achieve enlightenment in order to benefit beings and the wish to liberate beings once enlightenment has been achieved. The focus of the intention embraces both enlightenment and (the welfare of)

---

1.   One may, for example, recite set prayers that reflect the joy of the great benefit of the bodhisattva vow for oneself and then prayers that invite other beings to be joyful too, as something wonderful for their benefit has just happened.

sentient beings: on account of both of these, the bodhisattva has determination, courage and clarity of purpose.

This concludes the traditional ceremony for giving rise to the aspiration for supreme enlightenment.

the vow of bodhisattva practice

This is also taken in three steps: preparation, actual ceremony and conclusion.

A. PREPARATION

This is in ten parts:

- ▸ the supplicant requests the vow,
- ▸ the preceptor enquires about any general obstacles there may be to taking it,
- ▸ the preceptor explains about the gravest causes of breaking the commitment,
- ▸ the preceptor talks about the bad consequences of letting the commitment degrade,
- ▸ and about the good consequences due to keeping it,
- ▸ the accumulations are established,
- ▸ the preceptor enquires about any specific obstacles (to taking the vow),
- ▸ encourages the supplicant,
- ▸ encourages the special motivation in the supplicant and
- ▸ gives some summarised instruction.

B. THE ACTUAL CEREMONY

In order to arouse in the supplicant the proper disposition for taking this vow, the preceptor says:
"My good child, do you wish to receive the following commitments

from myself, bodhisattva .... and to follow whatever was the basis of training and right conduct of all the bodhisattvas of the past, through which they accomplished their training; to follow whatever will be the basis of training and right conduct of all the bodhisattvas of the future, through which they will train; and to follow whatever is the basis of training and right conduct of all the bodhisattvas presently in this world?"

This is asked three times of the supplicant who thrice agrees.

C.   THE CONCLUSION

This is in four parts. Having requested the preceptor to look kindly upon one:

► he gives an explanation of the benefits of gaining insight into supreme wisdom,
► he explains about not letting another know about the commitment without oneself having first considered the suitability or otherwise of that person,
► he gives a brief summary of the instructions (related to the vow) and
► offerings are made to the preceptor out of gratitude for his kindness. The roots of virtue are then dedicated.

This concludes the explanation of the vow of bodhisattva practice and thus concludes the explanation of taking the bodhisattva vow according to Dharmakirti's tradition.

VIII   The Benefits of Developing Bodhicitta

These are of two types: imaginable and unimaginable.

1.   IMAGINABLE BENEFITS

These are themselves of two types: those arising from giving rise to the application and those arising from the commitment to practice.

1a. Imaginable Benefits arising from the Aspiration Vow are eightfold:

i.   one will enter the mahâyâna,
ii.   the vow will serve as the basis for all the other aspects of bodhisattva training,
iii.   it will completely eradicate all faults,
iv.   this unsurpassable root will plant itself firmly in enlightenment,
v.   one will gain unsurpassable merit,
vi.   one will please all the Buddhas,
vii.   all beings will be benefitted and
viii.   one will quickly achieve true and perfect Buddhahood.

i. Even though the conduct of someone may be the very best possible, if that person has not given birth to bodhicitta he or she has not yet entered the Great Way (mahâyâna). If one has not entered the mahâyâna, it will not be possible to attain Buddhahood. One who has awakened the bodhisattva mind becomes a mahâyânist. Thus it says in the *bodhisattvabhûmi:*

> "As soon as this power has been awakened, one has entered the mahâyâna, the great path which leads to unsurpassable enlightenment."

ii. If someone does not have the *aspiration*, the longing to achieve enlightenment, there will be little point in observing the three domains of discipline which are known as *bodhisattva training*. However, for someone who does so aspire, the adoption of the three disciplines and subsequent training in those disciplines constitutes the very foundation for doing what is necessary to fulfil their aspiration. The *bodhisattvabhûmi* says:

> "Giving rise to this attitude is the basis for all the bodhisattvas' training."

iii. Virtue is the remedy for previous wrongs. The best of all virtues is the bodhisattva mind. Thus, once this remedy has been brought into play, it will cause the annihilation of all unfavourable elements.

> "Blazing like the fire at the age's end, this will definitely and instantly burn very great wrongs."

iv. When the waters—of loving kindness and compassion—moisten the ground—which the mind of a being—and when the root—the mind set on enlightenment—is well and firmly planted, branches full of leaves—the 37 factors favourable to enlightenment—will develop. Once the fruit—perfect Buddhahood—has ripened, there will arise great benefits and happiness for all beings. Thus when the bodhisattva mind has arisen, the root of Buddhahood will have been firmly planted. The *bodhisattvabhûmi* says:

> "The awakening of the bodhisattva mind is the root of unsurpassable, pure and perfect enlightenment."

v. Immeasurable merit will be obtained. The *vîradatta-grhapati-pariprcchâsûtra* says:

> "If whatever merit is generated by awakening the bodhisattva mind could be made into form, it would not only fill up the whole expanse of space but extend beyond."

vi. It will please all the Buddhas. The same sûtra says:

> "Were someone to fill as many Buddhafields as there are sand grains on the banks of the river Ganges with gems and most precious substances and to offer them to all the Tathâgatas and were another person, through compassion, to become dedicated to enlightenment, with hands joined, then it would be the latter who would have made the superior offering: it would be immeasurable."

vii. It will benefit all beings. The *gandavyûhasûtra* says:

> "It is like a foundation because it brings benefit to all beings."

viii. One will quickly become a really perfect Buddha. It says, in the *bodhisattvabhûmi:*

> "Once this mental attitude has arisen, one will dwell in neither of the two extremes[1] but quickly achieve really perfect Buddhahood."

---

1. The **two extremes** are the totally peaceful absorption of limited nirvâna and the ego-based confusion of worldliness.

1b. Imaginable Benefits which arise through the Bodhisattva Practice Vow are tenfold. These are the eight mentioned above and further:

- it brings constant benefit to oneself and
- it accomplishes the welfare of others, in all kinds of ways.

i.-viii. as above

ix. "Unlike before, once this commitment to bodhisattva practice has been undertaken there will be a mighty and uninterrupted flow of merit, as vast as space; even when one is asleep, has fainted, is not particularly exercising care etc."

x. It will dispel the sufferings of beings, bring them happiness and suppress their defilements. The *bodhicaryâvatâra* says:

> "To those who are deprived of happiness and experience many sufferings, it brings the satisfaction of many forms of happiness, eradicates sufferings and, further, dispels ignorance. Is there any virtue that can match this? Is there anywhere such a friend or such goodness?"

2.   UNIMAGINABLE BENEFITS

It will bring forth all the qualities that emerge between its taking and enlightenment: there is no way of calculating these.

IX   The Harmful Consequences of Rejecting Bodhicitta

Through this wrong action one will:
- be reborn in states of suffering,
- impair one's capacity to help others and
- delay considerably achievement of the bodhisattva levels.

i.   By not fulfilling the bodhisattva promise and by abandoning the commitment to enlightenment, one is effectively cheating all beings. One will be reborn in states of suffering due to the fruition of this deception. About this, the *bodhicaryâvatâra* says:

> "If the commitment has been made but the work not done, one will get what one deserves for having so cheated beings."

ii. "If someone has broken this commitment, the situation of all beings worsens."

iii. "Those who vacillate between strong breaches of commitment —the cause of downfall—and strong commitment to reach enlightenment, will experience serious delay in attaining the bodhisattva levels."

X The Causes of Relinquishing Bodhisattva Mind

These are considered in two areas: the causes for relinquishing the aspiration and the causes for relinquishing the practice.

▸ the commitment of aspiration will be relinquished by rejecting beings from one's intention, by adhering to the "four dark actions" or through adopting an attitude incompatible with (the aspiration).
▸ the commitment of practice will be relinquished, according to the *bodhisattvabhûmi*:

"...if one has committed the *great ensnaring*, i.e. the four offences which are like a state of defeat,[1] this is taught as breaking the commitment. It is further taught that a *medium ensnaring* or a *lesser ensnaring* will damage the vow correspondingly.

According to the *samvaravimśaka*:

"...furthermore, it is taught that relinquishing the aspiration also breaks the commitment to practice."

It is also taught, in the *rnam.par.gtan.la.dbab.pa.bsdu.ba.* that there are four causes for breaking the bodhisattva vow—the two mentioned above and further (3) to renounce the bodhisattva training and (4) to adopt aberrant views. Acarya Śantideva says:

"An incompatible mental attitude breaks the vow."

---

1. killing, stealing, sexual misconduct and lying.

XI How to Restore the Vow (if it has been broken)

If the *aspiration vow* has been broken, it can be restored by re-taking it. The *practice vow* may have been broken simply by the aspiration vow having been lost. If this is the case, then restoration of the latter brings about automatic restoration of the former. If the practice vow has been broken due to some other cause, it will have to be taken again. If it is lost due to the "states of defeat" which are the medium or smaller "ensnarings", then it suffices to disclose them with remorse. The *samvaravimsaka* says:

"The commitment needs to be restored. For a middling fault, one needs to confess to three; to one for the rest. Do not become confused by defilements; (keep) mind (pure) as I do."

This was the ninth chapter, discussing the proper adoption of bodhicitta,
from this Gems of Dharma, Jewels of Freedom

XII. INSTRUCTION FOR DEVELOPING BODHICITTA

These are the instructions relevant to:

▸ **development of bodhisattva aspiration** and
▸ **development of bodhisattva practice.**

Chapter Ten: Instructions for Developing Bodhisattva Aspiration

The synopsis for this section:

The aspiration instructions are summed up in five points: not to exclude beings from one's mind; to remain mindful of the qualities of bodhicitta; to establish the two accumulations; to repeatedly cultivate the bodhisattva attitude and to nurture the four white modes of action and relinquish the four dark ones.

Concerning these five points:

— the first is the means for not abandoning bodhicitta,
— the second is the means for preventing bodhictta degrading,
— the third is the means for strengthening bodhicitta,
— the fourth is the means to increase bodhicitta and
— the fifth is the means for not forgetting bodhicitta.

1. "Training never to exclude beings from one's intention"

This is explained as being the way of avoiding abandoning bodhisattva action. The *anavataptanâgarâja pariprcchâsûtra* says:

> "Were there to be one thing that a bodhisattva could possess which would contain fully every quality of the Enlightened One, who is endowed with the best of everything, what would that one thing be? It would be the aspiration never to exclude beings from one's intentions."

To exclude beings from one's intentions means the likes of the following: one person treats another unfairly and the latter, as a consequence, no longer feels any sympathy for the former, thinking such thoughts as, *Were there ever a possibility of helping you, I wouldn't; were there ever the possibility of saving you from harm, I wouldn't.* The latter has excluded the former from his or her compassionate intentions.

Does "excluding beings from one's thoughts" mean all beings or even just one being? Except for śrâvakas and pratyekabuddhas, no one excludes all beings from their mind—not even birds of prey or wolves. Thus, one who has mentally shut out just one being and not rectified that within two hours has broken the bodhicitta commitment. This means that those who exclude beings from their intentions while enacting bodhisattva conduct and thinking of themselves as bodhisattvas are completely mistaken. That would be like having killed one's only child yet still purchasing children's clothing.

Since it is quite possible to let drop the bodhisattva attitude even towards those who have been helpful, the risk of losing it towards those who are harmful is indeed high. Therefore, by paying special attention to being compassionate to the latter, one should try to help them and make them happy. That is the way in which the best of beings practise.

"Those who are hurt by others in return for the goodness they show them, yet, despite this, still act beneficially towards them, are the finest humans in the world: people who can return good for bad."

2. "Training to remain mindful of the qualities of the bodhisattva attitude"

This is the way to avoid its degradation. The *bodhipathapradîpa*:

"The benefits of developing the aspiration for enlightenment have been explained in the *gandavyûha* by Maitreya" etc.

Actually, that text explains the benefits of the development of the bodhisattva mind through 230 examples and it is said that all those benefits fall into four main categories:

a. "My good children: this bodhicitta mind is like the seed of all the Buddhas' qualities. As it dispels spiritual poverty it is like the God of Wealth." This and other examples illustrate the *benefits for the bodhisattva.*

b. The following two examples are given to illustrate the *benefit for* *others.* "As it provides excellent protection for all beings, it is like a refuge ... as it supports all beings, it is like the supporting earth."

c. These examples and others illustrate the benefit the vow brings in terms of *cutting away wrong views:* "As it defeats the enemy, the defilements, it is like a spear ... as it fells the mighty tree of suffering, it is like an axe."

d. These examples and others illustrate its benefit in causing the accomplishment of everything that goes in the right direction: "As it completely fulfils all intentions, it is like the wondrous vase ... as it makes all wishes come true, it is like a wish-fulfilling gem."

Through being mindful of the above benefits, one will come to value greatly the bodhisattva mind and to appreciate its excellence. When this has been achieved and thereafter maintained through practice, it protects bodhicitta from degradation. Therefore one should always be mindful of bodhicitta's benefits, even should it be just for a short while in every 2-hour period of the day.

3. "Training in establishing the two accumulations"

This is the way to strengthen bodhicitta. Of this, the *bodhipathapradīpa* says, among other things:

"The accumulations, the natures of which are virtue and primordial wisdom, are the cause for bringing this to full perfection."

Of these, the accumulation of virtue is the **skilful means** aspect (of accomplishment), comprising the ten virtuous ways of acting, the four modes of gathering beings etc. The accumulation of primordial wisdom is the profound **wisdom** aspect (of accomplishment), knowing that such (skilful actions are accomplished) within an utterly pure context.[1]

Thus, as establishing the two accumulations is that which

---

1. **context**: the context of action is generally sullied by *triplicity*, i.e. the triple notion of a subject, an object and their interaction. The context of action is pure, unsullied by triplicity, when—as here—virtue is accomplished without any idea of a bodhisattva doing good (subject), of sentient beings being benefitted (object) or of bodhisattva activity (interaction).

strengthens bodhicitta, one should always endeavour to accomplish them — even if it involves just reciting a brief mantra once during each two-hour period of the day. The *sambhâraparikathâ* says of this:

"A bodhisattva constantly thinks, "Which of the accumulations of virtue and primordial wisdom can I achieve today; what can I do to benefit beings?"

4. "Training repeatedly in bodhicitta"

This helps one's bodhicitta to increase. The *bodhipathapradîpa* says of this:

"Having given rise to bodhicitta as an aspiration, one should strive to increase it in every way."

This (striving) should be understood as applying to three areas of activity:

▸ training in the attitude which is the cause of bodhicitta,
▸ training in the bodhicitta attitude itself and
▸ training in the mentality of bodhisattva conduct.

a.   The attitude which is the cause of bodhicitta is always to be in a disposition of loving kindness and compassion towards sentient beings — or at least to engender such a thought once in every 2-hour period.

b.   The training in bodhicitta itself is (to cultivate) a longing to attain enlightenment in order to be able to benefit beings. This should be contemplated during the three periods of the day and the three periods of the night. Alternatively one can perform the longer bodhisattva ritual or else, at a minimum, recite the following prayer by the Great Atiśa once in every 2-hour period:

"Until enlightenment, I seek refuge in the Buddhas, in the dharma and in the supreme community. Through the virtue of whatever generosity and so forth[1] I accomplish, may I achieve buddhahood in order to benefit conscious beings."

---

1. **generosity and so forth**: i.e. the six pâramitâ. See later chapters.

c.   The training in the mentality relevant to bodhisattva conduct is twofold: developing the willingness to work for the benefit of others and developing the intention to purify one's own mind.

c1.   The first means dedicating one's body, possessions and whatever virtues one has established in the three times, to the service of others and to their happiness. It implies cultivating a willingness to give.

c2.   Developing the intention to purify one's own mind involves constant examination of one's conduct and also the elimination of defilement and bad action.

5.   "Training in abandoning the four dark actions and cultivating the four white ones"

This is the way to avoid forgetting bodhicitta. The *bodhipatha-pradīpa* says:

"In order to be able to remember this bodhisattva attitude in other existences, one should carefully observe the rules of training which have been explained."

Where have these rules of training been explained? In the sūtra taught at the request of Kasyapa — the *kasyapaparivartasūtra*, in which it says of the four dark actions:

"Kasyapa! A bodhisattva cultivating these four things will forget his commitment to enlightenment. What are these four? They are..."

To summarise them, the four dark actions are:

1.   To deceive a guru or person worthy of receiving offerings.
2.   To cause others to regret actions that should not be regretted.
3.   To speak improperly to a bodhisattva, i.e. one who has taken the bodhisattva vow.
4.   To cheat or deceive any sentient beings.

The four white actions are also given in that same sūtra:

"Kasyapa! Should a bodhisattva cultivate these four, in all future existences the bodhisattva mentality will definitely manifest from birth onwards; without any interruption this bodhicitta will never be forgotten, throughout the time until enlightenment. What are these four? They are..."

To summarise the four briefly they are:

1. Never to tell lies knowingly, even at the cost of one's life.
2. To establish all beings in virtue and further to establish them in mahâyâna virtue.
3. To consider a bodhisattva, i.e. one who has taken the vow, as being the Teacher, the Enlightened One, and to proclaim that person's qualities throughout the directions and
4. to constantly stay within a noble disposition of mind; one without any deceitfulness or trickiness towards any sentient being.

1. EXPLANATION OF THE FIRST DARK ACTION AND ITS OPPOSITE WHITE ACTION

If, with an intention to deceive, one has actually been deceitful towards anyone "worthy of offerings", i.e. a guru, an abbot, a dharma master or Buddhist held in respect, this breaks the bodhisattva vow, unless something is done to remedy the fault within two hours. It does not matter whether or not the person knew they were being deceived, whether or not the deception caused displeasure, whether it was a major or minor deception or whether the deceit actually worked or not; whatever the case the vow is broken.

The remedy[1] to this is the first white action, which is to avoid, at all times, the intentional telling of untruths — even at the risk of one's life.

2. EXPLANATION OF THE SECOND DARK ACTION AND ITS OPPOSITE WHITE ACTION

This occurs in relation to the virtuous actions of others. It involves trying to stir up remorse in them by getting them fixated

---

1. **remedy**: i.e. the remedy for this type of mind in general. The remedy referred to in the paragraph above is the immediate remedy, e.g. a purification practice such as Vajrasattva meditation, for a specific action. This double reference to the notion of remedy applies in the following three points also.

in notions of regret (for the good they have done). An example of this, in a case of generosity, would be that of a person who has been generous, i.e. done a good action, yet one tries to make him or her regret it by saying that in days to come the lack of funds created by their generosity will leave them a beggar and then what will they do? Whether they actually do regret what they have done or not, if this is not remedied in two hours it breaks the bodhisattva vow.

The remedy for this is the second white action: to establish all beings in virtue and in particular in the virtue of mahâyâna.

3. EXPLANATION OF THE THIRD DARK ACTION AND ITS OPPOSITE WHITE ACTION

This occurs through anger or hatred and involves talking about the faults of someone who has taken the bodhisattva vow. They may be ordinary faults or dharma failings, talked about to that person's face or indirectly, in a pleasant or unpleasant way. Whether the bodhisattva concerned was disturbed or not by what one has said, it will break the bodhisattva vow unless remedied within two hours.

The remedy is the third white action: to conceive of one who has taken the bodhisattva vow just as one would conceive of a Buddha and to let their qualities be known everywhere.

4. EXPLANATION OF THE FOURTH DARK ACTION AND ITS OPPOSITE WHITE ACTION

This entails intentionally trying to deceive anyone whomsoever. Unless remedied within two hours, this will break the bodhisattva vow, whether the person was aware of the deception or not and whether any harm was actually done or not.

The remedy is the fourth white action—"to act always with the noblest intentions towards beings"—i.e. intending to benefit them and this without concern for one's own welfare.

This was the tenth chapter, on how to develop aspiration bodhicitta, from this Gems of Dharma, Jewels of Freedom

INSTRUCTIONS FOR DEVELOPING
BODHISATTVA PRACTICE

The instruction is threefold: training in noblest **conduct, higher mind** training and training in the best and most profound **wisdom**. Of these, the *bodhipathapradîpa* says:

"One who abides within the commitment which is the very identity of practice bodhicitta and who very correctly trains in the three aspects of training in bodhisattva conduct will deepen their appreciation of the those three aspects of training in conduct."

▸   The training in noblest conduct is threefold, comprising *generosity, right conduct* and *forbearance,*
▸   the higher mind training is that of *meditation* and
▸   training in most profound wisdom is that of *prajña.*
▸   *Joyful perseverance* is that which fosters these three trainings.

The *mahâyâna-sûtrâlankâra* says:

"The Victorious One has most perfectly explained the six transcendent qualities (pâramitâ) in terms of the three trainings: the first is the first three, the last two are the last two and the third applies to all three."

The synopsis for this chapter is:

Training in practice bodhicitta can be summarised as sixfold: generosity, right conduct, forbearance, diligence, meditation and prajñâ.

Quoting the Sûtra Taught at the Request of Subâhu:

"Subâhu! In order for a bodhisattva mahâsattva quickly to achieve real and perfect enlightenment, the six transcendent qualities must be applied constantly and in all circumstances, until their utter perfection. What are those six? They are the transcendent perfection of generosity, the transcendent perfection of right conduct, the transcendent perfection of forbearance, the transcendent perfection of diligence, the transcendent perfection of meditation and sixthly the transcendent perfection of prajñâ."

One should understand the six transcendent qualities through two presentations which follow:

- ▸ the first (Ch. 11) is a summarised explanation or **overview,** treating them as a group, and

- ▸ the second (Chs. 12-17) is a **detailed explanation** of them one by one.

Chapter Eleven:
An Overview of the Six Pâramitâ

The synopsis for this chapter is:

"The six transcendent qualities are summarised through six topics: their definite number, definite order, essential characteristics, etymology, subdivisions and groupings."

1.   The Definite Number

There are six (pâramitâ). In terms of higher states of rebirth and liberation, there are three which lead to higher rebirth and three which lead to liberation. Of the three which lead to higher states: *the pâramitâ of generosity* will bring material prosperity, *the pâramitâ of right conduct* will bring a good physical existence and *the pâramitâ of forbearance* will bring a favourable entourage.

Of the three which lead to liberation:
the pâramitâ of diligence will bring increase of qualities,
the pâramitâ of meditation will bring mental peace and
the pâramitâ of profound understanding (prajñâ) will lead to profound understanding.

The *mahâyâna-sûtrâlankâra* says: "Higher states — the best possible prosperity, body and entourage."

2.   The Definite Order

2A   THE ORDER IN WHICH THEY DEVELOP IN ONE

Through generosity, one will be able to have a proper conduct, without concern for one's own material well-being. One who is endowed with right conduct will be able to cultivate forbearance. Through forbearance, one will be able to be diligent. Through diligence, profound absorption (samâdhi) can be developed in meditation. The mind that rests skilfully in samâdhi will know the essential nature of phenomena, just as it is.

2B   THE GRADUAL PROGRESSION FROM LESS TO HIGHER

The lesser are explained first and those founded in what is nobler are explained subsequently.

2C   THE GRADUAL PROGRESSION FROM OBVIOUS TO SUBTLE

The former are more obvious, being easier to explain and easier to put into practice. The latter, more subtle, require more advanced explanation and are more difficult to put into practice. The *mahâyâna-sûtrâlankâra* says of this:

"What comes later arises from a ground prepared by what comes before. Thus these come in their order, since some are inferior and others superior and some obvious and others subtle."

3.   The Essential Characteristics

There are four essential characteristics of bodhisattva generosity and the other pâramitâ:

- ▸ they diminish and remove those things which are unfavourable,
- ▸ they enable the development of primordial, non-conceptual wisdom (jñâna),
- ▸ they bring accomplishment of one's wishes and
- ▸ they bring beings to full maturity, through the three paths.

The *mahâyâna-sûtrâlankâra* says of this:

"Generosity curtails unfavourable elements, brings non-conceptual primordial wisdom, perfectly fulfils all wishes and brings beings to maturity in three ways..." etc.

4.   Etymology[1]

Since it clears away suffering, it is "generosity".[2]

Since it is the attainment of coolness, it is "right conduct".[3]

Since it forbears (what would cause) anger, it is "forbearance".[4]

Since it is application to that which is sublime, it is "diligence."[5]

Since it keeps the mind turned inwards, it is "meditation".

Since it causes awareness of that which is ultimate and meaningful, it is supreme awareness—prajñâ.

Since all of them transport one to the other shore of samsâra, i.e. to nirvâna, they are "transcendent virtues" (pâramitâ).[6]

---

1. This section refers to the etymology, or in fact to the definition, of the original Sanskrit names of the pâramitâ. This changed with translation into Tibetan and is currently again in process of change as appropriate Western language terms vie with each other to become generally accepted as best possible translations. See following notes.

2. The Skt. root *da* in *dâna* not only implies giving but also has an edge of meanings such as "removing", " cutting off" etc. Gampopa here, and for the following five pâramitâ, passes on a traditional, Indian explanation of the names of the pâramitâ, from a commentary to the *mahâyânasûtrâlankâra*.

3. *sila* means "cool" in Sanskrit. It makes sense to refer to Buddhist right conduct in terms of coolness, such as that offered by the shade of a tree, as it is a relief and a refuge from the oppressive Indian heat, analogous to the heat of passionate uncontrolled conduct, from which right conduct brings release. This simile lost some of its punch when it went to cold Tibet.

4. *ksanti* — often translated as patience, is, as the later chapter reveals, to do with coping with situations and being able to face up to difficulties. It has a sense of being able to bear a load, without cracking, and forbearance seems closer to this meaning than patience.

5. The definition of the Tibetan term has, like that of the English word "diligence", a feeling of joyous enthusiasm about it. In popular use, however, "diligence" has come to mean a more dutiful, forced type of effort: unfortunate since the very root of the word means "delight".

6. pâramitâ — is Sanskrit for "other shore".

5.   Subdivisions

Each of the transcendent virtues has six subdivisions — the generosity of generosity, right conduct of generosity etc. — thus making 36 subdivisions in all. The *abhisamayâlamkâra* says:

"The six transcendent virtues—generosity and so forth—each subdivide into six in terms of each other and in terms of being a complete means (for enlightenment)."

6.   Groupings

The six transcendent virtues fall into two groups: those of the two accumulations:

Generosity and *right conduct* belong to the accumulation of virtue.
Deep understanding (prajñâ) belongs to the accumulation of primordial wisdom (jñâna).
Forbearance, diligence and *meditation* belong to both.

Thus the *mahâyâna-sûtrâlankâra* says:

"Generosity and right conduct belong to the accumulation of virtue. Deep understanding (prajñâ) belongs to the accumulation of primordial wisdom (jñâna) and the remaining three belong to both."

This was the eleventh chapter, presenting the six transcendent virtues, from this Gems of Dharma, Jewels of Freedom

THE TRANSCENDENT VIRTUES PRESENTED
INDIVIDUALLY, IN DETAIL

Ch. 12: The Transcendent Virtue of Generosity

The transcendent virtue of generosity is summarised as sevenfold: reflections upon the fault of its absence and the qualities of practising it; its essential character; its different aspects; the essential characteristics of each aspect; how it can be increased; how it can be made pure and its consequences.

1. Reflections upon the fault of its absence and the qualities of practising it

A person lacking generosity will constantly suffer from poverty[1]. Rebirth among deprived spirits is possible and should even the person be reborn human, he or she will be poverty-stricken. The *prajnapâramitâsamcayagatha* says of this:

"The miserly will be reborn among deprived spirits. Even if reborn human, they will be poor."

It also says, in the *vinaya,*

"The deprived spirits answered Dro Shin Jay's question saying, *We are avaricious and miserly and we have not practised the slightest generosity – that is why we are condemned to this deprived spirit state.*"

This is what happens. Further, without generosity, one can neither help others nor 'achieve budddhahood:

"Those unaccustomed to giving are without wealth and have no power at all to gather beings to them — so no need even to

---

1. This refers principally to two things. One is the longer term consequences upon one's wealth, due to the play of cause and effect. The other is poverty not in terms of what one has but in terms of how satisfied one is with what one has. A "rich" person can feel very dissatisfied, i.e. poor, with all that he or she possesses whereas a "poor" person can feel satisfaction and contentment with very little.

consider their chances of reaching enlightenment."

The opposite of this is that generous people will be happy on account of having plenteous possessions throughout all their existences. The *prajñāpāramitāsamcayagāthā* says:

"Bodhisattva generosity severs the possibilities of rebirth as a deprived spirit. It will abolish poverty and destroy all defilements. The bodhisattvas' practice of their conduct will bring limitless and tremendous wealth."

In the *suhrllekha* it tells us:

"Practise generosity correctly; there will be no better friend for the next life."

Also the *madhyamakāvatāra* says:

"Everyone seeking happiness does not only want a happy human life regardless of wealth; they would like also to be well provided for. As the Enlightened One knew that such a life would only occur through the practice of generosity, it was about generosity that he first taught."

Furthermore, if one is generous, it will be easier to achieve enlightenment. The *bodhisattva-pitaka* says:

"Enlightenment is not hard to encounter for one who has been generous."

Also the *ratnameghasūtra* says:

"Generosity brings about the enlightenment of a bodhisattva."

Further, we find the drawbacks of a lack of generosity and the advantages of its practice discussed respectively in the *grahapati-ugra-pariprcchāsūtra* :

"What I have given is mine; what I have hoarded is not mine[1]. What has been given has purpose; what is hoarded is pointless.

---

1. This and the following points refer to the longer term consequences and in particular those in future lives.

That which has been given does not require protection; what is hoarded does. What has been given brings no anxiety; whatever is hoarded is accompanied by worries. What has been given shows the way to Buddhahood; what is hoarded shows the quick way to evil. Giving will bring great wealth and hoarding will not. Giving will never know the end of wealth; hoarding will exhaust it."

2.   Its essential character

Generosity means giving, with an unattached mind, that which has value. The *bodhicaryâvatâra :*

"What is the essence of generosity? It is to give things away through a generosity motivated by non-attachment."

3.   Its different aspects

There are three: material generosity, supportive generosity and dharma generosity. Of these:
material generosity strengthens others' physical existence,
supportive generosity strengthens the quality of their lives and
dharma generosity strengthens their minds.

Furthermore, the first two kinds of generosity bring well-being to others in this life whereas the gift of dharma brings well-being for (this and) future lives.

4.   The essential characteristics of each aspect

4A   MATERIAL GENEROSITY

This is itself of two kinds: proper and improper. The former is to be cultivated and the latter abandoned.

■ **4Ai.   Improper Material Generosity** is discussed through four aspects: improper motivation, inappropriate gifts, inappropriate receiver and an improper way of giving.

~ improper motivation ~

This can be either a wrong motivation or a lesser one. Giving out of **wrong motivation** means giving in order to harm others, to gain fame or because of competition. A bodhisattva should renounce all three. The *bodhisattvabhūmi* says:

"Bodhisattvas should not give in order that others be killed, tied up, punished, imprisoned or banished. Bodhisattvas should not give in order to acquire fame or be praised. Bodhisattvas should not give in order to compete with others."

Giving through **lesser motivation** means being generous through fear of poverty in future lives or because one intends it to be the cause of one's own future human or divine rebirth and future wealth. Bodhisattvas should give up these two types of motivation.

"Bodhisattvas should not give through fear of poverty. Bodhisattvas should not give in order to gain the support of Indra, a cakravartin or Iśvara."

The *bodhisattvabhūmi* also talks about other kinds of improper generosity, that should be renounced. They can be summarised as follows.

~ improper gifts ~

Bodhisattvas should not, if requested, give poison, fire, weapons etc. if they will bring harm to the person requesting them or to others. They should not respond to requests for snares, hunting devices and so forth; in brief, whatever may harm others. They should not give away their parents or use them as surety. They should not give away unconsenting spouse or offspring.

One who has much wealth should not give little. One should not give communal wealth.

~ inappropriate receivers ~

Even though demons with harmful intentions may beg one for one's body, one should neither give it nor parts of it to them. Neither should one give one's body to those who are under the sway of demons or to those who are mad or temporarily deranged.

Their need is not real; they are irresponsible and their words are for the most part nonsense. It is not generosity to give food and drink to those well satiated.

~ improper way of giving ~

It is not right generosity if one is unhappy to give, angry about the giving or giving with a disturbed mind. One should not give to the deprived in a state of contempt or disrespect for them; neither should one dishearten, threaten or deride the person begging.

■ **4Aii. Proper Material Generosity**

~ proper objects to give ~

This is explained in terms of "inner" and "outer" objects. The *inner* ones are body-related. The Sûtra Taught at the Request of Semay's Son says:

"If it is beneficial to give and if one's own attitude is pure, one can give a hand if a hand is required, a leg if a leg is required, an eye if an eye is required, one's flesh if that is what is needed, one's blood if that is required..."

Those who are bodhisattva-beginners and who have not yet truly realised the equality of self and others may dedicate their whole body but not give away parts of it. The *bodhicaryâvatâra* says of this:

"One should not give away one's body through an essentially impure motivation; that would be to give up the basis for great achievements for the good of others in this life and the next."

"The *outer* objects are the likes of wealth, grains, silver, gold, jewelry, ornaments, horses, elephants, children and so forth."

Lay bodhisattvas are permitted to give away whatever inner or outer gifts they possess. The *mahâyâna-sûtrâlankâra* says: "There is no bodhisattva who would not give away body and wealth."

Ordained bodhisattvas are allowed to give everything except their three dharma robes. The *bodhicaryâvatâra* says of this:

"Give everything except for the three dharma robes." This is because without one's three items of clothing it will be more complicated to work for the benefit of beings.

~ the receiver ~

There are four types of special receiver:

- those particularly designated by their qualities; gurus, the Three Most Precious Refuges etc.,
- those particularly designated by the benefit (they have brought us)—father, mother etc.,
- those particularly designated by their sufferings — the sick, the unprotected etc. and
- those particularly designated by the harm (they have done us) — enemies etc.

The *bodhicaryâvatâra* says, "Qualities, benefits..." etc.

~ the way the gift is given ~

One should give with the very best of intentions and accomplish the act of giving in the best possible way. The first of these, the *intention*, means giving through a motivation of compassion, i.e. in order to attain enlightenment and to benefit beings.

As for the second, *accomplishing the act in the best way:* "A bodhisattva should give joyfully, with respect, personally, at the right time and without harming others."

- *joyfully* means to be happy about giving during all three moments of the act: immediately before giving, while giving and to be unregretting afterwards.
- *with respect* means with respect for the receiver.
- *personally* means not appointing the task of giving to someone else.
- *at the right time* means when one has already acquired what is pledged.
- *without harming others* means without causing hardship in one's entourage or for those who actually possess the goods. Even though something may well be one's own property, should giving it away

bring tears to the eyes of those who partici pated in its acquisition, then one should not give it. One should not practise generosity by giving goods which have been stolen, burgled[1] or misappropriated.

The *abhidharmasamuccaya* says, "Give again and again, in order to fulfil wishes most perfectly."

Generosity should be impartial: this is advice related to the receiver. It means not being biased in one's evaluation about who should receive a gift.

One should give in order to fulfil wishes: this advice is related to the gift itself. It means giving that which corresponds most closely to the expectations of the receiver.

4B   SUPPORTIVE GENEROSITY

This is to give protection to those who are afraid: of robbers, thieves, beasts of prey, illness, water and so forth. The *bodhisattvabhûmi* says:

"The gift of fearlessness should be known as the provision of complete protection from lions, tigers, crocodiles, monarchs, robbers and thieves, water and so forth."

4C   THE GIFT OF DHARMA

This is explained through four points: listener, motivation, authentic dharma and presentation.

■ **4Ci.   The Person Taught**   This means explaining the Buddhist teaching to those who wish to hear it, have respect for both it and the one who expounds it.

■ **4Cii.   Motivation**   One should get rid of wrong motivations and resort only to good ones. To give up *wrong motivation* means to teach dharma without materialistic concern for honours, praise or fame. The *prajñâpâramitâsamcayagâthâ* says, "It is to be free from materialism when teaching beings dharma."

---

1. "burgled" and "stolen" refer respectively to things stolen by stealth and things stolen directly from the owner, as in a hold-up.

In the Sûtra Taught at Kasyapa's request, it says:

"The Buddha speaks highly of the gift of dharma being given with a pure mind unconcerned with material gain."

To *resort to good intentions* means that compassion should be the motivation for teaching dharma.

■ **4Ciii. Authentic Dharma**   This means teaching unerringly the unmistaken meaning of the sutras and other texts. The *bodhisattva-bhûmi* says,

"Giving the dharma means to teach the unerring dharma, to teach the appropriate dharma and to make sure that the fundamental points of training are well understood."

~ the way dharma should be presented ~

When someone requests dharma instruction, it is not fitting to explain things there and then. The Moonlight Sûtra says:

"Should someone request you to explain the dharma, first say that you have not studied it that extensively. Do not teach straight away. You should consider the suitability[1]. If you know the person to be a worthy vessel for a teaching, the dharma can be explained without a request being made."

The Buddhadharma should be explained in a clean and pleasant place. The *saddharmapundarîkasûtra* says:

"A well-arranged and spacious carpet should be spread out in a clean and pleasant place."

In such a place, the address should be given from a teaching throne: "Well-seated on an elevated dharma seat which is beautifully arranged with various pieces of cotton cloth." One should be clean, properly attired, neat and tidy and one should behave correctly while explaining the dharma. The *sâgaramati-pariprcchâsûtra* says:

---

1. of the person to receive the teachings they have requested

"One who teaches dharma should be neat and tidy and behave in a proper fashion. He should have bathed and be nicely attired."

When everyone has assembled and taken their seats and the person teaching has also sat on the dharma-seat, the latter should recite the mantra which overcomes the power of negative forces, so that their hindering power cannot spoil the teaching. The same sûtra gives:

"**Deyatta : shamay shamawati : shamita shatru : am kuray : mam kuray: mara jitay karota : keyauri : tejo wati : olo yani bishuddha nirmalay malapa nayay : kukuray : kha kha grasay : grasana : o mukhi para mukhi a mukhi shami dwani sarwa graha bandha nanay : ni gri hi tva : sarwa bara prawa dina : vimukta mara pasha : sarvi tva : Buddha mudra : anu gati ta : sarva maray : butsa rita pari shudday : biga shantu sarva mara karma ni**[1] : Ocean of Intelligence! If one recites the words of this mantra beforehand, no demons or negative forces within a radius of 100 paktsé will be able to come and harm the teaching; even were they to manage to come, they would be unable to create an obstacle. Then one should explain the dharma words clearly, articulately and in just the right amount."

5.   How generosity can be increased[2]

There are ways of transforming even a small amount of the above three types of generosity into something much greater. The *bodhisattva pitaka* says:

"Sariputra! Skilful bodhisattvas transform a little generosity into a great amount. Through the power of primordial wisdom (jñâna) it is elevated. Through the power of deep understanding

---

1. The mantra is represented here through an approximative rendering of how it sounds when pronounced in Sanskrit.

2. This point and the next point should be given very careful attention, because they are vitally important from a practice point of view and because they apply also to the following five pâramitâ. The texts for the other pâramitâ refer one back to this section rather than repeating the advice.

(prajñâ) it is expanded and through the power of dedication it is made immeasurable."

5A   "THE POWER OF PRIMORDIAL WISDOM ELEVATES IT"

This means understanding the total purity of triplicity, (by recognising) the giver to be like a conjuration, the gift to be like a conjuration and the receiver too to be just like a conjuration.

5B   "THE POWER OF PRAJNA EXPANDS IT"

Deep understanding (prajñâ), applied in order to give rise to a vast amount of merit, involves:

- at the outset giving in order to establish all beings in the state of Buddhahood,
- during the giving, being without attachment to the gift itself and
- at the conclusion being free of expectation of good future-life consequences from one's giving.

The *prajñâpâramitâsamcayagâthâ* says:

"Not conceiving of their giving as something substantially existent and never practising generosity in anticipation of its full karmic rewards—that is how the wise and skilful practise generosity, and even a little giving becomes great and immeasurable."

5C   "THE POWER OF DEDICATION[1] MAKES IT IMMEASURABLE"

This means dedicating such generosity to the ultimate enlightenment of every sentient being. The *bodhisattvabhûmi* says,

"Do not be generous with a view to the specific (personal) results of that act of generosity. Dedicate all generosity to the ultimate, perfectly pure and complete enlightenment of each and every sentient being."

Dedication not only increases (the results) — it makes them

---

1. This is not dedication in the sense of applying oneself dedicatedly to the task of generosity. It is dedication in the sense of targeting, investing, the wholesome consequences generated by an act of generosity.

inexhaustible. The sûtra taught at the request of the Arya "Inexhaustible Intelligence" says:

> "Venerable son of Śaridati! Should a drop of water be put in the ocean, it will not be consumed for endless aeons. Likewise when the roots of virtue have been dedicated to enlightenment, they will never become exhausted throughout all of one's journey to Buddhahood, the heart of one's quest."

6.   How generosity can be made pure[1]

To quote the *śikṣâsamuccaya* "Through applying voidness which has compassion as its very essence, virtue will be made pure." When the above-mentioned forms of generosity are supported by (realisation of) voidness, they will not become a cause for samsâra; when they are supported by compassion, they will not become a cause for the lesser way *(hinayana)*. Thus is generosity made pure because it solely becomes a cause for attaining non-abiding nirvâna[2].

In the Sûtra Taught at the Request of "Forehead Jewel", it is taught that generosity is marked with **four seals of voidness**. It says:

> "Practise generosity by applying four seals to it. Which are they? To apply the seal of the voidness of that which is inner, one's body; to apply the seal of the voidness of that which is outer, the gift; to apply the seal of the voidness of the subjective mind and to apply the seal of the voidness of the phenomenon of enlightenment. By having applied those four seals, generosity will really have been accomplished."

The support of **compassion** means being generous because one cannot bear the sufferings of beings, considered specifically or in general.

---

1. see note to point 5 above.

2. nirvâna which abides neither in samsâra nor in the limited attainment of peace of the hinayâna.

7.   The consequences of generosity

The results of generosity are both temporary and ultimate. *Ultimately,* through generosity, one will become totally enlightened. The *bodhisattvabhûmi* says:

"When bodhisattvas perfect the transcendent virtue of generosity, they truly become perfect Buddhas who have reached peerless, manifest and perfect enlightenment."

(In the meantime) the *temporary* results are that through material generosity one will have the most perfect wealth, without needing to plan for it. Through gathering beings to oneself, by being generous, one will be able to orient them towards the ultimate. The *prajñâpâramitâsamcayagâthâ* says:

"Bodhisattva generosity destroys the route to rebirth as a deprived spirit. It suppresses poverty and also cuts through defilement. As long as bodhisattvas practise the bodhisattva conduct, they will get vast and limitless wealth. Through being generous, they will bring every being in suffering to a more mature state."

The *bodhisattvabhûmi* says:

"Gifts of food will make one strong, gifts of clothes will bring a good complexion, gifts of steeds will provide the sure happiness and oil lamps offered will bring good eyesight."

Through supportive generosity, one will not be harmed by negative forces and obstacles. The *ratnâvalî* says,

"One who has protected the fearful from what makes them afraid will not be harmed by any negative forces and will become supreme among the mighty."

By giving the gift of dharma, one will soon meet the Buddhas, be close to them and attain everything wished for. The *ratnâvalî* says:

"Through giving the dharma to those studying it, and thereby diminishing their obscurations, one will become a companion of the Buddhas and swiftly attain that which one longs for."

Chapter Thirteen:
The Transcendent Virtue of Right Conduct

The transcendent virtue of right conduct is summarised as sevenfold: reflections upon the fault of its absence and the qualities of practising it; its essential character; its different aspects; the essential characteristics of each aspect; how it can be increased; how it can be made pure and its consequences.

1.   Reflections upon the fault of its absence and the qualities of practising it

■ Someone who possesses the quality of generosity but who **lacks right conduct**[1] will not be able to obtain the very best of physical existences among humans or gods. The *madhyamakâvatâra*:

"An individual who breaks his legs of right conduct may obtain possessions through generosity but will nevertheless fall into lower existences."

Further, one who lacks right conduct will not encounter the Buddhadharma. The Sûtra on Right Conduct says:

"Just as the blind cannot see form, so those without right conduct will not see dharma."

It is also the case that those without right conduct will not become free from existence in the three dimensions of samsâra. The same sûtra says:

"The legless cannot, no matter how they try, walk along a path. Likewise those without right conduct cannot become liberated."

Furthermore, someone without right conduct cannot attain

---

1. **right conduct**: This translation for the name of the second pâramitâ (Skt. *sila*, Tib. *tshul.khrims*) comes close to the definition of *tshul.khrims* given by the lineage masters and chosen by the early translators, who could not use "coolness" for *sila* (see note to earlier chapter). It means to take as one's personal code *(khrims)* of conduct, or definition of what is right, the way *(tshul)* of the Buddha.

enlightenment, because their path to Buddhahood is incomplete.

▪ On the contrary, however, someone who **has the qualities of right conduct** will attain the very best physical existence. The *prajñâpâramitâsamcayagâthâ* says:

"Through self-control one avoids the many forms of animal life and of the eight unfavourable states and one always finds the favourable ones."

Further, through right conduct one will penetrate the very foundation of all that is excellent and joyous. The *suhrllekha* says,

"Right conduct is taught as being the very foundation and basis for every quality, just like the earth is the basis for all animate and inanimate life."

Also, possession of right conduct is like having a fertile field where plentiful harvests of qualities can flourish. Therefore the *madhyamakâvatâra* says:

"As good qualities flourish on the field of right conduct, the fruition draws constantly nearer."

Further, one who has right conduct will find it opens many doors of meditative absorption. Thus the *candrapradîpasûtra* says:

"The attainment of profound absorption free from defilement is a beneficial quality which arises due to very pure right conduct."

Also, through right conduct, whatever one prays for will be accomplished. Thus the *pitâputrasamâgamanasûtra* says:

"It is through whatever right conduct one has observed that every prayer one makes comes true."

Moreover, right conduct makes it relatively easy to achieve enlightenment. The same sûtra says:

"Since purity of conduct brings so many beneficial qualities, it will not be difficult to achieve enlightenment."

There are the above and other benefits. The Right Conduct Sûtra:

"When conduct is right, Buddhas appear and one meets them. Observing right conduct is the finest adornment; a state of being endowed with every joy. Those of right conduct are praised in every world."

2.   Its essential character

It has four main qualities, described in the *bodhisattvabhûmi* as follows:

"One should know the essential character of right conduct as having four particularities. What are they? It needs to be adopted from another[1] very properly and purely. One's own intention should be exceedingly pure in every respect. Should it deteriorate, one would need to restore it. To prevent it from deteriorating, one should cultivate respect for it and remain very mindful of it."

The four particularities mentioned above can be summed up as covering two main areas: correctly adopting right conduct (the first) and properly keeping it (the other three).

3.   Its different aspects

It is threefold: right conduct as commitment (**vows**), as a build up of **dharma virtue** and as accomplishment of the **welfare of other** beings. The first of these stabilises the mind, the second brings the elements of one's own existence to maturity and the third causes other beings to achieve their full maturity.

4.   The essential characteristics of each aspect

4A   RIGHT CONDUCT OF OBSERVING VOWS

This is explained both in general and specifically.

■ **4Ai   The General Vows of Buddhism** are the seven kinds of "self-liberation" (prâtimoksa) vows. The *bodhisattvabhûmi* says:

---

1. "another" here means the preceptor.

"Right bodhisattva conduct related to ridding oneself of wrong activity means properly taking one of the **self-liberation vows:**

English	Sanskrit	Tibetan
full monk	bhiksu	dge.slong
full nun	bhiksuni	dge.slong.ma
quasi nun	śiksamânâ	dge.slob.ma
novice monk	śramanera	dge.tshul
novice nun	śramanerikâ	dge.tshul.ma
layman's precepts	upâsaka[1]	dge.bsnyen
laywoman's precepts	upâsikâ	dge.bsnyen.ma

These cover possibilities both for those following the monastic life and laypersons, as appropriate. The above commitments turn one away from harming others and away from involvement with those things which constitute the very bases for harming others. *Prâtimoksa* — "self-liberation" — vows, turning one away from harm, enable both those striving for their own enlightenment to work for their own welfare, and bodhisattvas to work altruistically. The *nârâyanapariprrchâsûtra* says:

> "Right conduct is not to be observed in order to gain royal status; nor for the sake of higher rebirth; nor for Indra or Brahmahood; nor for the sake of possessions; nor for the sake of physical well-being etc. Likewise right conduct is not to be observed through fear of the horrors of rebirth in hell; nor through fear of rebirth in animal states; nor through fear of the terrifying worlds of the Lord of Death. Not for these reasons is right conduct observed but in order to establish oneself in the way of the Buddha, to be able to strive for the welfare and the happiness of all beings."

---

1. This, and the female equivalent which follows, involves observing eight precepts: not killing, stealing, lying, taking intoxicants, committing sexual misconduct, wearing adornments, participating in revelry or eating after the appointed hour. There are two possibilities for the no sexual misconduct vow: brahmacarya upasaka, which involves complete celibacy and lay upasaka, which involves fidelity to one's spouse and abstinence in prescribed circumstances.

■ **4Aii   Specific Buddhist Vows**   In the tradition stemming from Dharma-master Śantideva, according to what is taught in the *akâsagarbhasûtra,* there are:

"Three root downfalls specific to monarchs, five specific to ministers and eight specific to dharma novices. Altogether these make 18 but there are (because of duplication) in fact 14 things to be overcome:

1. to steal that which belongs to the Three Precious Refuges,
2. to force others to abandon the dharma,
3. even though a monk's conduct may not be impeccable, to take his robes, have him beaten or imprisoned or oblige him to give up his commitment,
4. to commit one of the five worst actions[1],
5. to adhere to aberrant philosophy and
6. to destroy towns etc.

Of the above, 1 to 5 inclusive are root downfalls for a monarch and 1 to 4 and 6 are those of a minister. The eight specific wrong actions of dharma novices are:

1. to speak about voidness to those inadequately prepared,
2. to turn away from perfect enlightenment those who have entered the way to Buddhahood,
3. to practise mahâyâna yet completely renounce the self-liberation ethics,
4. to believe that the training yâna cannot bring about the elimination of desire etc. and to cause others to so believe,
5. to extol one's own qualities and denigrate others',
6. through seeking praise, respect or honour, to pretend one understands voidness when one in fact does not,
7. to have promised to do something virtuous and then go back on one's promise or to make offerings to the Three Precious Refuges and then take them back and
8. to give up meditation and absorption in that which is the

---

1. litt. "actions without interval" because the consequences happen immediately upon death.

highest reality in order to do ritual recitations.

The above are root downfalls and a prime cause for sentient beings ending up in the great hells."

In the tradition of Dharmakirti, according to what is said in the *bodhisattvabhūmi*, "It is taught that one needs to give up four types of action, comparable to a battlefield where one is defeated, and 46 kinds of wrongdoing." The four actions like a place of defeat are described in the *samvaravimśaka* "Twenty Vows" text, which is an abridgement of the *bodhisattvabhūmi* :

"1.   through longing for honour and respect, to praise oneself and denigrate others,

2.   through avarice not to practise material or dharma generosity to the suffering and helpless,

3.   to take harmful revenge, even though someone may have apologised and

4.   to abandon authentic mahâyâna and teach a semblance of dharma."

There are also the 46 faults such as "not making offerings to the Three Precious Refuges thrice daily, being carried away by one's desires" etc.

4B   RIGHT CONDUCT AS THE AMASSING OF VIRTUOUS QUALITIES

Once one has properly adopted the bodhisattva right conduct based on vows, one then needs to build up every possible and appropriate virtue of body and speech in order to progress towards great enlightenment. These are many. Taken together they are known collectively as the right conduct of amassing virtuous qualities. What are they? In the *bodhisattvabhūmi:*

"The following is to be understood as being the bodhisattva right conduct of amassing what is virtuous. Relying upon and abiding within the bodhisattva's right conduct, it is to apply oneself enthusiastically to study, contemplation, meditation and to remaining in solitude. It is to respect gurus and to serve them and to serve and care for the sick. It is to give excellently and proclaim good qualities; to appreciate the attributes of others and be forbearing with those who are scornful. It is to dedicate virtue to enlightenment and make earnest prayers to that end, to make offerings to the Three Precious Refuges and to strive to be diligent, to be ever caring and careful, to be mindful of the training and through awareness to keep to it, to guard the doors of one's senses and to know how much one should consume, not to sleep in the first and last parts of the night but to persevere in joining one's mind with what is wholesome, to rely upon holy individuals and dharma mentors and to examine one's own delusions, admit them and get rid of them. These sort of dharmas need to be practised, nurtured and brought to their maturity."

4C   RIGHT CONDUCT AS WORK FOR THE WELFARE OF OTHERS

In brief, it can be known as having 13 main aspects. What are they? In the *bodhisattvabhûmi* :

" 1. to support those who are doing worthwhile activities,
  2. to remove the sufferings of beings in torment,
  3. to teach those who lack skill how to cope intelligently,
  4. to appreciate what has been done and to benefit in return,
  5. to protect beings from what frightens them,
  6. to remove the distress of those who are suffering,
  7. to provide the needy with the provisions they lack,
  8. to very properly bring together a dharma following,
  9. to engage them in that which corresponds to their mentality,
  10. to make them happy through the very finest of qualities,
  11. to excellently annihilate (whatever needs removing),
  12. to inspire awe through exceptional abilities and
  13. to make them long for (the good and wholesome)."

Furthermore, both in order to instil confidence in others and to prevent their own conduct from degrading, bodhisattvas should get rid of (their own) impure physical, verbal and mental behaviour and only rely on what is pure.

~ purity of physical behaviour ~

One should avoid unnecessary wild behaviour—running, jumping and so forth. Purity means to remain relaxed and smooth with a kind expression on one's face: "Therefore be self-controlled and always have a smiling face. Get completely rid of that constant frown and dark looks. Become a friend to beings and be sincere towards them."

How should one look at others? "When looking at others, by knowing that it is through them that you will become a Buddha, look at them in a pleasant, kind way."

How should one sit? "One should not sit with legs outstretched or fidget with the hands."

How should one eat? "One should not eat with an overful mouth, noisily or with the mouth gaping."

How should one move around? "One should not be noisy and hasty when doing things like getting up from one's seat; neither should one slam doors. One should take pleasure in being quiet."

How should one sleep? "Oriented in whichever direction one prefers, one sleeps in the posture the Protector assumed when he passed into nirvâna."

~purity of speech ~

One should give up excessive or harsh speech. It says of *excessive speech,* in the *candrapradîpasûtra:*

"The immature are completely spoiled for dharma; the mind is no longer flexible and becomes rough; peaceful stability and profound insight are remote; such are the faults due to love of talking. There is no longer any respect for gurus; one begins to enjoy corrupt speech and through interest in the pointless, wisdom deteriorates; such are the faults due to the love of talking." etc.

About the faults of *harsh speech,* it says, in the *candrapradîpasûtra:*

"Whoever sees a mistake should not publicise it critically since, whatever was done, he will reap the same result."

In the *sarvadharmâpravrttinirdeśasûtra* it says:

"If one describes the lapses of a bodhisattva, enlightenment recedes into the distance. If one talks through jealousy, enlightenment recedes far into the distance." etc.

Therefore excessive and harsh speech are to be given up. How should one speak?

"When speaking, one's words should be meaningful to listen to, clearly expressed and beautifully chosen, liberated from involvement and aversions, smooth and in just the right amount."

~ *pure and impure mental behaviour* ~

Impurity here is explained in terms of both a desire for prestige and honours and an attachment to sleep and mental dullness. The *fault of craving prestige and honour* is explained in the *adhyâśayasam-codanasûtra:*

"Maitreya! A bodhisattva should examine how gaining prestige and being honoured gives rise to desire and attachment. He should know how gaining prestige and being honoured gives rise to anger and aversion. He should know how prestige and honours give rise to confused ignorance. He should know how gaining prestige and being honoured gives rise to underhandedness. He should consider how none of the Buddhas ever encouraged prestige or being given honours and he should examine how prestige and honours steal one's roots of virtue. He should consider how prestige and honours are like a prostitute trying to seduce her client." etc.

The thirst for prestige is never satiated. The *pitâputrasamâgamanasûtra* says:

"Like dream water in a dream: one may drink it but it cannot quench real thirst. So also may one obtain desired objects which please the senses, yet one will never feel satisfied."

Having considered the above, one should reduce one's desires and be satisfied with what one has.

About *the fault of enjoying sleep,* it is said: "Whoever comes to enjoy sleep and inertia will suffer considerable degradation in their understanding and their mental capacity will deteriorate too. Whatever arises from primordial wisdom will be constantly impaired." And "The understanding of one who comes to enjoy sleep and inertia will disintegrate through ignorance, laziness and indolence. That person will become prey to non-human forces and be harmed by them when meditating alone in the forests." etc.

Therefore the above forms of impure mental conduct should be abandoned. What are the pure ones? They are to have and maintain faith and the other qualities mentioned above.

5. How the power of right conduct can be increased

It is increased by the three powers mentioned above (generosity chapter): primordial wisdom, deep understanding and dedication.

6. How it can be made pure

This is accomplished through the two supports — voidness and compassion — mentioned above (generosity chapter).

7. Its consequences.

One should understand that there are both temporary and ultimate consequences of right conduct. The *ultimate result* is to attain enlightenment. The *bodhisattvabhûmi* says:

"A bodhisattva who has completely perfected the transcendent virtue of right conduct genuinely becomes a perfect Buddha, with peerless, true and perfect enlightenment."

The *temporary results,* whether one seeks them or not, are to possess the greatest happiness and well-being. The *bodhisattva pitaka* tells us:

"Sariputra! There will not be even one of the most wonderful splendours known to gods and humans that a bodhisattva who keeps such completely immaculate conduct will not be able to experience."

There may be these delights and joys of samsâra yet the bodhisattva will not be dazzled by them and will continue along the way to enlightenment. The *nârâyanapariprrchâsûtra* says:

"A bodhisattva endowed with such amassed right conduct would not be in any way corrupted even by the possessions of a universal monarch *(cakravartin)*. He would still exercise mindful care and long for enlightenment. He would not be detoured even through Indrahood. Then too would he exercise mindful care and long for enlightenment." etc.

Furthermore, those who keep right conduct will receive offerings from and be cared for by humans and non-humans alike. It says, in the same sûtra:

"The gods always respect those who keep the amassed virtues of right conduct; the naga will constantly express their appreciation of them; the yakśa will ever praise them; the gandharva will constantly make offerings to them; brahmins, princes, merchants and landowners will supplicate them, the Buddhas will constantly embrace them with their compassion and they will be empowered to worlds and the divine forces present therein." etc.

This was the thirteenth chapter, discussing generosity,
from this Gems of Dharma, Jewels of Freedom

Chapter Fourteen:

The Transcendent Virtue of Forbearance

The transcendent virtue of forbearance is summarised as sevenfold: reflections upon the fault of its absence and the qualities of practising it; its essential character; its different aspects; the essential characteristics of each aspect; how it can be increased; how it can be made pure and its consequences.

1. Reflections upon the fault of its absence and the qualities of practising it

■ In someone endowed with generosity and right conduct yet lacking forbearance, anger can still arise. Once anger has arisen, all the virtue created up to that time, through generosity, right conduct and so on, could be consumed there and then. Thus it says in the *bodhisattva pitaka:*

> "That known as 'anger' can overpower the roots of virtue established during a hundred thousand aeons."

The *bodhicaryâvatâra* also says:

> "Whatever one may have excellently practised—the generosity, offerings to the tathâgatas and so forth established during a thousand ages—can all be defeated by one burst of anger."

Furthermore, when anger has found a niche inside someone who lacks forbearance, it is like the festering wound of a poisoned arrow. The mind thus afflicted knows no joy, no peace and in the end one cannot even rest in sleep. Thus it is said,

> "Mind in the grip of anger's affliction cannot enjoy the experience of peace. It cannot experience joy or a feeling of well-being. Thus one cannot sleep and becomes unreliable."

And

> "...in brief, there is no such thing as someone happy through anger."

It is also the case that anger dwelling inside someone lacking forbearance will also show on the outside as a violent demeanour.

Through this, friends, relatives and employees all become vexed and tired with one; even gifts of money or valuables cannot persuade them to put up with one's anger any longer. Thus it says:

"Friends and loved ones grow tired; even when lured by generosity, they can no longer stand it."

Furthermore those lacking forbearance present opportunities to negative forces *(mâra)*, which then create obstacles for them. Therefore the *bodhisattva pitaka* says:

"A mind under the influence of anger is prey to negative forces and encounters obstacles."

Moreover, by lacking forbearance, the six transcendent virtues which together form the path to Buddhahood are not all six complete; thus one will not attain enlightenment. Therefore the *prajñâpâramitâsamcayagâthâ* says:

"Where there is anger and no forbearance, how can there be enlightenment?"

- The opposite of the above is to possess forbearance. It stands supreme among all the roots of virtue. It is said:

"There is no evil comparable to anger and nothing so difficult as to be forbearing. Therefore one should cultivate forbearance most earnestly using all sorts of means."

Besides, if one is forbearing one attains all sorts of felicity and well-being in everyday circumstances. Therefore it is said:

"Whoever manages to overcome anger through self-control will be happy in this and other (lives)."

Furthermore, by possessing forbearance, one will attain enlightenment. Thus it says in the *pitâputrasamâgamanasûtra* :

"*Anger is not the way of the Buddhas*, as is said. It is by cultivating loving kindness in all circumstances that enlightenment will arise."

2. Its essential nature

It is to be unperturbed by anything. The *bodhisattvabhūmi:*

> "It is not to be destabilised by anything whatsoever, through dwelling solely in compassion, without materialistic concern. In brief, the essential nature of a bodhisattva's forbearance should be known as this."

3. Its different aspects

Forbearance is of three main types:

- remaining undisturbed by harm done by others,
- acceptance of suffering and
- that when aspiring to a definite understanding of phenomena.

Of these,

▸ the first is to forbear through analysing the nature of beings who make trouble,

▸ the second is to forbear through analysing the essential nature of suffering and

▸ the third is to forbear through a discerning analysis of the unerring nature of phenomena.

The first two aspects cultivate forbearance in terms of what is relative and the third in terms of the ultimate.

4. The essential characteristics of each aspect

4A FORBEARANCE IN THE FACE OF HARM FROM OTHERS

This means practising forbearance towards those who either do what one does not want them to or who prevent oneself from doing what one wants to do—those who strike, insult, get angry at or deeply resent and so forth either oneself or one's own. What does *to forbear* actually mean in such circumstances? Forbearance means remaining unperturbed or not harming in retaliation or not brooding on the event, whichever is appropriate.

4Ai According to Dharma-Master Santideva's teachings, one should be forbearing by applying (the advice quoted in the following nine points, i.e. by meditating as follows):

~ consideration of the fact that the other person,
the one doing the harm, is out of control ~

Reflect: "Those who do me harm have lost control of themselves, through anger, as did Devadatta[1] to the Buddha. Anger is such that self-control is lost when that which one does not like manifests. Since (aggressors) are not in control of their acts, it is inappropriate to retaliate." Therefore it says:

"Thus being all under some influence they are, by that very fact, not in control of themselves. Knowing this one will not become angry towards realities which are but illusions."

~ consideration of the fault of one's own karma ~

Reflect: "The harm that I am experiencing now is a hurt arising through something very similar that I did in a previous existence. Therefore it is not fitting to retaliate against someone else for the mistakes of my own bad karma." Hence it is said:

"By my having harmed sentient beings in former times in just this sort of a way, it is meet that this harm should come to me now through others' violence."

~ consideration of the fault of one's physical existence ~

Reflect: "If one did not have this body then the other's weapons and so forth would have nothing to harm. The actual hurt occurs through the presence of this body and, from that point of view, it is not right to retaliate." Thus,

"Their weapon and my body are both causes for this suffering.

---

1.   Devadatta, Buddha Sakyamuni's cousin, performed many evil acts through the competitive jealousy he felt towards the Buddha.

Without this body, what would there be for them to be angry at?"

~ consideration of the fault of one's mind ~

Reflect: "This mind of mine did not take on a really good body — one that could not be harmed by others. By having taken a lesser, vulnerable body, it is afflicted by harms. Therefore, since it is my own mind that caused such a body to be mine, it is not right to retaliate against someone else."

"A human body is like a sore — it cannot bear to be touched and is pain ridden. As it was I who took on this province of passions, with whom should I get angry for the harms it encounters?"

~ consideration of how there would be no difference in fault ~

Reflect: "Some, through ignorance, do harm; others, through ignorance, get angry at them. How could one of them be faultless? In fact, they are both at fault."   As this is the case, one should reject what is faulty and instead practise forbearance.

~ consideration of the usefulness (of the harm) ~

(In practice,) development of forbearance is dependent upon (encountering) something harmful. Through cultivating forbearance, evil is purified and the accumulations are perfected. Through perfecting the accumulations, there will be enlightenment. Therefore through the very fact of harm there is great usefulness and for this reason one should practise forbearance. "On account of the forbearance which occurs because of these, many of my evils are purified." etc.

~ consideration of the great kindness (the harmer does one) ~

One will not be able to achieve enlightenment without the transcendent virtue of forbearance. The cultivation of forbearance cannot be achieved without there being someone causing harm.

Therefore this harmful person, being a support of dharma, is extremely kind and, furthermore, forbearance should be practised when there is this harm.

"I should rejoice about my enemies because they are supports for my bodhicitta practice. By achieving it, through them, the result of forbearance will be for them. By first relating to them in this token manner, they become a cause of forbearance."

~ consideration of how enlightened beings would be pleased ~

"Furthermore, the Buddhas are friends who never vacillate and who benefit us immeasurably. What way is there to repay their kindness other than to respect beings?"

~ consideration of the tremendous benefits (of forbearance) ~

"Those who show respect in many ways thereby cross most excellently to the other shore."

4Aii According to the (tradition of Santideva, in the) *bodhisattvabhûmi*,

It says that one develops forbearance by cultivating five notions. They are: "The notion that the one who harms is one's dearest friend; the notion that these are only phenomena, the notion of impermanence, the notion of suffering and the notion of completely embracing all beings to oneself."

~ the notion of the harmer being one's dearest friend ~

These beings who are at present causing harm were not like this in former lives. Then they were one's parents, relatives or teachers and there is not one of them who was not formerly one's mother. In that sense, they have been helpful and beneficial to a degree that no one could ever calculate and hence it is not right to retaliate against the present sort of trouble they are making. Through relating to the situation in these terms, one makes oneself forbearing.

~ the notion of what is happening being merely phenomenal ~

The harm that is taking place is (a relative situation the very nature of which is) dependent upon the circumstances (of the moment) and is no more than just notions, just phenomena. *There is really no entity, no being, no life-form, no person—not even the slightest trace of one—being abusive, hitting, grudging or making obstacles to me.* One practises forbearance through thoughts like these.

~ the notion of impermanence ~

Sentient beings are impermanent: they possess the characteristic of mortality and the greatest harm that can befall them is to lose their lives. Thus, one can practise forbearance by contemplating the notion that there is no need to kill them since they will die anyway by the very nature of their existence.

~ the notion of suffering ~

Every sentient being is afflicted by the three types of suffering. One cultivates forbearance of harm, through the notion of suffering, by thinking that one should be removing sufferings and not creating further ones.

~ the notion of completely embracing all beings to oneself ~

"Since I have taken the bodhisattva commitment, I should be working for the welfare of all sentient beings": so thinking, one should hold every sentient being very dear to one's heart — with the same fondness that one has for one's own spouse. Thus one creates forbearance through the notion that it is not fitting to retaliate to trivial harms done by someone one treasures so dearly.

4B FORBEARANCE AS ACCEPTANCE OF SUFFERING

This means accepting joyfully and without regret all the sufferings involved in achieving highest enlightenment. It says in the *bodhisattvabhūmi:* "It is to accept the eight sorts of suffering such as those due to the place in which one stays and so forth."

The main points of these eight are to accept, joyfully and without getting discouraged, whatever difficulty, tiredness, heat, cold, hunger, thirst, mental stress and other sufferings the following entail:

- seeking dharma robes, alms and so forth if one is following the noble life,[1]
- making offerings to and respectfully serving the Most Precious Refuges and gurus,
- studying the dharma,
- explaining it,
- reciting texts,
- meditating,
- striving in meditation during the first and last parts of the night instead of sleeping and
- working for the welfare of others, in the 11 ways mentioned above etc.

A parallel of such appreciative acceptance is to be found in the way one is glad to receive a painful treatment — such as blood-letting or moxibustion — in order to be cured of a serious illness. The *bodhicaryâvatâra* says of this:

> "The suffering of my achieving enlightenment is understandable. It is like the suffering inflicted on the body by surgery to rid it of an unbearably painful internal sickness."

Someone who accepts the suffering involved in dharma development, and who manages to swing the battle with samsâra and defeat the enemy, the defilements, is a truly great hero. There are some people renowned in the world as heroes but there is really no comparison, since they only defeat ordinary enemies, who by their very mortal nature would be slaughtered by death anyway. What they achieve is simply like hitting a corpse with a weapon. The *bodhicaryâvatâra* says,

> "By slaughtering one's reservations about any sort of suffering, one defeats the enemies — anger, hatred and so on. The one who achieves that victory is a real hero; the rest kill corpses."

---

1.   a monk or nun, novice or fully-ordained.

4C FORBEARANCE AS ASPIRATION TO CERTAINTY ABOUT PHENOMENA.

The *bodhisattvabhûmi* says that this is to aspire to eight attributes —the Most Precious Ones' qualities etc. It is also to practise forbearance in the face of, and to aspire to the meaning of, the unique identity, the very nature of voidness of both types of entity[1].

5. How forbearance's power can be increased

It is increased by the three powers mentioned above (generosity chapter): primordial wisdom, deep understanding and dedication.

6. How it can be made pure

This is accomplished through the two supports—voidness and compassion—mentioned above (generosity chapter).

7. Its consequences

One should understand that there are both temporary and ultimate consequences of forbearance. The *ultimate result* is to attain enlightenment. The *bodhisattvabhûmi* says:

"Vast and immeasurable forbearance will result in great enlightenment. By relying upon this, bodhisattvas will become purely, most excellently and perfectly enlightened."

In the meantime the temporary consequences, even though they are not purposely sought for, will be to have, in every future existence, a beautiful body, no illness, fame and acclaim and a long life and to possess the attributes of a universal monarch. Thus the *bodhicaryâvatâra* says:

"Through practising forbearance in the face of worldly burdens one will attain beauty and the likes, absence of illness and acclaim. Through these, an exceedingly long life and the delights of a universal monarch will be obtained."

---

1.   personal entity and phenomenal entity.

Chapter Fifteen:

The Transcendent Virtue of Diligence

The transcendent virtue of diligence[1] is summarised as sevenfold: reflections upon the fault of its absence and the qualities of practising it; its essential character; its different aspects; the essential characteristics of each aspect; how its power can be increased; how it can be made pure and its consequences.

1. Reflections upon the fault of its absence and the qualities of practising it

Even though one may have the qualities of generosity and so forth, if one has no diligence, one will waste time. Where there is time-wasting,[2] virtue is not accomplished, there is no ability to benefit others and one will not attain enlightenment. Therefore the *sâgaramatipariprcchâsûtra* says:

"One who wastes time is without generosity...(etc.) ...and is without profound understanding. One who wastes time performs no actions to benefit others. Enlightenment is very far, exceedingly far indeed, for one who wastes time."

Possession of diligence, which is the contrary of time-wasting, prevents all the white qualities from becoming tainted and fosters their increase. The *prajñâpâramitâsamcayagâthâ* says:

"Through diligence, good qualities will not become tainted and one will discover the Buddhas' treasure of infinite primordial wisdom."

---

1. **diligence** — none of our attempts to find a truly adequate yet not unwieldy translation for *btson.'grus* have yet succeeded. Expressions such as "joyous perseverance", "enthusiastic application" would give the feel of the notion that is being conveyed, yet they are long and do not work in all circumstances. There is a need to convey the sense of joy and enthusiasm along with that of constancy and effort. "Diligence" does in fact have a sense of joy, etymologically. Unfortunately it has lost that implication in modern usage.

2. **time wasting** here means not using one's life as fully and as usefully as it could be lived. The Tibetan *la.lo can* generally means "laziness" but in this chapter it is used much more broadly to embrace all the tendencies, combatted by the pâramitâ of forbearance, which attenuate the intensity of life's positive potential.

Furthermore someone endowed with diligence will be able to get across that mountain which is the destructible complex[1]. Thus the *mahâyâna-sûtrâlaṅkâra* says:

"Through diligence one goes beyond the destructible complex and is liberated."

Moreover, through possessing diligence the attainment of enlightenment will be rapid. Therefore the *mahâyâna-sûtrâlaṅkâra* says:

"Through diligence one will become supremely enlightened as a Buddha." The *sâgaramatipariprcchâsûtra* also says:

"Ultimate, totally pure and perfect enlightenment is not difficult for those who practise diligence. Why is this? Sagamati! Whoever has diligence has enlightenment."

The *pûrnapariprcchâsûtra* says in a similar vein,

"It will not be difficult for enlightenment to come to one who constantly exerts himself with diligence."

2.   Its essential character

It is to delight in virtue. Thus the *abhidharmasamuccaya* says,

"What is diligence? The remedy for time-wasting, it is to have a mind that genuinely delights in virtue."

The commentary to the *mahâyâna-sûtrâlaṅkâra* also says that its very nature is *to take utter delight in virtue*. It is *the remedy to time-wasting*, time-wasting being its opposite and impeding condition. Time-wasting is threefold: time-wasting as idleness, time-wasting as underestimating one's capacity and time-wasting as involvement with lowly pursuits.

---

1. **destructible complex**: an unwieldly name used to describe the main philosophies based upon a notion of self. There are twenty main categories based on four ways of associating a notion of self with any of the five aggregates (skandha). The name comes from the fact that the notion of self is, deludedly, one of a lasting, overall entity when in fact the actual thing that the delusion is projected onto is not lasting but constantly destroyed and not unique but complex, e.g. thinking of one's body as oneself.

2A TIME-WASTING AS IDLENESS

This means being attached to the pleasures of letting the mind drift, through sleep, idling in bed and lounging around: these are to be given up. Why give them up? Because there is no time to spare for such things in this life. It is said:

"Monks! Understanding will dim. Life will be cut off. The creative power of life will be cast away. Even the Teacher's Doctrine will be destroyed, for certain. Why is it that you do not practise with diligence and unflinching discipline?"

Quoting the *bodhicaryâvatâra*:

"Death will come so swiftly. Between now and then one must establish the accumulations."

One may think that it will suffice to establish the accumulations (of virtue and wisdom) at the time of death but when that moment comes, there will be no time to establish anything. As it says:

"Right now get rid of time-wasting. There is no time to spare: do whatever possible!"

One may feel falsely confident thinking that death will not happen before one has completed one's virtue. That is an unreliable notion. As is said:

"A confident mind is out of place. The Lord of Death does not work in terms of what has or has not been done. Therefore no one, sick or healthy, should feel certain about this precarious existence."

Therefore, by whatever means possible, one should cease wasting time through idleness, casting it off as one would throw off a snake that had slithered onto one's lap or in the same way as one would extinguish one's hair on fire. Thus the *bodhicaryâvatâra* says:

"Just as you would hurriedly jump up if a snake crept onto your lap, so likewise when sleep and idleness creep in, swiftly counteract them." And the *suhrllekha* says:

"When hair or clothes suddenly catch fire, one does one's utmost to put them out. So also should one strive hard to do whatever will prevent rebirth. Nothing else is as important as that."

2B   TIME WASTING IN TERMS OF UNDERESTIMATING ONE'S POTENTIAL

This is a defeatist attitude whereby one feels, *how could a lesser person like myself ever achieve enlightenment, even if I made great efforts?* There is no need to discourage oneself in that way; in fact, one needs to get rid of the waste of potential caused by such an attitude. If one wonders why such discouragement is unnecessary, (take heart from the scripture) which says:

"If they develop the power of diligence, even bees, flies, bluebottles, worms or whatever insect it may be will achieve enlightenment, so hard to attain! That being the case, how could one such as myself, born as a human full of potential and with an understanding of what is beneficial and what is harmful, not achieve enlightenment, provided that I do not forsake the bodhisattva conduct?"

2C   TIME WASTING THROUGH INVOLVEMENT WITH LOWLY PURSUITS

These are one's involvements with unvirtuous activities such as overcoming enemies and amassing possessions etc. As those are the very real cause of suffering, they are to be given up.

3.   The different aspects of diligence

Diligence is threefold: armour-like diligence, applied diligence and diligence as insatiability. The first is the most excellent attitude. The second is the most excellent activity. The third is what carries the first two through to their conclusion.

4.   The essential characteristics of each aspect

4A   THE ARMOUR OF DILIGENCE

One wears the armour of the attitude, *from this moment onwards and until every sentient being has been established in the highest enlightenment, I will never lay aside diligence in virtue.* It is said in the *bodhisattva pitaka:*

"Sariputra! Wear this as an inconceivable armour: until the furthermost end of samsâra, whatever it may be, never relax diligence dedicated to enlightenment."

The Sûtra Teaching Diligence also says:

"Bodhisattvas should wear this armour in order to gather beings to them. Since the number of beings is incalculable, the wearing of the armour should also be without limit."

The *aksayamatipariprcchâsûtra* also says:

"Enlightenment cannot be sought counting the number of cosmic ages: wearing the armour during that many ages and not wearing it for that many others. The inconceivable armour must always be worn."

The *bodhisattvabhûmi* says:

"If, in order to liberate one single being from suffering, I have to abide nowhere else but in hell for a thousand cosmic ages, this fills me with joy. It does not matter how much or how little time it takes or how much or how little suffering it involves. Such an attitude is the bodhisattva's armour-like diligence."

4B APPLIED DILIGENCE

This has three aspects:

- diligence in getting rid of defilement,
- diligence in accomplishing virtue and
- diligence in working for the welfare of others.

~ diligence in getting rid of defilements ~

Desire and the other defilements, as well as the actions they motivate, are the root of suffering. Therefore, they are prevented from arising through a prolonged action, both specific and global. The *bodhicaryâvatâra* says:

"When amid the hordes of the amassed defilements, keep firm your stance in a thousand ways: be like a lion among foxes. Do not let the hosts of the defilements injure you."

Is there in fact some example of the vigilance and discipline that one needs? It is said:

"Someone correctly observing the discipline should be as vigilant as a terrified person whose life is threatened: like someone carrying a pot full of mustard oil or a person held at swordpoint."

~ diligence in the practice of virtue ~

This involves striving hard in the practice of the six transcendent virtues, without any regard for one's own life or physical well-being. How should one strive? One should strive by means of five aspects of diligence: diligence as continuity, diligence as enthusiasm, diligence as being unshakeable, diligence as being undeterred and humble diligence.

1. diligence as continuity means working uninterruptedly. Of this the *ratnameghasûtra* says, "Since bodhisattvas apply diligence to every aspect of their daily lives, nothing can cause them regret about what their body or their mind does. That is how they apply it and that is called the bodhisattvas' diligence of continuity.

2. diligence as enthusiasm means acting joyfully, appreciatively and rapidly. As it is said, "Since this task has got to be completed, plunge into it like an elephant scorched by the midday sun plunges into a pool."

3. diligence as being unshakeable means not being detracted from one's task by any of the harms caused by one's own thoughts, defilements or sufferings.

4. diligence as being undeterred means not changing one's mind when seeing others' violence, brutishness, aggressiveness, degenerate views and so forth, as is recounted in the Sûtra of Arya Vajra Victory Banner.

5. humble diligence means practising the above forms of diligence without a haughty mind.

~ diligence in accomplishing the welfare of others ~

This is to make effort in the 11 fields such as supporting activities that are unsupported etc.

4C   DILIGENCE AS INSATIABILITY

This means striving after virtue in a way that knows no satisfaction until enlightenment is reached. As is said, "If one never has enough of sensorial pleasures, akin to honey on a razor's edge, how could one ever have enough of the peaceful reward (found) in the happiness of the full maturation (of diligent actions)." [1]

5.   How diligence's power can be increased

It is increased by the three powers mentioned above (generosity chapter): primordial wisdom, deep understanding and dedication.

6.   How it can be made pure

This is accomplished through the two supports — voidness and compassion, mentioned above (generosity chapter).

7.   Its consequences

One should understand that there are both temporary and ultimate consequences of diligence. The *ultimate result* is to attain enlightenment. The *bodhisattvabhûmi* says:

"Bodhisattvas, through perfectly completing the transcendent virtue of diligence, truly became perfect Buddhas, are truly becoming perfect Buddhas and will truly become perfect

---

1. The full maturation referred to here means a good rebirth, due to good karma. This section does not mean that one should feel dissatisfied with the final result—the total peace and happiness of Buddhahood (it could not, since karma and its maturation is always concerned with samsâra and samsâra alone). It is simply warning us against settling into being satisfied with the comfortable feeling of having good karma and leading a relatively good life. It is not that that is wrong but that it drastically limits the good we could be doing ourselves and others. It also betrays a poor understanding of the dimension of the task in hand—enlightenment for ourselves and all beings.

Buddhas with highest utterly pure and perfect enlightenment."

The temporary result is the attainment of the finest existential happiness during those periods when one is in the world. Thus the *mahâyâna-sûtrâlankâra* says, "Through diligence one attains the existential activity for which one wishes."

This was the fifteenth chapter, on the transcendent virtue of diligence, from this Gems of Dharma, Jewels of Freedom

Chapter Sixteen:

The Transcendent Virtue of Meditation

The transcendent virtue of meditation[1] is summarised as sevenfold: reflections upon the fault of its absence and the qualities of practising it; its essential character; its different aspects; the essential characteristics of each aspect; how its power can be increased; how it can be pure and its consequences.

1. Reflections upon the fault of its absence and the qualities of its practice

Whoever has the qualities of generosity and so forth but not that of meditation can be overpowered by distractions, and so will be wounded by the sharp fangs of the defilements. Thus the

---

1. meditation (Tib. *bsam.gtan* Skt. *dhyâna*) This term does not cover everything implied these days by the word meditation. The Tibetan literally means mental stability/thought process stability. As explained in detail in this chapter, the general idea is to take control of one's mental processes so as to remove confusion and suffering and to create peace and happiness, mainly through developing concentration meditation.

bodhicaryâvatâra says: "Humans whose minds are quite distracted live between the fangs of the defilements."

Furthermore, without meditation clear cognition[1] will not arise. If clear cognition has not arisen one is not completely able to benefit others[2]. The *bodhipathapradîpa* says:

"If one has not achieved stabilised peace,[3] there will be no emergence of clear cognition. Through thus being without clear cognition there is no ability to work for the benefit of beings."

Moreover, profound wisdom will not arise in one who does not possess (skill in) meditation; without profound wisdom one will not attain enlightenment. Thus the *suhrllekha* says:

"There is no profound wisdom where there is no meditation."

The contrary is to be endowed with (skill in) meditation. Through it one will reject craving for lesser things, clear cognition will emerge and many doors of profound absorption (samâdhi) will be opened in one's mind. Thus the *prajñâpâramitâsamcayagâthâ* says:

"Through meditation, lower sensations are rejected and one truly achieves intelligence, clear cognition and profound absorption."

Furthermore, through being skilful in meditation, profound wisdom will develop and this will cause every defilement to be overcome. Thus the *bodhicaryâvatâra* says:

---

1. **clear cognition** When the mind is focussed and stable through meditation, it is unencumbered with thoughts and has a crystal clear lucidity that endows it with clairvoyance, clairaudience, knowledge of others' minds, knowledge of the past and the ability to produce extraordinary phenomena. Please note that these are very different sorts of clairvoyance etc. than the uncertain instinctive abilities possessed by some people.

2. **unable to benefit others** — because one does not know what is really provoking their present situation: the complexities of their subconscious, the influence of past lives etc. Also one has no idea of what unexpected events may happen to them.

3. **śamatha** is meditation which brings stability and release from the power of habitual thoughts and defilements. The Tibetan *zhi.gnas* conveys the meanings *peace/pacification* (*zhi*)—meaning that defilements and thoughts are not disturbing—and *stability* (*gnas*) due to the mind resting in absorption on its object of concentration. See below in this chapter.

"Through the profound insight of one who is excellently skilled in *samatha*, it is known that defilements are totally overcome."

Moreover someone skilled in meditation will have insight into the ultimate meaning and therefore give rise to compassion for sentient beings. Thus the *dharmasangītisūtra* says:

"Through settling the mind in meditation, there will be insight into the ultimate, just as it is. Through insight into the ultimate, just as it is, bodhisattvas will enter into a state of great compassion for sentient beings."

Besides, through meditation one will be skilful in establishing in enlightenment all those who are training under one's guidance. Thus the *mahâyâna-sûtrâlankâra* says:

"Also, through that very meditation, one establishes all individuals in the three types of enlightenment[1]."

2.   Its essential character

Its very nature is that of *samatha* (stability and peace):[2] the mind resting inwardly and one-pointedly on virtue. Therefore the section of the *bodhisattvabhûmi* dealing with the essential definition of meditation says:

"It is a mind (turned) inwards, one-pointedly resting in virtue."

That sort of meditation is attained through eliminating the factors which are incompatible with it—powerful distractions. Hence the first priority is to get rid of total distraction. This involves *isolation*, inasmuch as the body needs to be isolated from social busyness and the mind needs to be isolated from thoughts. Thus the *bodhicaryâvatâra* says:

"With body and mind isolated, thoughts will not arise."

---

1. ...of the śravaka, pratyekabuddha and the bodhisattva.

2. See note earlier in this chapter for a description of these two elements of śamatha.

2A   ISOLATING THE BODY FROM SOCIAL BUSYNESS

This is treated through six topics: the essential characteristics, causes and harmfulness of social busyness and the essential characteristics, causes and benefit of isolation.

2Ai   The essential characteristic of social busyness is to be distracted through the company of one's children, spouse, acquaintances or possessions.

2Aii   The cause of social busyness is attachment, i.e. attachment to people such as one's spouse, household etc., attachment to material things such as food, clothing etc. and attachment to reputation and respect such as other people's praise etc. Through such attachments one cannot get away from social busyness. Thus it is said, "Because of attachment and through craving for material possessions, one cannot let go of the world."

2Aiii   The harmfulness of social busyness should be known as being both general and specific.

~ the general harm caused by social busyness ~

As it says in the *adhyâśayasamcodanasûtra*:

"Maitreya! Social busyness has twenty shortcomings. What are they? One is not in control of oneself physically, one is not in control of oneself verbally, one is not in control of oneself mentally, the defilements flourish, one is polluted by worldly talk, one is open to negative influences, one is given over to inattentiveness, one will gain no results in samatha and vipaśyanâ meditation[1]..." etc.

~ the specific harms of social busyness ~

Through the harm caused by **attachment to people**, one will not achieve enlightenment. The *candrapradîpasûtra* says:

"Indulging one's desires, one becomes attached to children and

---

1. **samatha, vipaśyanâ** See definitions later in chapter, p. 224.

spouse and relies on the despicable home(life), and thereby never attains highest and excellent enlightenment."

The *bodhicaryâvatâra* also says of this:

"Through attachment to beings, the highest purpose is completely blotted out."

One should therefore get rid of attachment to those people. As is said:

"Neither do they benefit one nor does one benefit them; so steer well clear of the immature!"

About the benefits of casting off these attachments, the *candrapradîpasûtra* says:

"Perfect enlightenment is not hard to find for those who, having rid themselves of clinging to spouse and offspring and, fearing domestic life, have genuinely shaken free from it."

The harm caused by **material attachments and attachment to reputation** is twofold: one cannot guarantee keeping them and they involve suffering. It says of the first, in the *bodhicaryâvatâra*:

"What will become of the wealth and fame that one has amassed is quite unknown."

Of the second it says:

"Whatever the object of one's attachment, it will come back to one a thousandfold as suffering."

2Aiv The essential characteristic of isolation is to be free from social busyness.

2Av The cause of isolation is to abide in solitude in a secluded place. A *secluded place* would be the likes of funeral grounds, forests, caves, meadows and so forth. To qualify as a secluded place it should be one "earshot" away from worldly habitations, i.e. a distance of 500 bowspans.[1] It says in the *abhidharmakośa:*

"A place is considered to be secluded when it is out of earshot, i.e. 500 bowspans away..."

2Avi The benefits of isolation. When someone has abandoned social busyness and gone to stay in isolation, for the sake both of enlightenment and other sentient beings, the benefits are manifold: it is the best way to serve and respect enlightened beings, one's mind will get out of samsâra, one will shake free of the eight worldly concerns, defilements will not be fostered and meditation will become part of one's being. These will be explained point by point.

~ it is the best way to serve and respect the Buddhas ~

To take only seven paces towards a hermitage with the intention of staying in retreat in order to benefit beings through bodhicitta, is far more pleasing to the totally pure and perfect Buddhas than offerings of food, drink, flowers and so on. Thus the *candrapradîpasûtra* says:

"Food, drink, robes, flowers, incense and garlands are not what best serve and honour the Victor, the finest being of all. Whoever, longing for enlightenment and saddened with the evilness of conditioned life, takes seven paces towards a place of retreat with the intention of staying there in order to benefit beings has far greater and better merit than those who make such offerings."

---

1. **secluded place**—The Tibetan term gön.pa, *dgon.pa,* meaning "secluded place", has become the everyday word for monastery. As can be deduced from the definition which follows in the text, many monasteries do not fulfil the criteria defining seclusion. The term gives a sense both of isolation and protection.

*~ one's mind will shake free from samsâra and
the eight worldly concerns¹ and defilements will not be fostered ~*

The same sûtra tells us that, "Likewise when one becomes constantly dissatisfied with conditioned (life), there is not the slightest longing for the world and tainted things will not be fostered at all."

*~ that which is needed more than anything else
—profound absorption—will swiftly develop ~*

The same sûtra says, "Give up enjoyment of towns and cities and always turn to retreat in the forests. Be single-minded at all times, like a rhinoceros, and it will not be long before the best profound absorption is attained."

2B   THE NEED TO ISOLATE THE MIND FROM THOUGHTS

While staying in retreat, one should contemplate, thinking, "Why exactly did I come to this hermitage? I came to this isolated place in fear and in awe of places, such as towns and cities, where there is distraction. Fleeing them, I came to retreat." What was so frightening there? The *grhapatiugrapariprcchâsûtra* says:

"I was afraid and in awe of social busyness. I was afraid and in awe of material success and honours. I was afraid and in awe of corrupting friends. I was afraid and in awe of those who teach bad ways. I was afraid and in awe of desire, anger and confusion. I was afraid and in awe of the mâra (demon) of the aggregates, the mâra of defilements, the mâra of death and the mâra of seductive pleasure. I was in awe and fear of the three (lower states of possible rebirth)—animals, deprived spirits and hell-beings. Through such awe and fear did I come to retreat."

---

1. **eight worldly concerns** These are attachment to, or being affected by, the following pairs of opposites—gain/loss, fame/infamy, praise/blame and happiness/unhappiness.

One should then examine oneself, thinking: "Through being in awe and afraid of those things I am in retreat but what are body, speech and mind doing right now?"

▸ Counteract (wrong physical activity) by contemplating, "If while in retreat my *body* is killing, stealing etc. then there is no difference between myself and beasts of prey, hunters, thieves and robbers. Is this really accomplishing my initial purpose in coming here?"
▸ Counteract (wrong speech activity) by examining speech and contemplating, "If while in retreat I chatter, slander, misuse speech etc. then there is no difference between myself and peacocks, parrots, songbirds, larks and so forth. Is this really accomplishing my initial purpose in coming here?"
▸ Counteract (wrong mental activity) by examining mind and contemplating, "If while here in retreat I have thoughts of desire, anger and jealousy, then I am no different from wild animals, baboons, monkeys, bears, mountain bears and the like. Is this really accomplishing my initial purpose in coming here?"

Thus, when body and mind are both isolated, distractions will no longer arise and, being now undistracted, one can enter into meditation. Then one needs to train the mind.

2C   THE NEED TO TRAIN THE MIND

One needs first to reflect upon which defilement is the greatest and then to contemplate in a way which remedies it:

▸ the remedy for desire is to meditate on the unpleasant,
▸ the remedy for anger is to meditate on loving kindness,
▸ the remedy for ignorance is to meditate on interdependence,
▸ the remedy for jealousy is to meditate on the similarity of self and others,
▸ the remedy for pride is to meditate on changing place with others and
▸ if all the defilements are equally gross or in the case of excessive thought, one practises breath meditations.

2Ci If desire is the predominant defilement, as a remedy one should meditate on the unpleasant as follows. First one contemplates, thinking of bodies as being (composed of) 36 impure substances such as flesh, blood, skin, bones, marrow, serum, bile, phlegm, mucus, saliva, urine etc. Then one goes to funeral grounds and observes corpses—fresh ones, 2-day old ones, 3-day old ones, 4-day old ones and 5-day old ones. One observes their decay, their complete transformation and how they become black and eaten by small beasts. Then one reflects, "...my own body is also of that nature, a similar phenomenon, and I have not yet transcended such a condition."

When observing new corpses, the flesh still intact, being brought to the funeral ground or those where there is just the muscle structure as interwoven fibres or those broken down into many pieces or when one observes skeletons of those dead many years previously, of which the bones are shell-coloured or pigeon-coloured, one meditates as above, thinking "...my own body is also of that nature, a similar phenomenon, and I have not yet transcended such a condition..."

2Cii If anger and malice are predominant, one cultivates loving kindness as a remedy as follows. In general there are three aspects of loving kindness, as mentioned in an earlier chapter. The aspect developed in this context is loving kindness focussed upon sentient beings. First one considers someone naturally very dear to oneself and gives rise to thoughts of bringing about that person's well-being and happiness. Through this, one achieves a corresponding feeling of loving kindness (towards that person). This feeling of love is then extended towards a mixed group of people[1]. It is next expanded to embrace ordinary people; then to one's acquaintances; then to those living in one's town and finally to include everyone living in all ten directions of the compass[2].

---

1. People dear to oneself, those to whom one is indifferent and those one does not like.

2. The eight points of the compass + zenith + nadir.

2Ciii If dull-mindedness is predominant, as a remedy one meditates on interdependent origination as follows. It says, in the *sâlistambhasûtra* ("Rice Shoot" Sûtra):

> "Bhikkhus! Whoever understands this rice shoot understands interdependent origination.
>
> Whoever understands interdependent origination understands the nature of phenomena.
>
> Whoever understands phenomena understands Buddhahood."

There are *two ways of presenting interdependence*:

‣ in the order in which it arises—the interdependent origination of samsâra and

‣ in the order through which it is counteracted—the interdependent origination of nirvâna.

The former has two aspects: inner and outer interdependent origination, the first of which is discussed here in terms of prime cause and conditions.

inner interdependent origination of samsâra in terms of prime causes

> "Monks! Through the existence of this, this will arise. Through this having arisen, (then) this arises. That is how it is. Through the condition of ignorance, there will be creations ... etc. (up to) ... there will be birth and through that condition there will be ageing and death, sufferings and lamentations, pain, mental stress and upsets. That is how this great cluster of nothing but misery is produced."[1]

"This" refers to the sense dimension, in terms of dimension of existence, and to womb birth, in terms of states of birth.

1. The first (link) established is the condition of **"ignorance"**, i.e. a non-recognition of that unique nature (tathâtagarbha) which ought to be known, due to the influence of which

---

1. This is an edited form of the 12 links of interdependence, of which only the first and last are given here. The following section will furnish the missing elements.

2.   there is the actual doing of tainted[1] action, be it virtuous or non-virtuous. This is known as **"creation** due to the condition of ignorance".

3.   The mind polluted by the seed-like potentials imprinted in it by such actions is known as **"consciousness** due to the condition of creations". Through the power of action mind is

4.   transformed into something quite aberrant and joins up with the procreative elements in the mother's womb to become the various stages of embryo and then foetus. This is known as **"name and form**[2] due to the condition of consciousness". Through the development of this

5.   the various sense faculties—of sight, smell etc.—become complete. They are known as the **"six perceptual gateways** due to the condition of name and form."

6.   When these various sense faculties, such as sight and so on, meet up with their corresponding objective fields through the corresponding consciousness[3], this tripartite meeting causes an actual experience of the object. This is known as **"contact** conditioned by the six perceptual gateways". According to the nature of this contact there arises

7.   feeling, in the sense of a pleasant, unpleasant or indifferent experience. This is known as **"feeling** due to the condition of contact".

8.   Attachment to that feeling, craving and powerful craving for it, is known as **"craving** conditioned by feeling". Through such

---

1. The taint is "triplicity", i.e. subject-object-interaction. The *dualistic* delusion of subject and object which results from ignoring the true unique nature of mind automatically becomes *triplicity* by the cross-fertilisation of subject and object illusions.

2. name and form is a sort of codeword for the five aggregates. In the early stages of the embryo there is some form but barely any presence of the other four aggregates, which are there *nominally*, as genetic coding and karmic potential, but not *actually*, e.g. there can be no visual consciousness because no eye is yet formed.

3. E.g. the faculty of vision enters into contact with visible form through visual consciousness, the faculty of taste enters into contact with flavours through gustative consciousness etc.

craving there is a

9.   striving in order either not to lose the experience or to bring it back. This is known as **"grasping** conditioned by craving". Due to this striving one

10. performs actions—physically, verbally or mentally—which generate rebirth. This is known as **"becoming**, conditioned by grasping".

11. Whatever existence composed of the five aggregates is generated by those actions is known as **"birth** conditioned by becoming". Through having been born,

12.   the development and maturity of the actual existence is ageing and its destruction is **death.** These are **"ageing and death** due to the condition of birth".   Through confusion and ignorance, death is accompanied by craving and attachment, and misery as an inner torment. **Lamentations** are the verbal expression of that misery. **Pain** is the unpleasant sensation due to the existence of the nexus of the five senses. **Mental distress** is the pain in the mind resulting from various sorts of mentation. Other such problems are **upsets**—a term relating to the subsidiary defilements.

The above interdependent factors should be understood as falling into three distinct groups:

- ► ignorance, craving and grasping are **defilements,**
- ► creations and becoming are **action (karma)** and
- ► the other seven factors—consciousness etc.—are **suffering.**

The *pratītyasamutpādahrdayakārikā* says:

> "The 12 specific links should be understood in terms of three groups. These interdependent origins taught by the Sage most properly fall into three categories——defilement, action and suffering. The 1st, 8th and 9th are defilement, the 2nd and 10th are action and the remaining seven are suffering."

Further, the above is exemplified as follows: *ignorance* is like the sower of a seed, *action* (karma) like a field, *consciousness* like the seed itself, *grasping* like moisture, *name and form* like a shoot and *the remaining links* are like the branches and leaves (of the plant).

Were ignorance not to occur, creation and so forth could not concretise ... etc. up to ... and if birth were not to occur then ageing and death could not concretise. However, it is because of the presence of ignorance that creations etc. do actually happen ... etc. through to ... and because of the existence of birth that ageing and death will actually happen.

In these processes, ignorance does not plot, thinking, *I will manifestly establish creations,* nor do the creations have a mind which thinks, *We were made to manifest by, and created by, ignorance* ... etc. Likewise birth does not plot, thinking, *I will manifestly establish ageing and death* nor do ageing and death consider themselves actually brought into being by birth.

Nevertheless, it is through the existence of ignorance that creations and so forth are manifestly established and will occur and, likewise, through the existence of birth that ageing and death are made manifest and will happen. This is how to view *inner interdependent origination in terms of prime causes.*

inner interdependent origination is also linked to secondary causes – "specific conditions"

This is because it comprises the six elements: earth, water, fire, air, space and consciousness:

▸ the **"earth element"** is that which makes the body's firmness and actual material existence.

▸ the **"water element"** is that which performs the task of holding the body together.

▸ the **"fire element"** is responsible for the transmutation of food, drink and so forth.

▸ the **"air element"** is that which performs the task of moving the breath in and out.

▸ the **"space element"** applies to the inner cavities of the body.

▸ the **"consciousness element"** itself comprises of the five sense consciousnesses and the tainted mental consciousness.

Without the above six conditions, a body cannot come into being; furthermore the presence of all six inner elements is universal and hence comprises everything.[1] It is due to them that the body will have its actual manifest existence.

In these (processes), the six elements do not think, *I will establish the body's firmness* etc. and neither does the body think, *I am generated by these specific conditions.* Nevertheless, it is through these specific conditions that the body occurs in all the ways it does.

One may wonder if the full development of the 12 factors of interdependence is completed in this life. The *daśabhumikasūtra* says:

"Creation due to the condition of ignorance applies to what happened in former times. The (links) from consciousness up to feelings apply to the present. Craving through to becoming applies to the future. Everything else emerges inexorably from that."

counteracting the above – the interdependent origination of nirvāna

Through realising the true nature (*dharmatā*) of all phenomena to be voidness, ignorance is stopped. Through its cessation, (all the other links) through to ageing and death will be stopped in their due order.[2] As is said:

"By stopping ignorance, karmic creation is stopped" ... etc. to ... "by stopping birth, ageing and death and misery and lamentations, pain, mental stress and upsets are stopped. That is

---

1. It is not that the six elements are simply the specific bodily functions mentioned here—leaving many other functions and phenomena still to be accounted for in the human body, or in the wider body which is the universe. The elements—despite their primitive names—represent a far-reaching and radical sixfold analysis of anything and everything: they are the six main elements which constitute everything. For instance, from a "physics" point of view, they represent respectively: matter (earth), bonding/gravity (water), thermodynamics (fire), kinesis (air/wind), dimension (space) and consciousness. See "Working With the Elements" by Dr Akong Tulku Rinpoche & Edie Irwin, Kagyū Samyé Ling.

2. Through absence of link 1, link 2 cannot happen. Through absence of link 2, link 3 cannot happen etc.

how this great cluster of nothing but misery will cease."

2Civ If jealousy is predominant, one meditates on the similarity of oneself and others as a remedy. Just as one longs for happiness for oneself, so do other beings long for happiness for themselves. Just as one does not want suffering oneself, neither do other beings want to suffer. (Thus thinking,) one cultivates the same care for others as one has for oneself. The *bodhicaryâvatâra* says:

> "From the very outset one should make efforts to meditate on the similarity of self and others. One should protect all beings as oneself through the similarity of their happiness and suffering and one's own."

2Cv If pride is predominant, the remedy is to meditate on substituting oneself for others. Immature beings suffer in a samsâra that they themselves have created through a motivation of caring for themselves alone. Buddhas, motivated by their care for others and acting solely for the welfare of others, have attained enlightenment. Thus it says:

> "Immature beings act out of self-interest. The Sages act for the good of others. (Just) consider the difference between these two!"

Therefore cast off egotism by understanding cherishing oneself to be a fault. Treat others as yourself by understanding cherishing others to be a quality. Thus the *bodhicaryâvatâra* says:

> "Through understanding ego to be faulty and others to be an ocean of qualities, cultivate a rejection of egotism and a commitment towards others."

2Cvi If all the defilements are equally present or if there is too much thought, one trains in breathing meditations as a remedy. These are the six (main) types of practice such as counting the breaths and so on, presented in the *abhidharmakośa* :

> "There are held to be six: counting, following, resting, thinking, transformation and utter purity."

There are also practices in which the defilements are neither eliminated, used nor transmuted. Such is the way of the mantrayâna or of the tradition and instructions of Marpa and his spiritual sons, which should be learnt directly (from a qualified teacher). They are to be understood through "uniting with the innate essence"[1] and the Six Practices of Naropa.

All the above (points Ci-Cvi) represent the various stages of mental training that lead one to meditative concentration and stability.

3.   The different aspects of meditation itself

There are three: meditation which procures tangible well-being, meditation which gives rise to good qualities and meditation which acts for the benefit of others. The first of these makes one's mind a suitable vessel, the second produces enlightened qualities in one who is already a fit vessel and the third works for the benefit of beings.

4.   The essential characteristics of each aspect

4A   MEDITATION WHICH PROCURES TANGIBLE WELL-BEING

According to the *bodhisattvabhûmi*,

"This is the meditation of bodhisattvas: it is free from all thoughts, it gives rise to excellent mastery of mind and body, it is supremely peaceful in the very best way, it is without arrogance, it is without involvement with experiencing the "taste" of meditation and it is free from any notion (of an object of meditation)—these (qualities) are what should be understood by *well-being during practice*."

i.   **free of all thought** means that it remains fully concentrated without any interference due to the discursive intellect producing ideas of existence, non-existence etc.

---

1. This is another name for mahâmûdra.

ii.   gives rise to excellent mastery of mind and body means the destruction of every bad condition that one's body or mind might adopt.

iii.   supremely peaceful in the very best way means that it enters such a condition naturally.

iv.   without arrogance refers to an absence of the defilements of views[1].

v.   without involvement with experiencing the taste of meditation refers to an absence of the desire defilement.[2]

vi.   free from the notion (of an object of meditation) means free from experiencing sense objects such as form etc.

That which serves as the gateway into all these is the concentration meditation of the four *dhyâna*—the 1st dhyâna, the 2nd dhyâna, the 3rd dhyâna and the 4th dhyâna. Of these, the 1st dhyâna is accompanied by thought and analysis, the 2nd dhyâna by joy, the 3rd dhyâna by happiness and the 4th by equanimity.

4B   MEDITATION THAT PRODUCES GOOD QUALITIES

This is of two kinds: exceptional and common. The **exceptional** meditations, immeasurable and inconceivable, are the various profound absorptions belonging to the ten powers. Since the śrâvaka and pratyekabuddha are not even aware of the names of such meditations, how could they ever actually engage in them? The **common** ones are the likes of the *complete liberations, surpassings, gateways of exhaustion, excellent specific intelligences* etc., which are also common to the śrâvaka. Even though they are said to be held in common, they are in fact common in name only, and not the same meditation in actual practice.

---

1. This topic is clearly explained in the abhidharma teachings on the main and subsidiary defilements. The defilements concern *views, philosophies* and *opinions* which do not concur with natural reality. Furthermore there are the dogmatisms, self-righteousness, distorted religious beliefs etc. which grow out of mistaken views.

2. The text (Rumtek xylographic edition) mistakenly reads *srid.pa'i.nyon.mongs* (worldly defilement) instead of *sred.pa'i.nyon.mongs*, as Khenpo Tsultim Gyamtso pointed out.

4C   MEDITATION THAT WORKS FOR THE WELFARE OF OTHERS

Whichever concentration meditation is resorted to, there can be countless physical emanations. These meditations operate for the benefit of beings in 11 ways, such as supporting beings according to their needs etc.

Then there are also the very well known śamatha and vipaśyanâ. What are they? *Śamatha* (stable peace) is mind resting within mind due to most excellent profound absorption. *Vipaśyanâ* (profound insight) follows on from this: it is an excellent discerning appreciation of phenomena which understands what is and what is not to be done. The *mahâyâna-sûtrâlaṅkâra* says:

"Through abiding in the most excellent, mind is made to rest within mind and there is supreme discerning appreciation of things. These are (known respectively as) śamatha and vipaśyanâ."

Śamatha represents concentration meditation itself and vipaśyanâ is the deep understanding (prajñâ) facet of (that experience).

5.   How meditation's power can be increased

It is increased by the three powers mentioned above (generosity chapter): primordial wisdom, deep understanding and dedication.

6.   How it can be made pure

This is accomplished through the two supports — voidness and compassion — mentioned above (generosity chapter).

7.   Its consequences

One should understand that there are both temporary and ultimate consequences of meditation. The ultimate result is to attain enlightenment. The *bodhisattvabhûmi* says:

"Through completely perfecting the transcendent virtue of meditation, bodhisattvas truly became perfect Buddhas, are truly becoming perfect Buddhas and will truly become perfect Buddhas—with highest, utterly pure and perfect enlightenment."

In the meantime (through meditation) one will attain the body of a god beyond the sense dimension. Master Nagarjuna says:

"Through the four dhyâna through which one completely gets rid of involvement with the senses and happiness-suffering, one attains a similar lot to that of the gods in the Purity, Luminous, Increased Virtue and Great Result heavens."

This was the sixteenth chapter, on the transcendent virtue of meditation, from this Gems of Dharma, Jewels of Freedom.

Chapter Seventeen:

The Transcendent Virtue of Wisdom (prajñâpâramitâ)

The transcendent virtue of wisdom (prajñâ) is summarised as sevenfold: reflections upon the fault of its absence and the qualities of practising it; its essential character; its different aspects; the essential characteristics of each aspect; that which is to be known, the need to cultivate it and its consequences.

1.   Reflections upon the fault of its absence and the qualities of its practice

If a bodhisattva constantly abides within the transcendent perfections from generosity through to meditation yet lacks the transcendent virtue of wisdom, he or she will never attain the state of omniscience. Why is this? The (first five pâramitâ) are like a group of blind people without a guide and hence unable to go to the city they wish to visit.

Thus the *prajñâpâramitâsamcayagâthâ* says:

"How could even a trillion blind persons ever reach the city, without a guide and not knowing the way? Without wisdom to show them the way, the five eyeless pâramitâ are without a guide and unable to reach enlightenment."

Contrarily, when they possess wisdom, all the wholesome aspects of bodhisattvas' virtue—generosity etc.—are transformed into the path to Buddhahood and they will attain the state of omniscience, just like the crowd of blind persons being led by their guide to the city. Thus the *madhyamakâvatâra* says:

"Just as the whole group of blind persons are easily led to the place of their choice by one sighted person, so similarly are the poor-sighted qualities led to victory by wisdom."

The *prajñâpâramitâsamcayagâthâ* says:

"By thoroughly understanding the nature of phenomena through wisdom, one will completely transcend the three dimensions of experience."

This being so, one may consider that wisdom alone might suffice and that skilful means—generosity and so forth—are not needed. This is not the case. The *bodhipathapradîpa* says:

"It has been taught that 'wisdom lacking skilful means or skilful means lacking wisdom—whichever it may be—is bondage.' Therefore do not abandon this combination."

Exactly what bondage occurs if one practises wisdom or means on their own? A bodhisattva who resorts to wisdom without skilful means will fall into the partial nirvâna considered to be peace by the śrâvaka and become utterly bound and never reach non-abiding nirvâna. According to the theory of the three capacities (*yâna*), one will be bound to that condition lastingly. According to the theory of a single yâna, one would be bound to that state for 80,000 major aeons.

On the other hand, if a bodhisattva resorts to means without wisdom, he or she will never get beyond the state of immaturity and will be bound to samsâra and samsâra alone. In the *aksayamatipariprcchasûtra* it says:

"With wisdom lacking means, one is tied to nirvâna. With means lacking wisdom, one is tied to samsâra. Therefore the combination of both is needed."

It also says, in the *vimalakîrtinidesasûtra*:

"What is bondage for bodhisattvas and what is their liberation? Their bondage is wisdom not supported by skilful means whereas their liberation is wisdom supported by skilful means."

Hence, to practise either skilful means or wisdom on its own is to dice with demons *(mâra)*. The *sâgaranânâgarâjapariprcchâsûtra* says:

"The works of mâra (demons) are two: means without wisdom and wisdom without means. Those should be recognised as the work of mâra and rejected."

Further, let us exemplify these: just as someone wishing to reach the town of his choice needs a combination of eyes to inspect the way and feet to cover the distance, so also do those going to the city of impartial nirvâna need the integrated combination of the eyes of wisdom and the feet of skilful means. The *gayasîrsasûtra* says:
"In brief, mahâyâna is twofold: means and wisdom."

Wisdom will not arise of its own accord. For example, a small amount of wood may be ignited but it will never become a powerful, enduring blaze: yet a good quantity of extremely dry branches stacked together can be ignited to make a mighty, long-lasting blaze that is inextinguishable. Similarly, if only a small amount of wholesome action has been established, great wisdom will not arise but when vast amounts of the great merits of generosity, right conduct and so forth have been established, a great wisdom will emerge and this will burn away all the obscuring defilements.

Therefore it is necessary to resort to generosity and so forth, even be it just for the sake of wisdom itself. The *bodhicaryâvatâra* says:

"The Victor has taught that all these factors[1] are for the sake of wisdom."

2. Its essential character

The essential character of wisdom is an accurate, discerning appreciation of phenomena. Thus the *abhidharma-samuccaya* says:

"What is wisdom (prajñâ)? It is an accurate discerning appreciation of phenomena."

3. Its different aspects

The commentary to the *mahâyâna-sûtrâlaṅkâra* gives three kinds of wisdom: worldly wisdom, lesser supramundane wisdom and best supramundane wisdom.

4. The essential characteristics of each aspect

4A WORLDLY WISDOM

This is the wisdom arising from the four domains of knowledge: the sciences of healing, logic, linguistics and creative skill.

4B LESSER SUPRAMUNDANE WISDOM

This is the wisdom that arises through the study, contemplation and meditation of the śrâvaka and pratyekabuddha. It is to realise the self-perpetuating aggregates to be impure, ridden with suffering, impermanent and devoid of any entity.

4C GREAT SUPRAMUNDANE WISDOM

This is the wisdom that arises from mahâyâna study, contemplation and meditation. It is the awareness that every

---

1. The first five pâramitâ.

phenomenon is, by its very nature, void, unborn, without foundation and without root. Thus it says in the 700-verse version of the *prajñâpâramitâ* :

"To understand that every phenomenon has no existence as something born[1]; that is the *prajñâpâramitâ*."

The *prajñâpâramitâsamcayagâthâ* also says:

"One who thoroughly understands every phenomenon to be without own nature is a person who practises the supreme *prajñâpâramitâ*."

The *bodhipathapradîpa* says:

"One will fully understand 'wisdom (prajñâ)' by understanding voidness, the very nature of which is realisation that the aggregates, elements and perceptual gateways are unborn."

5.   That which is to be understood

Of the three types of wisdom mentioned above, the one that needs to be understood is the third type—best spiritual wisdom. It will be presented through six topics: refutation of belief in substantial reality, refutation of belief in unreality, the mistake of believing in non-existence, the mistake of both beliefs, the path of liberation and the nature of liberation—nirvâna.

5A   REFUTATION OF BELIEF IN SUBSTANTIAL REALITY

Atiśa made an analysis of this point among his major reasonings in the *bodhipathapradîpa*, where he says, "It is illogical for something existing to arise[2]; for non-existents also, like sky flowers[3]..." In the

---

1. "Born" has a more precise meaning than one would guess from the term itself. It means generated, i.e. arisen, or produced, as something *independent, having own nature and lasting*. Although things may arise in our awareness, the experience of them always depends on various factors, has only a relative nature and changes.

2. **arise** This means the same as "born". See previous note. (continued...)

teachings on the gradual path he says that all substantial realities, or beliefs in substantiality, are contained in the two sorts of self entity and that both those entities are by their very nature (de)void (of true existence).

5Ai The two types of entity What then are the two sorts of self entity or mind? They are called "entity of individual beings" and "entity of phenomena" (self entity and phenomenal entity for short).

What is the "entity of an individual being" or "individual's mind"?

There are many views on this. In fact, what is referred to as a *person* is actually an unbroken continuum of self-reproducing aggregates accompanied by intelligence, a mischievous and cunning thing, always thinking and scheming, moving and scattering about. About this the *mdo.sil.bu* says:

"The term *individual,* applied to a continuum, is in fact constant movement and scattering."

Once the *individual* is believed to be a lasting and unique entity there will emerge involvement with, and clinging to, notions of *I* and *self.* It is that involvement which is known as *the individual entity* or *mind.* Through the notion of self, defilements will be generated. Through the defilements, action (karma) will be generated. Through action (karma), suffering will be generated. Thus, all sufferings and evils have ego-delusion, or mind, as their root. Therefore the *pramânavartikâ* says:

"When *I* exists, *other* will be known. Through the I-and-other pair comes clinging and aversion. Through the complex interaction of these will arise all harm."

What is phenomenal self-entity?

Phenomena (*dharma*) means the outer perceived world and the

3.(...continued)
3. **sky flower** This term, and others such as a barren woman's child or tortoise's fur, are used to show a contradiction in terms, here the notions of *arisal* and *non-existence* etc.

inner perceiving mind. Why are those (two aspects) called phenomena? Because they possess their own specific characteristics. Thus the *mdo.sil.bu* says, "The holding of specific characteristics is called *dharma*."

The term *phenomenal self entity* is applied to delusions which take both the percept and the perceiver as concrete realities, and to the subsequent involvement with those realities.

5Aii Analysis of the fact that both types of entity are by their very nature voidness[1]

Refutation of individual self entity

Dharma Master Nâgârjuna says, in his *ratnâvalî* : "*I* and *mine* deviate from ultimate reality." This means that, from the point of view of ultimate reality, those aspects of self entity do not exist.

(self is invisible to those who are aware of the total truth)

If individual self entity—ego—really existed it should equally be there when ultimate truth is "seen", yet when a mind with insight into the truth sees the essential nature, there is no "self". Therefore it does not have any ultimate existence[2]. The *ratnâvalî* says:

---

1. **voidness**—No one English word seems properly to convey the various meanings of the Sanskrit *sunyata,* the Tibetan *stong.pa.nyid.* "Emptiness" is too hollow and graphic. "Void" evokes, too much, an image of cosmic space. "Voidness" has the advantage of being clumsy enough to make one think twice. The main point is to express the meaning of something being de**void** of the substantial reality it seems to have. The realities apparent to the mind are myriad. They share a common point, which is to be themselves devoid of the particular reality they each seem to have relatively. However, it is important to realise that that does <u>not</u> mean that they share a common reality — a void which would be a state, a condition; something that could be experienced—like the wood common to wooden objects. Voidness is not a thing, a state, a tangible reality. It is a nature. When one refers to a mirage being devoid of true reality, it does not mean that its true reality is a void.

2. This is not a negation of the relative existence of self, or ego. It points to the fact that personality is only relative—never something that exists permanently, ultimately, in its own right. This is why it is compared to mirages, conjurations and dreams. They all have a certain relative reality, provoked by circumstances, but no ultimate existence whatsoever.

"Why? When the ultimately pure is fully recognised, just as it is, these two will not arise."

In that text, *recognising the ultimately pure, just as it is* refers to insight into the truth. (Dualistic) mind or *these two* which *will not arise* means that there will not be perception of "I" or "mine".

(origins of mind)

Were an own mind or a self to exist, it could be examined as originating from itself, from something else or through the three phases of time[1].

It does not arise from itself because (as far as the process of origination is concerned) its production must have either already happened or not yet happened. If it does not yet exist, it cannot possibly serve as a cause (for its own production) and if it does already exist, it cannot possibly become (its own) result. Thus something *producing itself* is a contradiction.

It does not arise from others because they are substances, (different) things (from it).[2] Why can they not be *causes*? A "cause" only exists with respect to a result and, as long as there is no result, there is no cause. As long as there is no cause, no result can manifest either. This is similar to the previous argument.

It does not arise from a combination of the above since both concepts are faulty, as explained above.

It does not arise from the three facets of time: it is not a product of the *past*, because the past, like a seed gone rotten, has no longer any power. It is not produced by the *future* — that would be like the child of a barren woman. It is not a product of the *present* because it is illogical that it could be both creation and creator (in the same instant).

---

1. These were, and often still are, the main philosophical notions associated with the origin (in the long term or in each instant) of self or soul.

2. Just as darkness cannot come from a flame, which is by nature light.

Thus the *ratnâvalî* says:

"On account of it not being obtained from itself, something other, a combination or the three times, belief in a self will be consumed."

"Not obtained from" means not generated by.

(location of the self)

There is yet another way to consider this. One should examine whether or not this "self" exists in the body, in the mind or in a name. The *body's* nature is that of the four prime elements: the body's solidity is the earth element, its fluids are the water element, its warmth is the fire element and its breathing and movement constitute the water element. The four elements possess neither self nor own mind just as the four outer elements—earth, water and so on—are without mind or self.

Does the self exist in the *mind* then? Mind has no existence whatsoever, for neither oneself not anyone else has ever seen it. If mind has no actual existence, then self as mind can have no actual existence either.

Does self or one's own mind exist in the *name*? A name is merely something given haphazardly; it has no substantial existence and bears no relation to a self.

Thus the three reasons presented above demonstrate that personal self entity or mind has no true existence.

Refutation of phenomenal entity

This is in two parts, demonstrating the non-existence of percepts and the non-existence of the perceiving mind.

(Non-existence of percepts [perceived reality]: two views)

As for the first, some believe in the substantial existence of percepts. The **Vaibhâsika** hold there to be minute particles of matter which exist substantially; they are round and partless. The grouping of these particles constitutes objects such as material form and so forth. As the particles agglomerate, there are interstices. They presently appear as something homogeheous just as do a yak's tail or a pasture of grass. The minute particles do not drift apart because the karma of beings causes them to bond as they do. The **Sautrântika** hold that when such partless particles conglomerate, they are in contact without interstices yet without being actually joined.[1] These are the views of those (two main traditions) but neither is really the case.

(Non-existence of percepts: are "particles" unitary or multiple?)

If a particle (as conceived of by the two traditions above) is *unitary* then would it not have sides (directional dimension)? If so, would it not have relative east, west, north, south, top and bottom parts. This makes six sides and destroys the contention of it being unitary. If it had no directional dimension (sides) (there would be no way for atoms to join and agglomerate, hence) all matter would be, by nature, a sole atom. This is evidently not the case either. The *vimśatikâkârikâ* says:

> "If one particle is joined to six (others), the particle has six different parts, making it unfractionable yet sixfold. If those six are one, then substance is only one particle."

Are particles *multiple*? If one unfractionable particle could be proved to exist, it would be reasonable to propose that many of them could conglomerate to make multiple entities but since the existence of an unfractionable unit (as postulated) cannot be proved, multiples of them cannot be proved to exist either.

As a consequence, since particles have no substantial existence, an outer substantial reality composed of particles of such a nature

---

1. The Rumtek xylograph reads *'byar.la.ma.reg.par.* Khenpo Tsultrim Gyamtso rectified this to *reg.la.ma.'byar.ba.*

cannot exist either[1].

(Non-existence of percepts: the correct view)

One may wonder, "What then is this (world) which is actually manifesting right now?" It is an image in the mind, which appears to the mind as being an outer world. This is because of delusion. If one asks, "How can one know that is so?" the answer is that it can be known through scriptural authority, reason and examples.

The **scriptural authority** can be found in the *buddhâvatamsaka* where it says,

"My children! The three domains of existence are just mind."

Also in the *lankâvatârasûtra* where it says:

"Mind disturbed by conditioning will manifest convincingly as what appear to be objective realities. They are mind itself and not something endowed with objective existence. Thus external objects are mistaken perception."

Reason can be presented in the form of the syllogism: "Those things which appear as external [*subject*] are illusory manifestations of mind [*proposition*] since that which has no true existence is present and manifest [*reason*] as, for instance, human horns or a visualised tree [*example*]. Such manifestations are simply illusory projections of the mind because:

1. they do not appear as what they really are—changing appearances

---

1. Several points need to be made here. The first is that this is a specific refutation of the ideas of a substantial universe made of atoms as postulated by the Vaibhasika and the Sautrântika. It is not a refutation of all ideas (including modern ones) of a gross universe made of particles. This having been said, it does provide us with tools for investigating more recent theories — particle theory etc. — using the notions of differentiation in respect to spatial reality in the sense of first having to prove the lasting existence of basic "building blocks" before accepting the existence of a grosser world supposedly made of those building blocks. The idea is not to refute their relative manifestation but to show that there is <u>only</u> relative manifestation and that those particles or multiple realities have no ultimate, independent lasting existence. These arguments seem very valid in the light of late 20th century scientific thought, which recognises the interference effect due to the presence of the observing mind and which is trying to puzzle out a minute reality of unstable particles.

brought about by certain causes and conditions,

2. appearances can transmute and disappear, through the power of imagination and

3. the way things manifest is different for each of the six types of being.

Examples of such a process would be dreams, magical conjurations and the like.

(Non-existence of the perceiving mind)

Some—**pratyekabuddha** and **cittamatrin**—consider the subjective, perceiving mind really to exist, as something apperceptive and self-illuminating. They hold such a view but it is inaccurate for three reasons: mind does not exist when examined in terms of moments of time, mind does not exist since no one has ever witnessed it and mind does not exist since there is no objective reality.

(Non-existence of the perceiving mind: when examined in terms of time)

The apperceptive, self-illuminating mind that they postulate: is it present in one instant or several?[1] Were it truly to exist in each instant, would that instant be temporally fractionable[2]? If it were so, this would refute its existence as a unique existing unit of mind. If it were not so, (the idea of sequences) of many instants becomes absurd[3]. Thus the *ratnâvali* says:

---

1. In their conception of mind, mind exists as indivisible instants of time. The refutation here, based on notions which would today be called differentiation and integration, demonstrates the impossibility of indivisible <u>real</u> moments of time, i.e. having determined, independent character.

2. i.e. is there an earlier part of the instant and a later part?

3. If instants have no beginning and end, there is no way that one can precede another to make a sequence of mind moments. The only other possibility would be for everything to take place in a single moment: equally absurd.

"One must examine the instant: just as it has an end, it has a middle and a beginning. Since an instant is thus threefold, the world cannot exist as instants."

Without the existence of the threefold division of time, the (true existence of the) instant is refuted by its being insubstantial. Through the instant being unproven, the existence of mind (composed of such instants) is also unproven.

(Does mind) exist as multiple (instants)? Were one instant to be proven it would be reasonable to postulate an accumulation of many instants but since the existence of one instant is not proven, the idea of mind as multiple instants is not demonstrated either.

(Non-existence of the perceiving mind: since it has never been witnessed)

Seek out the location of "mind"—in the body, outside of it and between the two; seek it high and low. Examine most thoroughly to determine whether it has any form or colour whatsoever. Seek until there is a certain outcome, whatever it may be. Search for it according to the guru's instructions—such as how to change the object of inspection. When, no matter how one seeks, mind is never seen, never encountered, and no substantial characteristic such as colour or something visible is to be found, it is not the case that mind exists but one has not yet been able to find it or witness it. If it cannot be seen, no matter where one seeks it, it is because the investigator is the investigated and the seeker is beyond the scope of his or her own intellect, beyond the scope of words, thoughts, ideas or expression. That is why the *kâśyapaparivartasûtra* says:

"Kasyapa! Mind is found neither within, without nor in between. Kasyapa! Mind cannot be investigated, cannot be shown, cannot be used as a basis, cannot appear, cannot be known and has no abiding. Kasyapa! Mind has never, is never and will never be seen, even by any of the Buddhas."

In the "Sûtra which Perfectly Grasps Dharma" it says:

"Therefore mind is a contrivance, a fake. Once fully understood as not being something existent, it will no longer be perceived as a real essence. Devoid of any essence, phenomena are without any real existence. I have properly taught that all conventional phenomena are thus by nature. Whoever is wise and skilled will cultivate the Middle Way through overpowering the two extremes. Phenomena are devoid of any essence. That is the way of enlightenment and that is my teaching."

The *dharmatâsvabhâvaśûnyatâcalapratisarvâlokasûtra* says:

"Every phenomenon is, by its very nature, unborn, essentially non-abiding, free from the extremes of acting and action and beyond the scope of thought and non-thought."

Since no one has ever witnessed "mind", it is pointless discussing whether it is or is not apperceptive and self-illuminating. Thus the *bodhicaryâvatâra* states:

"Since it has never been seen, at any time, even by a few, to talk about it being self-illuminating or not self-illuminating is as meaningless as discussing the elegance of a barren woman's child."

Tilopa said:

"Marvel! This self-cognisant primordial wisdom (jñâna) is beyond verbal expression. It is not the domain of the intellect."

(Non-existence of the perceiving mind: since no objective reality exists)

Further, since, as was explained above, visual forms and so forth—the outer objective reality—cannot be proved to exist, then the inner mind which perceives them cannot be shown to exist either. In a section of the *dharmadhâtuprakrtiasambhedanirdeśa* it says:

"Investigate whether this thing you call "mind" is blue, yellow, red, white, maroon or transparent; whether it is pure or impure, "permanent" or "impermanent" and whether it is endowed with form or not. Mind has no physical form; it cannot be shown. It does not manifest, it is intangible, it does not cognise, it resides neither inside, outside nor anywhere in between. Thus it is utterly pure; totally non-existent. There is nothing of it to liberate; it is the very nature of dharmadhâtu."

Furthermore, the *bodhicaryâvatâra* says:

"When there is nothing to be known, what is the point of speaking of knowledge?" and
"It is certain therefore that without the presence of something knowable, there can be no knowledge."[1]

Through the above points, it has been demonstrated that the perceiving mind, a subjective mind, has no ultimate existence. This concludes the section discussing the belief in reality.

5B   REFUTATION OF BELIEF IN NON-EXISTENCE

If the two types of self entity have no authentic existence as real things, could they be non-existent, unreal? In fact, they do not even exist as unrealities. Why? Were one or the other to have existed in the first place, as something real, and then to have ceased existing, it would be suitable to postulate (the idea of) non-existence.[2] However, since neither the two kinds of self entity nor the "mind" ever had substantial existence in the first place, they cannot be classed in either of these extreme definitions of *existing* or *non-existing*. Saraha said:

"To believe in reality is to be like cattle! But to believe in unreality is even more stupid."

---

1. e.g. without anything to be seen, there cannot be seeing. When there is no sound (within hearing distance) then there can be no hearing awareness (of that sound).

2. The idea here is that a non-thing can only be defined in terms of the original thing itself. Once an elephant has been clearly defined and established, one can go on to define a non-elephant or things which are un-elephantine. If no real elephant had ever been found in the first place, to go on to define no-entities related to it would be absurd. Although things do exist relatively, because of illusions which manifest through interdependence, nowhere can anything be found ultimately to exist—all by itself—lastingly. Since existence cannot be established, to go on to definitions of non-existence is impossible.

The *lankarâvatârasûtra* says:

"Externals are neither existent nor non-existent; mind cannot be truly apprehended either. The characteristic of the unborn is the perfect riddance of all these views."

The *ratnâvali* says, "When no real things are found, how can there be unrealities?"

5C EXPLANATION OF THE MISTAKE OF BELIEF IN NON-EXISTENCE

If belief in existence is the root of samsâra, will those who hold a view of non-existence be liberated from samsâra? In fact, this mistake is even worse than the one explained above[1]. As Saraha said:

"To believe in reality is to be like cattle! But to believe in unreality is even more stupid."

It also says in the *ratnâkuta:*

"Kaśyapa, the view of personality — even if it is as big as Mt Meru — is easy (to abandon): not so for a view of voidness due to pride." And further:

"Faulty views concerning voidness will be the downfall of those of little wisdom."

In the *mûlamadhyamakakârikâ* it says: "Those who believe in voidness are said to be incurables." Why are they incurable? Take the example of a purgative: if both the blockage and the medicine are eliminated, the patient will recover. If the blockage is removed but the patient fails to cleanse the purgative itself from his system, he may not recover and may even die. Likewise, belief in substantial reality is eliminated by cultivating the notion of voidness but if the person clings to voidness and makes it a "view", the "master of voidness" will annihilate himself and be on his way to

---

1. i.e. belief in real existence.

the lower states[1]. The *ratnâvali* says:

"A realist goes to the higher states; a nihilist to the lower ones."

Thus the latter mistake is worse than the former.

5D   EXPLANATION OF THE MISTAKE OF BOTH BELIEFS

In fact, belief in existence and belief in non-existence are both mistakes because they are beliefs which have fallen into the two extremes of permanence and nihilism. The *mûlamadhyamakakârikâ* says:

"To say *it exists* is the view of permanence and to say *it does not exist* is the view of nihilism."

To fall into the extremes of permanence or nihilism is confused ignorance and while there is such confusion there will be no liberation from samsâra. The *ratnâvalî* says:

"To believe in assertions that this world, which is like an optical illusion, either 'exists' or 'does not exist', is confusion and ignorance, through which there will be no liberation."

5E   EXPLANATION OF THE PATH TO LIBERATION

One may wonder, "What then can bring liberation?" One will be liberated by the **middle way**[2], which does not abide in

---

1. Someone who believes in substantial reality and understands something of karma, cause and effect, will at least make efforts to create causes for a good future rebirth and lead a good life. Someone attached to nihilistic ideas of voidness will not consider it worth the effort to create good karma and will be carried into animal rebirths by the conditioned stupidity of his or her mind.

2. **Middle way**   In this section we are given a real definition of Buddhism's famous "Middle Way", so often wrongly described, even by Buddhists themselves. It is "middle" because it avoids all philosophical extremes, and in particular those of permanentists and nihilists. It is <u>not</u> a compromise between extremes. If one extreme is black and the other white, the Middle Way is <u>not</u> grey. It is a solution that avoids falling into the extremes of black and white. It is a solution that avoids the intellect's simplistic need to define, when that which is in question is indefinable; or when the definitions proposed are mistaken or inadequate. When Lord Buddha taught the Middle Way, it was not to make Buddhists

(continued...)

extremes. The *ratnâvalî* says:

"Those who fully understand the truth, just as it is [1], and do not depend upon the two [2] will become liberated [3]." And "Thus one who does not resort to the two [4] is liberated."

[1]   that each and every phenomenon is and always has been unborn
[2]   permanence and nihilism
[3]   from samsâra   [4] extremes of eternalism and nihilism[1]

The *mûlamadhyamakakârikâ* says:

"Therefore the wise do not dwell on existence or non-existence."

What is this "Middle Way" which abolishes the two extremes? The *ratnakûta* answers:

"Kasyapa! What is the correct way for bodhisattvas to approach phenomena? It is this. It is the Middle Way; the correct, discerning appreciation of phenomena. Kasyapa! What is this Middle Way which is a proper discerning appreciation of phenomena? .... Kasyapa! 'Permanence' makes one extreme. 'Impermanence' makes a second extreme. Whatever lies between these two extremes cannot be analysed, cannot be shown, is not apparent and is totally unknowable. Kasyapa!   This is the 'Middle Way, which is a correct, discerning appreciation of phenomena'. Kasyapa!   'Self' is one extreme. 'Selfless' is a second extreme ... etc. ... Kasyapa! 'Samsara' is one extreme. 'Nirvana' is a second extreme. Whatever lies between these two extremes cannot be analysed, cannot be shown, is not apparent and is totally unknowable. This is the 'Middle Way which is a correct, discerning appreciation of phenomena'."

2.(...continued)
compromisers but to help them seek the real truth about the nature of what they experience, beyond the simplistic stories about reality which the discursive mind tries to propose.

1. These four comments appear in this way in the xylographic text; they are not the translators'.

Also, Master Śantideva has taught:

"Mind can be found neither inside, outside nor elsewhere. It is not a combination and neither is it something apart. It is not the slightest thing. The very nature of sentient beings is nirvâna."

Therefore, even though one may practise this Middle Way which does not consider things in terms of the two extremes, the middle itself is never something which can be examined. It abides beyond the intellect, free from understanding which believes sense data to be this or that. Atiśa has said:

"...likewise the past mind has stopped, is destroyed. The future mind is unborn and has not yet occurred. The present mind is exceedingly hard to investigate, is colourless, without form and, like space, without concrete existence."

The *abhisamayâlankâra* also says:

"It is not in the extremes of this shore or that. It does not abide between them. It is held to be *prajñâpâramitâ* on account of its *prajñâ* which (recognises) the sameness of all times."

5F   AN EXPLANATION OF THE NATURE OF NIRVANA: THE NATURE OF LIBERATION

If all samsâra's phenomena have no true existence, either as things substantial or insubstantial, then is "nirvâna" something which has substantial or insubstantial reality? Some philosophers do consider nirvâna actually to have some concrete existence. However, this is not correct, as the *ratnâvalî* explains:

"Since nirvâna is not even insubstantial, what could its substance be?"

Were nirvâna something substantial, it would have to be a composite product and that which is a composite will eventually disintegrate. Hence the *mûlamadhyamakakârikâ* states:

"Were nirvâna to be substantial, it would be a composite

product." etc.

However, it is not even the case that it is something insubstantial. The same work says:

"There is no existence of anything insubstantial in it."

Well then, what is it? "Nirvâna is the exhaustion of all perception of substantial existence and insubstantial existence. It is beyond the scope of the intellect and ineffable." The *ratnâvalî*:

"The end of all notions of substantial or insubstantial reality: that is 'nirvâna'."

It also says, in the *bodhicaryâvatâra*:

"Whenever substantiality or insubstantiality no longer dwell before the intellect, in that moment, through the absence of other forms and within non-objectification, there will be most excellent peace."

The *brahmapariprcchâsûtra* says:

"'Parinirvâna' means the complete pacification of every distinctive characteristic, and freedom from any sort of fluctuation."

The *sadharmapundarîkasûtra* says:

"Kasyapa! Nirvâna is the complete assimilation of everything into sameness."

Therefore nirvâna, besides being the pacification of all mental engagements, is also the absence of any true phenomenal existence, such as coming into being, cessation, something eliminated or something attained. The *mûlamadhyamakakârikâ* states:

"No abandoning, no acquiring, no nihilism, no eternity, no cessation, no arising: this is nirvâna."

Since nirvâna is without any arising, cessation, relinquishment or acquisition whatsoever, there is nothing of it which one creates, fabricates or modifies. Therefore the "Space Jewel Sûtra" says:

"Nothing to remove from this; not the slightest thing thereon to add. Properly beholding the nature; when truly seen—perfect liberation."[1]

Therefore although the terms "what is to be known is one's own mind" or "what is to be known is prajñâ — finest awareness" are employed in the context of analytical investigation, what prajñâ or mind actually is, is beyond knowledge or verbal expression. As the *suvikrânti-vikramaparprcchasûtra* says:

"As the *prajñâpâramitâ* cannot be expressed through anything phenomenal, it transcends all words."

Furthermore, in "Rahula's Praises to the Mother[2]" it says:

"I prostrate to the mother of all the Victors of the three times: the *prajñâpâramitâ* inexpressible in word or thought; unborn, unceasing, the very essence of space; the field of experience of discerning, auto-cognisant primordial wisdom."

6.   The need to cultivate this mind / prajñâ

Now, since all phenomena are voidness itself, one may wonder whether or not it is necessary to cultivate this awareness. Indeed it is necessary. For instance, even though silver ore has the very nature of silver, the silver itself will not be apparent until the ore has been smelted and worked on. Likewise all things have always been by their very nature voidness, beyond every form of conceptual complication, yet nevertheless there is a need for awareness of it to be developed since beings' experience it in various material ways and undergo various sufferings. Therefore, having become aware of what was explained above, there are four ways to cultivate this awareness: preliminary practices, meditation, post-meditation and the signs of familiarity (with voidness).

---

1. This very famous quote is picked up in several treatises, notably the *mahayanottara-tantrasastra* where its meaning is developed. See "Changeless Nature" KDDL.

2. The "Mother" in question is the *prajñâpâramitâ*.

6A   THE PRELIMINARIES

These involve settling the mind into its natural, relaxed state. How does one achieve this? By following what it says in the 700-verse version of the *prajñâpâramitâ*:

"Dear sons, dear daughters! Rely on solitary meditation and delight in the absence of busyness. Sitting cross-legged and not projecting any specific notions, cultivate awareness and so forth..."

and by doing the mahâmûdra preparatory practices.

6B   THE ACTUAL METHOD OF MEDITATION

One needs to do this according to the mahâmûdra system of guidance. One lets the mind settle free from even the slightest mental effort to posit, negate, adopt or reject. Tilopa says:

"Do not ponder, do not think, do not be aware, do not cultivate, do not analyse—leave mind to itself."[1]

Also, about letting the mind rest:[2]

"Listen child! Whatever thoughts you may have, within this (state of rest) there is no one bound, no one free. Therefore, o joy! Shedding your fatigue, rest naturally, without contrivance or distraction."

Nâgârjuna has also said:

"An elephant that has been trained, like a mind which has entered a relaxed state, has stopped running to and fro and (remains) naturally calm. Thus have I realised and hence what need do I have of a teaching?" and

---

1. This very famous advice from Tilopa is frequently developed in terms of time. In that case, the first three injunctions relate respectively to past, future and present and can be interpreted, "Do not ponder (the past), think about (the future) or be aware (of the present)..."

2. The following phrase is attributed to Saraha.

"Don't adopt an attitude or think in any way whatsoever. Don't interfere or contrive but leave mind loose in its own nature. The uncontrived is the unborn true nature. This is to follow in the wake of all the enlightened ones of the three times."

The "Lord of Retreat"[1] has also said:

"Do not see fault anywhere. Practise that which is nothing whatsoever. Do not foster longing for signs of progress and the like.[2] Although it is taught that there is nothing whatsoever to meditate on, do not fall under the sway of inactivity and indifference. In all circumstances, practise with mindfulness."

In the "Achievement of the Very Point of Meditation" it says,

"When meditating, one does not *meditate* on anything whatsoever. To call it 'meditation' is simply a terminological convention."

As Saraha said:

"If there is involvement with anything, get rid of it. Once realised, it is everything; no one will ever know anything else."

In the words of Atiśa:

"It is profound, uncomplicated Thatness: lucid and uncreated, it never arose, will never cease and is primordially pure. It is the dharmadhâtu, without middle or end, which by its very nature is nirvâna. Behold it with the fine eye of mind, undistorted by concept and without the blurs of sluggishness or agitation." And "Settle awareness free of conceptual complication in the dharmadhâtu which is itself free of conceptual complication."

If one can settle mind in the way described above, one will be employing an unerring method for cultivating the transcendent virtue of profound wisdom—the *prajñâpâramitâ*. The version of the

---

1. Shawaripa

2. Signs of progress in the understanding of voidness: in fact the actual word used is "warming" (to the experience of voidness). See "paths" chapter which follows.

prajñâpâramitâ in 700 verses says:

"To cultivate *prajñâpâramitâ* means neither engaging in, holding onto nor rejecting anything. To cultivate *prajñâpâramitâ* means not to abide in anything whatsoever. To cultivate *prajñâpâramitâ* means not thinking about or focussing on anything whatsoever."[1]

The (version of the) *prajñâpâramitâ* in 8,000 verses says:

"To cultivate the *prajñâpâramitâ* involves cultivating nothing whatsoever." And
"To cultivate the *prajñâpâramitâ* is to cultivate space."[2]

How can one "cultivate space"? The same sûtra tells us:

"The *prajñâpâramitâ* is even less of a conceptual nature than is space."

The *prajñâpâramitâsamcayagâthâ* says also,

"To apply the sublime *prajñâpâramitâ* means not thinking of either that which arises or that which does not arise."

In the words of the great master "Lord of Speech"[3]:

"Do not think about the thinkable. Do not think about the unthinkable either. By thinking neither about the thinkable nor the unthinkable, one will see voidness."

How does one see voidness? As it says in the *dharmasangîtisûtra*:

"The seeing of voidness does not involve sight." And

---

1. **cultivate** The Tibetan term *sgom* has a root meaning of developing the habit of doing something/becoming familiar with something. Thus it means to cultivate or develop and it is the main general term in Tibetan for "meditate"/"meditation", since the main point of meditation practice is to become familiar with the true way things are. Whereas a Tibetan seeing the term *sgom* will have these three meaning — develop, cultivate and meditate — resonating simultaneously in his or her mind, in English [these terms bring up different subconscious associations] and one or another has to be picked according to the context.

2. See preceding note.

3. Manjushri?

" Victorious, Accomplished and Transcendent One! Not to see any thing is to see excellently." And

"Without seeing any thing whatsoever, the one and only nature is seen."

The "Small Middle Truth" also says:

"It says in some exceedingly profound discourses that not-seeing is to see that."

The *prajñāpāramitāsamcayagāthā* also remarks:

"People talk in terms of seeing space. How one does 'see' space? One should investigate this point. The Tathagata taught the way to see phenomena as being like that."

6C   THE INTER-MEDITATION PHASE[1]

While viewing everything which occurs in between (meditation sessions)[2] as illusory, one should establish every wholesome merit one can, through the practice of generosity and so forth. As the *prajñāpāramitāsamcayagāthā* says:

"Whoever understands the five aggregates[3] to be like an illusion will no longer fabricate aggregates and illusions. To practise the total peace which is free of all sorts of cognition; that is to practise the sublime *prajñāpāramitā*."

The *samādhirājasūtra* says:

"Although magicians conjure up forms, making horses, elephants, carts and all sorts of things, nothing of what appears is actually

---

1. i.e. in-between meditation sessions, often called the "post-meditation" phase or state.

2. In between formal sessions if one is a beginner; in between moments of lucidity whenever they happen if one has some experience of voidness.

3. The five main areas of experience: form, feeling, cognition, mental activity and consciousness. All facets of relative experience can be categorised into one or another of these groups. In fact, the 4th aggregate, mental activities or mental events, contains all the others; they are abstracted on account of the importance they hold for most people.

there. Know that all things are likewise."

It is said in the "Very Point of Conduct": "The mind is attentive to no-thought, yet the amassing of wholesomeness never ceases."

Through such familiarity (with the wisdom of voidness), the meditation and inter-meditation phases will become indistinguishable and free from self-consciousness[1].

"There will be no more self-consciousness in terms of *I am meditating* or *I arise from meditation.* Why? Because there is awareness of the very nature of things."

– (the practice of prajñâpâramitâ comprises and transcends all other virtues) –

To be immersed, even for a short moment, in *prajñâpâramitâ*–the ultimate, voidness—constitutes an incomparably greater virtue than to spend aeons receiving dharma teachings, reciting (scriptures) or planting roots of goodness in the form of generosity and similar wholesome actions. In the *tattvaprakâsa* (the Buddha) states:

"Sariputra, the merit of one who has practised meditation of profound absorption in Thusness[2] for merely the duration of a finger-snap is greater than that of one who studies for a cosmic age. Sariputra, for this reason you should earnestly instruct others to practise meditation on Thusness. Sariputra, all the bodhisattvas who have been predicted as being future Buddhas also abide solely in that meditative state."

---

1. **self-consciousness** *rlom.sems* literally means arrogance or haughtiness but can take on a much broader meaning. Here it covers all habitual attempts of the discursive mind to create an identity. The truth of there being no fixed personality is evident due to the wisdom of voidness.

2. **Thusness** has been used for simplicity. There are many epithets for the ultimate truth: thusness, suchness, voidness etc. Although they all refer to a single thing, the inherent purity of mind, their terminology emphasises one or another facet of it. "Thatness" refers to it being the goal; "Thusness" presents it as everyone's true nature etc. The particular one used here gives a meaning of "one-and-onlyness".

It is also stated, in the "Sûtra Which Develops Great Realisation":

"It is more meaningful to practise meditative concentration for a session than to protect the lives of humans of the three dimensions."

In the "Great Head Mound Sûtra" it states:

"It is of greater merit to cultivate the true meaning of things for a day than to study and reflect for many cosmic æons. Why is this so? Because it takes one far away from the road of births and deaths."

In the *śraddhâbalâdhânâvatâramudrâsûtra* it says:

"There is greater merit in a yogi's session of voidness meditation than there would be if all beings in the three dimensions spent their whole lives using their possessions to accumulate virtue."

It is taught that if the meaningful point of voidness is not kept in mind, other virtues will be unable to gain one liberation." The *sarvadharmâpravrttinirdeśa* :

"One may observe right conduct for a long time and practise concentration meditation for millions of æons, but, without realisation of this highest truth, those things cannot bring liberation, according to this teaching. Whoever understands this nothing at all will never cling to anything at all."

In the "Ten Wheels, Essence of Earth" scripture it states:

"Familiarity with profound absorption cuts through doubts. Other than that, nothing has that capacity. Since the cultivation of profound absorption is supreme, skilful sages practise it assiduously." Furthermore:

"The positive result of meditating for a day far exceeds that of writing out, reading, studying, reciting or explaining the teachings for æons."

Once the key point of voidness, as described above, has been assimilated, it includes absolutely everything, without exception

It is **to take refuge**. This is taught in the *anavataptanâga-râjapariprcchâsûtra*:

"Bodhisattvas are aware that every phenomenon is without entity, without being, without life and without personality. To see in the way the Tathâgatas see—not as forms, not as names and not as specific phenomena—that is to have taken refuge in the Buddha with a mind unpolluted by materialism. The very defining essence of the Tathâgatas is the dharmadhâtu[1]. Dharmadhâtu is *that which pervades everything*. Thus, seeing it as that which accompanies the domain of all phenomena is to take refuge in the dharma with a mind unpolluted by materialism. Whoever is familiar with the dharmadhâtu as being uncreated, with the fact that the Śrâvakayâna is founded in the uncreated, and with the non-duality of the created and the uncreated, takes refuge in the sangha with a mind unpolluted by materialism."

It is also to **give rise to bodhicitta.** The "Sûtra of Great Bodhicitta" says:

"Kasyapa! Every phenomenon, like space, is without specific characteristic; primordial lucid clarity and utter purity. That is 'to give rise to bodhicitta'."

---

1. The word *dharma* is used severally in Sanskrit; in fact, it is accorded ten definitions. Sometimes it is the general word for "thing" or "phenomenon" and sometimes it means "dharma" in the modern Buddhist sense etc. The ideas being developed here, in a typically laboured but logical way, hinge upon these meanings of dharma. Dharmadhâtu could be interpreted as "The domain or realm or space in which phenomena happen". It is the very nature of mind which can give rise to anything of samsâra or nirvâna — the primordial space in which mind's drama takes place. The text shows how Buddhas have pure, primordial space as their essence whereas beings have it, of course, but cluttered with deluded and confused notions, which create their life experiences, their "phenomena" (dharma).

Although the **visualisation stage**[1]**, meditation on divine forms and mantra recitation** are spoken of, it is taught that if there is this (awareness of voidness) then all those are complete within it. Where is such a thing taught? It is said in the Hévajra tantra:

"Without meditation, without meditator; without deities and with no mantras either − in the uncomplicated nature, deities and mantras are truly present; the sattvas Vairocana, Aksobhya, Amogasiddhi, Ratnasambhava and Amitâbha."

The *śri-sarvabuddhasamâyogadâkinîjâsamvara-nâma-uttaratantra* says:

"Cast images and the like will not produce a yogi. Yet the yogi who strives excellently in bodhicitta will become the deity[2],"

whilst the *vajraśekhara-mahâguhyayogatantra* says:

"The intrinsic characteristics of every mantra are to be the mind of all the Buddhas, to (help one) achieve the essence of dharma and to embrace the dharmadhâtu in the right manner: such are taught to be the intrinsic characteristics of mantras."

Fire-offerings are also included in it. As the *amrtaguhyatantrarâja* says:

"What are fire offerings for? They are made in order to bestow the highest spiritual accomplishments and to overcome thoughts.

---

1. *bskyed.rim* This is sometimes called the "development stage" or "visualisation stage" of vajrayana sadhana. It refers to the stage of practice dealing with relative reality, in which, identifying with primordial purity, one visualises, makes offerings, invites presences, recites mantras etc. The other stage is *rdzogs.rim* during which one remains in ultimate reality, without artifice of any sort.

2. It should be noted, by readers unfamiliar with vajrayana practice, that *deity* does not refer to any real god but to sublime deomorphic symbols, representing enlightened qualities such as love, compassion, wisdom, skill in helping others, generosity, self-control etc. etc. Although Buddhism does teach about the existence of gods as sentient beings, they are simply better-off worldly beings, and not to be venerated, invoked or emulated as models of perfect spirituality. It might be better to translate the term *lha* as "sublime mind" in this context, but this would not render the straightforward simplicity of the original word — very useful in presenting the truths of Buddhism in lands where people were used to notions of local and cosmic gods.

Burning wood and so forth does <u>not</u> constitute a fire offering."

The **path in terms of the six pâramitâ** is also complete in it. The Vajra Samâdhi Sûtra says:

"When not departing from voidness, the six *pâramitâ* are united."

According to the *brahmaviśesacintipariprcchâsûtra* :

"To be without intention is generosity. Not to dwell on all sorts of things is right conduct. Not to make specific distinctions is forbearance. Absence of adoption and rejection is diligence. Non-attachment is meditation. No-thought is wisdom." The "Essence of Earth Sûtra" also states:

"The meditation of the wise and skilful on the teaching of voidness does not resort to or dwell upon anything wordly. It abides nowhere in any existence. It is the observance of most virtuous right conduct."

It is said in the same sûtra:

"All phenomena are of one taste, being equally void and without any specific characteristics. Therefore a mind which does not dwell upon or become attached to anything whatsoever is (practising) forbearance; through this, benefit will increase greatly. The wise who practise diligence have cast far away every attachment. The mind that neither dwells on nor clings to anything whatsoever should be known as a 'field of finest virtue'. To practise profound absorption in order to bring happiness and well-being to every form of conscious life is something which removes a great burden and which clears away every polluting defilement. Such are the characteristics of the truly wise and capable."

It also represents **prostrations**. The "Sky Jewel Sûtra":

"Like water poured into water and like butter poured into butter, such is this primordial wisdom which is intelligent of itself, by itself. Such magnificent seeing in itself makes prostration to this."

It also represents **the making of offerings**. The *pitâputrasamâgamanasûtra* says:

"To resort to the dharma of voidness and aspire to that which is the domain of experience of the Buddhas: that is to make offerings to the Enlightened Teacher and such offerings are unsurpassable."

Also, in the *amrtaguhyatantrarâja* it says:

"Pleasing are meaningful offerings but not so offerings of incense and the like. By making the mind perfectly workable[1], one makes the great and pleasing offering."

Furthermore, one who possesses this *prajñâpâramitâ* **atones[2] for past errors**. In the *karmâvaranavisuddhi* it says:

"You who are desirous of atonement, sit straight and behold the immaculate. Immaculately beholding the immaculate is the purest, noblest way to regret."

It also comprises **observance of moral rules and commitments**. As is said in the *susthitamatidevaputra-pariprcchâsûtra*:

"When there is no longer self-consciousness in relation to commitment and non-commitment[3], that is the right conduct of

---

1. Often "workable" would mean that one's mind does what one's noble bodhisattva intentions want it to do, rather than it simply being a product of confused conditioning. In this context "workable" means familiar with voidness in all circumstances.

2. Several ideas related to purification of past misdeeds (see previous chapter on taking the bodhisattva vow) are alluded to in this paragraph. One atones for past errors through, among other techniques, regret — often through confession prayers whereby one faces up to one's past and feels natural remorse for the harm and mistakes therein. Here, the facing up to voidness in itself atones because recognition of voidness's truth compensates for all errors, the common first cause of which is an ignorance of the pure and perfect condition of voidness.

3. Self-consciousness here means thoughts of self, projections of personality, in the sense of conceiving of oneself as someone who observes commitments etc. in order to improve conduct. To settle the mind in the non-ego, non-phenomenality, of voidness is the highest conduct. There is a further implication, well explained in *abhidharma* (see *mkhas.jug* KDDL),
(continued...)

nirvâna; that is the purest right conduct."

The "Ten Wheels Sûtra" also says:

"Someone may be considered to be a layperson, living at home
with head and beard unshaven. He may not wear monk's robes
and may not even observe the rules of right conduct. But if he
possesses the very quality of mind of a Realised Being, that
person is indeed a monk in the ultimate sense."

It also comprises all three stages of wisdom: **study,
contemplation and meditation**. As is said in the "Tantra of
Supreme Non-Abiding":

"Having eaten the food of the uncontrived, which is naturalness,
whatever one's philosophy, one will be satisfied. The immature,
lacking realisation, rely on phraseology. Everything is a
characteristic of one's own mind."

Saraha said, moreover:

"It is to read, it is to seize the meaning and it is to meditate. It
is also to assimilate the meaning of the treatises. There is no view
capable of demonstrating it."

It also comprises **torma offerings and similar dharma
activities**. The *amrtaguhyatantrarâja* says:

"When one has encountered the very nature of mind, offerings,
torma and so forth—all different types of activity and deed—are
contained therein."

Well, if solely familiarising oneself with the (universal) essence,
the nature of mind, comprises all those things, what was the reason

---

3.(...continued)
concerning commitment, or bonding, relative to a certain reality. Sometimes these bonds
and commitments are artificial — as is the case with vows taken — and sometimes they are
a natural by-product of practice, e.g. someone well absorbed in loving kindness meditation
is alienated from harming life by the very nature of his or her universal love, without needing
to take a formal vow. Likewise voidness has natural morality "built in".

for teaching so many graduated techniques? These evolved to guide those less gifted beings who are still confused about the nature of things. The "Sûtra Which Ornaments the Radiance of Jñâna" says:

"Explanations of causes, conditions and interdependence as well as teachings on the graduated path were given as means for the confused. In terms of this spontaneous dharma, what graduated training can there be?"

In the *mahâsamvarodayatantrarâja* it says:

"Thus is attained an eternally liberated identity[1]: an identity comparable to the vastness of space."

In the "Space Jewel Sûtra" it is said:

"Until one dwells in the ocean of dharmadhâtu, the stages and levels are held to be different. Once one has entered the ocean of dharmadhâtu, there is not even the slightest traversing of stages and levels."

Illustrious Atisa has said:

"When a mind is stably settled in the one, one does not give priority to physical and verbal virtues."

6D   SIGNS OF DEVELOPMENT

The signs of prajñâ's development are increased attention to virtue, a diminution of defilement, the arising of compassion for sentient beings, earnest application to practice, a rejection of all distractions and no more attachment to or craving for the things of this life. Therefore it is said, in the *ratnâvalî* :

---

1. A very interesting play on words. The "identity" is *mahâ atma*—great atma or great identity. Having removed all limited notions of self, soul or atma, the profound teachings finally present the true nature of mind, voidness, as the universal identity of everyone and everything. See "Changeless Nature" KDDL.

"Through familiarity with voidness one attains attentiveness to all that is virtuous."

7. The consequences of prajñâpâramitâ

These should be understood as being twofold: the ultimate result and the temporary consequences. The ultimate result is to attain enlightenment. Thus the 700-verse *prajñâpâramitâ* teaches:

"Manjushri! Through practising the *prajñâpâramitâ*, bodhisattva mahâsattvas will rapidly and genuinely become perfectly enlightened in peerless, unsurpassable perfect Buddhahood."

In the meantime, every good and excellent thing will occur. As it is said, in the *prajñâpâramitâsamcayagâthâ*:

"Whatever delightful, happy things are encountered by bodhisattvas, śravaka, pratyekabuddha, gods or any being— they all derive from the supreme *prajñâpâramitâ*.

This concludes the seventeenth chapter, concerning prajñâpâramitâ,
of this Gems of Dharma, Jewels of Freedom

Chapter Eighteen:
The Phases of the Path

After one has first developed the intention to achieve supreme enlightenment, step by step one will traverse the phases and levels of the bodhisattva path. The following synopsis outlines the phases of the path:

The phases of the path are well discussed through these five — the phase of accumulation, the phase of integration, the phase of insight, the phase of cultivation and the phase of complete accomplishment.

According to the *bodhipathapradípa* treatise, these five are as follows. The first, the **phase of accumulation**, is well taught (therein) as being first the teachings which form the foundation, laid through becoming familiar with dharma instructions suited to one's capacities, be they lesser or middling. These are followed by development of the two aspects of bodhicitta: aspiration and application. Then one strives to establish and amass the two accumulations. It next teaches how the **phase of integration**[1] occurs through an understanding acquired progressively through the subphases of "warming" etc. The phases of **insight, cultivation** and **complete accomplishment** are taught through the "achievements of (the levels of) Supreme Joy" etc.

---

1. **integration** with the wisdom inherent to voidness.

1. The Phase of Accumulation

The *phase of accumulation* represents all the efforts that those endowed with the mahâyâna potential have to make in the practice of virtue, from the moment they first set their mind on supreme enlightenment and receive some advice and instruction from a teacher until such time as "warming[1] to primordial wisdom" occurs. This phase of the path is itself subdivided into four, according to whether it is brought about by understanding, aspiration, longing for the sublime or attainment.

Why is it called the "Phase of Accumulation?" It is so called because of its activities, which serve to gather and establish the accumulations of virtue and so forth in order to make (one's mind) a suitable vessel in which can arise realisations such as those of "warming" etc. They are also referred to as *roots of virtue compatible with liberation.*

During that particular period, one cultivates twelve—i.e. three sets of four—(of the 37) factors of enlightenment. They are the Four Trainings in Mindfulness, the Four Right Practices and the Four Supports of Miraculous Manifestation. [2]

Of these, the **Four Trainings in Mindfulness**, which constitute the lower stage of the phase of accumulation, involve developing mindful awareness of what is *physical*, mindful awareness of *feelings*, mindful awareness of what is *mental* and mindful awareness of *phenomena.*

The **Four Right Practices**, which constitute the middle stage of the phase of accumulation, are: to get rid of existing evils and non-virtues, never to give rise to evils and non-virtues that are presently

---

1. warming — This has nothing to do with heat yoga, a practice specific to vajrayâna Buddhism. It applies to the first part of the phase of integration (see below) in which one first warms to the real meaning of voidness. This is explained through the analogy of someone on a cold night, attracted by a bonfire. At one point he will be close enough to start feeling the heat of the thing he has been aiming for for some time.

2. These are literally "The Four Legs of Miracles". They represent the training in profound absorption which leads to a clear, perfectly concentrated and peaceful mind. This mastery of mind is the basis from which can be manifested whatever appearances are necessary to help others gain confidence in the universal truths; hence the present translation "Supports of Miraculous Manifestation".

absent, to give rise to virtuous remedies not yet present and to assure the increase of those virtues which are already developed.

The **Four Supports of Miraculous Apparition,** which constitute the upper stage of the phase of accumulation, are: profound absorption through longing, profound absorption through diligence, profound absorption through intention and profound absorption through analysis.

2.   The Phase of Integration

This follows on from the proper completion of the phase of accumulation. It is the birth of "the four subphases of definite breakthrough in understanding which is conducive to realisation of the Four Truths". The four subphases are called: *warming, summit[1], forbearance[2]* and *the highest worldly point[3]*.

Why is it called the "Phase of Integration"? Here "integration" refers to integration into a direct realisation of truth[4]. During the subphases of *warming* and *summit,* **five faculties** are employed: the faculties of trust, diligence, recollection, deep absorption and profound wisdom. In the subphases of *forbearance* and *highest worldly*

---

1. The image here calls to mind the qualities of a mountain peak, from which there is a high and panoramic view. Furthermore, the earth, which in this case represents the defilements, has gradually diminished to a point, whereas space, representing voidness, becomes more and more present. At the peak, one stands betwixt heaven and earth, phenomena and voidness.

2. See previous chapter on forbearance. The third type of forbearance related specifically to dharma forbearance and the skill needed to face up to voidness and its implications.

3. This is the end of, and the highest point of, samsâra. After this subphase, there will be no more samsâric rebirth. The whole quality of experience will change. The subsequent Phase of Insight has nothing to do with worldliness, as the following chapter makes clear.

4. In the *abhidharma* teachings we discover these five phases of the path as being the general template of liberation for all Buddhists, be they Theravadin or Mahâyâna. The definition given here, of "integration with the truth", applies equally to all the yâna. The Phase of Integration leads up to the phase of lasting, liberating insight: the Phase of Insight. Truth can be taken as the Four Noble Truths, which point to the fundamental natures of everything. In mahâyâna buddhism the actual insight takes place in a single period during which there is irreversible insight into the ultimate void nature of everything. In other forms of Buddhism, this insight, mainly into the voidness of ego, takes place in 16 consecutive periods, four for each truth. Whichever is the case, it is important to understand that all the mental preparation for the insight takes place in this Phase of Integration, whereas the actual experience of integration itself happens in the Phase of Insight.

point, these become **five powers**: the powers of trust, diligence, recollection, deep absorption and profound wisdom.

3.   The Phase of Insight

This follows on from the subphase the *highest wordly point*. It is the combination of *śamatha* (stable peace) and *vipaśyanā* (profound insight) focussed on the Four Truths of the Realised.[1] In relation to (the 1st Truth, that of) suffering, there are (aspects of insight known as) "forbearance of awareness of the nature of suffering", "awareness of the nature of suffering", "subsequent[2] forbearance of awareness of the nature of suffering" and "subsequent[3] awareness of the nature of suffering". There are four such aspects[4] for each Truth. The insight has for identity the 16 instants[5] of forbearance and awareness.

---

1. **Four Truths of the Realised** — litt. "Four Truths of the Noble (*arya*)", often translated as the Four Noble Truths. These are Realised Beings' truthful, i.e. direct and undistorted, insights into the nature of existence. Only a mind enjoying the plenitude of voidness can appreciate the truth as it appears at this level. To call the everyday, intellectualised presentations of the Four Truths that one finds in so many Buddhist books "the Four Noble Truths" detracts somewhat from the main point: real truth is a most sublime experience proper to such pure beings. It is the result of tremendous preparation and not solely an intellectual understanding of general truisms relevant to worldly life as we know it.
The same comment about the translation of *arya* also applies to the Eightfold Path of the Noble, the eight qualities of which which form part of the 37 factors of enlightenment (see relevant note in section on Phase of Cultivation below). Once one understands something of the profound relationship with reality that it represents—all hinging on the first point, perfect view—the more commonplace representations of the eightfold path, although offering useful guidelines for life, are but a pale and limited reflection of the main point.
For those unfamiliar with them, the Four Truths are these: 1. of the suffering inherent to all creations, 2. of the causes of all those sufferings, 3. of the cessation of suffering and 4. of the path of training which brings such cessation.

2. The first forbearance involves understanding the suffering of the sense dimension of existence. The subsequent forbearance furthers this understanding to incorporate the sufferings of the form and formless dimensions.

3. See note immediately above.

4. Two forbearances of awareness and the two awarenesses themselves.

5. four for each truth x four truths = 16. The word "instants" does not necessarily mean a short time span of a few seconds or less. It is a term based in the notion of time and relativity; time is denoted by the passage of events. These 16 are perfect absorptions that are each a complete time period of realisation. Being complete in themselves and engineers of each other, "their nature is that of sixteen instants".

Why are those referred to as the "Stage of Insight?" Because at that stage one gains, for the first time, authentic insight into the Truths of the Realised. During that stage, one is endowed with the

seven aspects of enlightenment:

1. right mindfulness
3. right diligence
5. right proficiency
7. right equanimity.

2. right discerning appreciation
4. right joy
6. right profound absorption &

4. The Phase of Cultivation

It is what follows on from the arisal of the Phase of Insight. It has two aspects: the worldly[1] way and the transcendent way.

4A THE WORLDLY WAY OF CULTIVATING MEDITATION

This comprises the 1st, 2nd, 3rd and 4th worldly meditations (dhyâna) and the (four formless absorptions) through the perceptual gateways of limitless space, limitless consciousness, nothing whatsoever and neither cognition nor absence of cognition. There are three purposes in doing these meditations:

1.   they destroy the defilements which still remain to be removed through meditation,
2.   they enable one to achieve the exceptional qualities of the limitless meditations etc. &
3.   they represent a basis for the transcendent way of meditating.

4B THE TRANSCENDENT WAY OF MEDITATING

This consists of cultivating *samatha* and *vipaśyana*, focussed on the two aspects of primordial wisdom (*jñâna*), along with their

---

1. **worldly** inasmuch as the results of doing such meditation will be a better worldly rebirth rather than liberation from the world.

accompanying qualities.[1]

During the Phase of Insight (see above) there were four types of awareness or forbearance for each of the four Truths. Of these 16 facets of insight, the eight forbearances are proper to the Phase of Insight and suffice. The eight awarenesses however require deeper familiarity and this is what is developed through the Phase of Cultivation, through continued practise of the profound absorptions of the   four *dhyāna* and three of the formless meditations, along with their accompanying qualities.

Cultivating familiarity with a realisation of the essential nature—the *dharmatā*–(of things) belongs to the aspect (known as) "awareness of dharma" whereas cultivating familiarity with realisation of primordial wisdom belongs to the aspect (known as) "awareness in terms of subsequent realisation."[2] The (remaining formless meditation of) the perceptual entrance of neither cognition nor absence of cognition is solely a wordly meditation since it vacillates and is quite unclear.

Why is it called, "The Phase of Cultivation"? Because one cultivates[3] familiarity with meditation (which rests) within the unique universal essence, realised through the Phase of Insight. During this stage one is endowed with the **eightfold path of the Realised**[4]:

---

1. The following paragraphs, almost incomprehensible to those unfamiliar with a thorough explanation of the relationship between the Four Noble Truths and meditation, express, very concisely and from a technical point of view, what takes place during this phase. Apologies for the unwieldiness—even a simple thing such as taking a few steps becomes complicated when described from the point of view of anatomy!

2. A satisfactory explanation of the meanings of this sentence would require more than a footnote. The reader is referred ideally to the intimate advice on meditation given at the right time by his or her meditation teacher. Further information can be obtained through study of abhidharma texts such as Mipham Rinpoche's "Entering the Ways of the Wise".

3. See note 21 in chapter on prajñâpâramitâ.

4. See note above on the Four Truths of the Realised. This famous eightfold path is based upon right view — the non-conceptual and perfect view that is spontaneously present through the mind's immersion in its true, void nature. This is the first of the eight. The remaining seven represent the pure way in which something of this sublime view can be communicated to others, through skilful manipulation of concepts, setting an example etc.

(continued...)

1. right view,   2. right concept,
3. right expression,   4. right limits of action,
5. right livelihood,   6. right effort,
7. right mindfulness and   8. right profound absorption.

5.   The Phase of Complete Accomplishment

This occurs after the vajra-like profound absorption. Its nature is awareness—of all generation processes being exhausted and of non-arising[1]. As far as the vajra-like profound absorption is concerned, its *elimination stage* at the end of the Phase of Cultivation is included in its *preparatory* and *obstacle-removing stages*[2]. That particular profound absorption (*samâdhi*) is known as "vajra-like" on account of it being unimpeded, durable, stable, homogeneous and pervading. These are explained as follows:

▸ it is *unimpeded* since no worldly activity can be a cause which might unsettle it,

▸ it is *durable* since none of the obscurations can damage it,

▸ it is *stable* since no thought can trouble it,

▸ it is *homogeneous* since it is of unique taste and

▸ it is *pervading* since it is focussed upon the ultimate nature common to each and every thing that is knowable.

Following the vajra-like samâdhi, there is an *awareness of exhaustion of generation*. This is primordial wisdom focussed upon the Four Truths in terms of the universal causes of (suffering's) origination being exhausted. There is also *awareness of non-arising*. This is primordial wisdom focussed upon the Four Truths when resultant

---

4.(...continued)
When this point is appreciated, the reader will understand the poverty of many portrayals of the eightfold path, which give it as every Buddhist's guide to living. Despite its undeniable usefulness and proven validity, it is a poor reflection of the true eightfold path.

1. See explanation which follows a little later in the text.

2. A proper appreciation of this sentence would require considerable understanding of the development of voidness meditation through the ten bodhisattva levels, with a particular regard to the increasing subtlety of what is removed and what remains as a fine obstacle to meditation at each level.

sufferings[1] have been eliminated. Alternatively (one could say that) the primordial wisdom relevant to exhaustion of causes and non-arisal of results is awareness of exhaustion and non-arisal.

Why are those referred to as the "Phase of Completion"? Because training has been completed and it is the stage where the journey to the citadel of enlightenment has reached its end.[2] At that stage there are **ten qualities without training**. They are (the eight qualities of the eightfold path) non-training right view through to non-training right profound absorption, plus non-training total liberation and non-training immaculate primordial wisdom. These ten factors, in which there is no more training to be achieved, form five groups of **untainted aggregates:**

1. **right conduct**—training-free right expression, action and livelihood,
2. **profound absorption**—training-free right mindfulness and profound absorption,
3. **highest wisdom**—training-free right view, concept and effort,
4. **perfect liberation**—training-free total liberation and
5. **primordial wisdom insight of total liberation**—training-free immaculate primordial wisdom.

This concludes the eighteenth chapter, concerning the phases of the path, of this Gems of Dharma, Jewels of Freedom

---

1. i.e. knowing that all consequences—of past ignorance and negative action—have been eliminated from one's mind and can never reappear.

2. The phrase for Phase of Completion in Tibetan literally means "path gone to its end".

Chapter Nineteen:
The Levels of the Path

Do those five phases of the path exist as spiritual levels? Yes:

The levels comprise these thirteen: the beginners' level, the level of practice due to aspiration, the ten bodhisattva levels and the level of buddhahood.

According to the *bodhipathpradīpa*: "...one will attain Joy Supreme and so forth..." Joy Supreme is the name of the first bodhisattva[1] level. The words "and so forth" apply to the two levels below it and the ten above it.

1. The Beginners' Level

This applies to the period when one is in the Phase of Accumulation. It is so called because it is what brings one's immature being to maturity.

2. The Level of Practice Due to Aspiration[2]

This corresponds to the period when (one is in) the Phase of Integration. It is so called because its activity aspires only to the meaning of voidness.

---

1. In this context *bodhisattva* means one who has irreversible realisation of voidness and not anyone who has taken the bodhisattva commitment.

2. Even though this second level can apply to what would generally be considered very advanced Buddhists, the fact of aspiration being the main motive for practice is stressed because authentic and lasting realisation of voidness has not yet happened. There can be myriad experiences clarifying the meaning of voidness and a very clear conceptual appreciation of voidness at this level, but the authentic realisation of voidness, which amounts to release from samsâra for ever, is yet to happen at the 1st bodhisttva level which follows this preparatory level of voidness investigation.

During this phase the following are crushed so as not to occur:[1]
1.   those factors, such as avarice etc., which are incompatible with the *pâramitâ*,
2.   the defilements which will be eliminated through (the Phase **b** Insight and
3.   the various arbitrary conceptual frameworks which represent a blockage to true awareness.

3.   The Ten Bodhisattva Levels

These are the levels from "Joy Supreme" through to "Cloud of Dharma".   The *daśabhûmikasûtra* says:

"My good children!   These ten are the bodhisattva levels: the bodhisattva level of 'Joy Supreme' ..."

Joy Supreme—the first of the ten levels—corresponds to the Phase of Insight, in which voidness is genuinely realised. The second through to the tenth levels are the Phase of Cultivation, during which one cultivates the insight into the true nature realised during the first level. These ten bodhisattva levels should be understood both in general and specifically.

3A   GENERAL POINTS CONCERNING THE TEN BODHISATTVA LEVELS

There are three: their nature, the definition of *bhûmi* (Skt. for "level") and the reason for a tenfold division.

3Ai   The Nature of the Levels   They comprise the continuum of training—both in wisdom (prajñâ) which directly realises the absence of self-entity in phenomena, and in the profound absorption which accompanies and fosters this wisdom.

3Aii   Etymology   They are called "grounds" (*bhûmi*[2]) because they

---

1. At that stage, these negative factors are reduced and do not occur so much, but they will only be definitely removed at later stages, during the Phases of Insight and Cultivation.

2. bhûmi (Skt. = Tib. *sa*) means "earth", "ground", "level", "area" or "state". In the following section, the bodhisattva levels are portrayed using these metaphors. An accurate translation as "bodhisattva grounds" has been dropped in favour of "bodhisattva levels", as the latter sounds less strange and is in common usage in Buddhist centres.

serve as bases for all the qualities associated with that particular level and the state it represents. Furthermore, each one serves as the foundation which gives rise to the next one. The following examples show the appropriateness of this term: all the qualities of primordial wisdom are present and utilised within them, thus they are like oxen's fields[1]. Also, they are like places where horses are exercised, since one traverses them astride primordial wisdom. Lastly they are like fields, since they are the foundations upon which grow all the qualities associated with primordial wisdom (jñâna).

3Aiii The Reason for a Tenfold Division   They are ten on account of their particularities of mastery.[2]

3B   SPECIFIC POINTS ABOUT EACH BODHISATTVA LEVEL

These will be presented through nine particularities for each level: name, etymology, mastery, practice, purity, realisation, completed elimination, birthplace and ability.

1st Bodhisattva Level

PARTICULAR NAME   "Joy Supreme"

PARTICULAR ETYMOLOGY Those who have achieved this level feel immense joy, because enlightenment is close and benefit for sentient beings is really being accomplished: hence its name, "Joy Supreme". Thus it says, in the *mahâyâna-sûtrâlankâra*:

> "Upon seeing that enlightenment is close and that the good of beings is accomplished, there will arise the most supreme joy. For that reason it is called 'Joy Supreme'."

PARTICULAR MASTERY This level is achieved through mastery of ten qualities, such as having intentions which are never deceitful, no

---

1. In which the oxen live and are nourished.

2. Although one could make endless distinctions and classification, the major differences in special qualities defined in the section immediately following this show how these ten represent the major changes that take place between first integration into voidness (1st level) and the totally perfect and pure mastery of it following the 10th level.

matter what domain of action or thought one is engaged in. Thus the *abhisamayâlaṅkâra* says: "Through ten aspects of training mastered, the 1st level will be attained."

PARTICULAR PRACTICE Although bodhisattvas at this level practise all ten *pâramitâ*[1], it is said that they place particular emphasis on the practice of the *pâramitâ* of generosity, on account of their wish to bring contentment to all beings. Thus the *daśabhûmikasûtra* says:

"From the outset of the first level, of all ten *pâramitâ*, great emphasis is given to the *pâramitâ* of generosity, but this does not mean that the others are not practised."

PARTICULAR PURITY As is said in the *daśabhûmikasûtra*:

"On the first level, Joy Supreme, there is very vast vision; through the power of prayers many buddhas will be seen, many hundreds of buddhas, many thousands of buddhas ... etc. ... many hundreds of millions of Buddhas will manifest. Upon seeing them, one makes offerings with a great and noble intention and expresses great respect ... etc. ... one also makes offerings to their sangha. One dedicates all these roots of virtue to unsurpassable enlightenment. One receives teachings from these Buddhas, takes them to heart and remembers them. These teachings are practised earnestly and beings are brought to maturity through the four modes of attraction."

In such a way, and for many æons, they make *offerings* to the Buddhas, dharma and sangha and *are cared for* by them. They *bring beings to spiritual maturity*. Thus, through these three causes, all their roots of virtue are made very great and very pure.

"For instance, the degree of refinement and purity of good quality gold, and its ability to lend itself to any desired use, will depend on the amount of work the goldsmith has put into its smelting. Like this, the roots of virtue of bodhisattvas on the first level are perfectly refined, completely pure and fit for any use."

---

1. In the previous chapters we became familiar with the six parâmitâ. The ten, which will be outlined, one by one, corresponding to the ten bodhisattva levels, are the previous six plus those of skilful means, wishing prayers, powers and primordial wisdom.

PARTICULAR REALISATION   In general, realisation is one and the same during the actual meditation phase throughout the ten levels. The differences are in respect to the inter-meditation phase and it is this aspect which will be considered relevant to each level. On this 1st level, *dharmadhātu* is (realised as being) omnipresent and this provides full realisation of the identity of self and others. Therefore the *madhyântavibhāga* speaks of "omnipresence".

PARTICULAR ELIMINATION COMPLETED   In terms of the defilement obscurations, all of the 82 *defilements to be overcome through insight* have been eliminated. Of the three types[1] of cognitive obscuration, it is ones comparable to a rough outer skin which are eliminated. One is also without five types of fear or anxiety. These are described in the *daśabhûmikasûtra*:

> "What are the five fears present until one achieves the level of Joy Supreme? They are fear of not gaining one's livelihood, fear of not having a good reputation, fear of death, fear of the lower states of existence and anxiety about being stuck among many worldly people. At that level these are all annihilated."

PARTICULAR BIRTHPLACE   Bodhisattvas on this level are mostly born as universal monarchs (*čakravartin*) in Jambudvípa[2]; there they remove the pollution of beings' avarice. The *ratnâvalî* says that, "as a full consequence[3] of this, they become a mighty ruler of Jambudvípa". Although this is the special particularity of birth mentioned, through their pure intention to benefit others they are able to manifest themselves anywhere, in any way needed to train

---

1. This is a reference to prajñâpâramitâ, which describes three main types of cognitive obscuration, clouding a full and true vision of the ultimate. Their grosser and subtler aspects are compared respectively to the rough outer skin of a fruit, its flesh and its kernel. They are the likes of belief in external reality, belief in views and beliefs in permanence.

2. The Buddha taught many public teachings according to the accepted cosmology of his day, based on a central mountain with four major surrounding continents, of which Jambudvípa is that of our world. In other teachings, it is made clear that perceived reality varies infinitely from type of being to type of being, from age to age and from individual to individual. All these factors are taken into account when giving teachings.

3. Full consequence: please refer back to karma chapter. These are the consequences of action in terms of rebirth states.

beings, as was well taught through the *Jâtaka* stories[1].

PARTICULAR ABILITY "Bodhisattvas at this level of Joy Supreme exert themselves diligently through aspiration. At best, in an instant, a short moment, just a fraction of time, they can:

1. attain a hundred profound absorptions and experience their stable fruition,
2. see a hundred Buddhas,
3. most properly be aware of those buddhas' blessings[2],
4. shake a hundred world systems[3],
5. visit a hundred Buddhafields,
6. illuminate a hundred world systems,
7. bring a hundred sentient beings to full maturity,
8. live for a hundred æons,
9. be excellently aware of the past and future up to a hundred æons past or hence,
10. open a hundred gates of dharma,
11. manifest a hundred emanations anywhere and
12. manifest each of these physical forms as being accompanied by a hundred other bodhisattvas."

2nd Bodhisattva Level

PARTICULAR NAME   "Immaculate"

PARTICULAR ETYMOLOGY   This level is known as "Immaculate" since it is unstained by violations of right conduct.

"Being free from stains due to violations of proper conduct, it is known as 'the Immaculate State'."[4]

---

1. The Jâtakamâla scripture describes the previous lives of the Buddha, when as a bodhisattva he lived hundreds of lives dedicated to helping others, sometimes taking birth as a human, sometimes as an animal etc.

2. i.e. transmission of realisation.

3. With the truth of their teachings.

4. This and the etymologies for the remaining levels all come from the *mahâyâna-sûtrâlannkâra.*

PARTICULAR MASTERY   This level is attained through eight kinds of mastery, such as those over right conduct, actions etc.

"Right conduct, the accomplishment of action, forbearance, supreme joy, great compassionate love etc."[1]

PARTICULAR PRACTICE   Although bodhisattvas at this level practise all ten pâramitâ, they are said to place particular emphasis on the practice of the pâramitâ of right conduct.

PARTICULAR PURITY   As previously explained[2], three causes make the roots of virtue created by these bodhisattvas very powerful and very pure.

"To take an example, fine gold retreated and resmelted by a goldsmith will be rid of all impurities, even more so than before. Likewise, the roots of virtue of the bodhisattvas on the 2nd level are also purer, more refined and more workable than before."

PARTICULAR REALISATION   On this level, dharmadhâtu is understood as being the highest and most significant thing. They think, "I will strive at all times and in all ways in the training through which it is really, fully achieved." Thus it is said[3], "Highest thing..."

PARTICULAR ELIMINATION COMPLETED   For this 2nd level, and on through to the 10th level: in terms of the defilements, only the nuclear potentials of the sixty *defilements that need to be eliminated by cultivation* have not been removed and remain present. However, their activated forms have been crushed. In terms of the cognitive obscurations, the inner layer, like the flesh of a fruit, is eliminated[4].

PARTICULAR BIRTHPLACE   Many of the bodhisattvas on this level become universal monarchs holding sway over the four worlds in a cosmic system. There, they turn beings away from the ten vices

---

1. This and the remaining quotes on the masteries are from the *abhisamayâlaṅkâra*.

2. Above, for the 1st bodhisattva level.

3. Here and after, quoted from same source as point 7 above.

4. See explanation above of this same analogy relevant to elimination on 1st bodhisattva level.

and establish them in the ten virtues. Thus:

"Through the full maturation of this, one will become a ćakravartin who benefits beings through possessing the seven precious and illustrious attributes."

PARTICULAR ABILITY   In one instant, a short moment, a fraction of time, they can enter into a thousand meditative states and so forth[1].

3rd Bodhisattva Level

PARTICULAR NAME   "The Illuminator"

PARTICULAR ETYMOLOGY   It is known as "The Illuminator" because in that state the light of dharma and profound absorption is very clear; furthermore, it illuminates others with the great light of dharma. Thus it is said:

"It is the illuminator because it makes the great radiance of dharma."

PARTICULAR MASTERY   This level is achieved through having developed five things, such as an insatiable appetite for studying (dharma). As is taught:

"Insatiable with respect to dharma study, they impart teachings without material concern."

PARTICULAR PRACTICE   Although bodhisattvas at this level practise all ten pâramitâ, they are said to place particular emphasis on the practice of the pâramitâ of forbearance.

PARTICULAR PURITY   As explained previously, three causes make the roots of virtue of these bodhisattvas very great and very pure.

"To take an example: if very fine gold is hand polished by a skilled goldsmith, this removes any defects and impurities yet

---

1. The same as for the last point concerning the 1st bodhisattva level but multiplied here by a factor of 1,000 instead of 100.

does not reduce the original weight of the gold itself. Likewise, the roots of virtue, established in the three periods of time by these bodhisattvas, remain undiminished and become very pure, very refined and fit for any use."

PARTICULAR REALISATION   Bodhisattvas on this level understand the teachings of Buddhadharma to be the favourable condition conducive to (realisation of) *dharmadhātu* being the noblest reality: in order to study just one verse of teaching they would pass through a fire pit as large as a gigacosmos.[1] Therefore: "...the favourable condition, that which is the very best ..."

PARTICULAR ELIMINATION COMPLETED   [see 2nd level]

PARTICULAR BIRTHPLACE   Most bodhisattvas on this level take birth as Indra, King of the Gods; they are skilled in counteracting desire and attachment related to the sense dimension:

"They are skilful great masters of the gods, who counteract desire and attachment in the sense realm."

PARTICULAR ABILITY   In an instant, a short moment, a fraction of time, they can enter one hundred thousand meditative states etc.

4th Bodhisattva Level

PARTICULAR NAME   "Radiant"

PARTICULAR ETYMOLOGY   It is called "Radiant" because the brilliance of primordial wisdom, endowed with the qualities favourable to enlightenment, radiates everywhere and has consumed the two obscurations.[2] Thus:

"It is like a light (because) it thoroughly consumes the factors incompatible with enlightenment. Thus endowed, this level is *radiant with light*, because the two have been consumed."

---

1. **gigacosmos** — something like 10^9 solar systems such as our own. It is a thousand sets of one thousand sets one thousand small cosmic systems.

2. Although these two reasons for brilliance — presence of wisdom's light and absence of obscuration — are not without relation to each other, they are quoted as two separate reasons for such a name.

PARTICULAR MASTERY This level is achieved through ten factors, such as remaining in solitude etc. Therefore:

"Remaining in forests, with little desire, satisfied with what they have, pure in behaviour, observing vows..." etc.

PARTICULAR PRACTICE Although bodhisattvas on this level practise all the ten pâramitâ in general, it is said that they place particular emphasis on that of diligence.

PARTICULAR PURITY As explained above, three causes make the roots of virtue of these bodhisattvas extremely great and pure:

"To take an example: fine gold fashioned into a piece of jewelry by a skilled goldsmith cannot be surpassed by other pieces of gold, as yet unworked. In a similar way, the roots of virtue of bodhisattvas on this level are not outshone by those of bodhisattvas on lower levels."

PARTICULAR REALISATION Bodhisattvas on this level have truly realised that there is nothing whatsoever to really cling to. Thus all craving, even for dharma, is quenched; "...the fact that there is nothing to really cling to and..."

PARTICULAR ELIMINATION COMPLETED (see 2nd level)

PARTICULAR BIRTHPLACE Most bodhisattvas on this level take birth as a king of gods in the Dispute-Free heaven. They are skilled in dispelling mistaken philosophies based on a notion of the "destructible complex"[1] being permanent. Thus:

"They become divine monarchs in the Dispute-Free heaven and are skilled in totally defeating views of the destructible complex, where these are predominant."

PARTICULAR ABILITY In one moment, a short instant, a fraction of time, they can enter a million profound absorptions etc. etc.

---

1. One or more of the five aggregates. These views are based on an idea of a lasting self, composed of one or more of these aggregates.

5th Bodhisattva Level

PARTICULAR NAME   "Difficult to Practise"

PARTICULAR ETYMOLOGY   On this level one strives to help beings achieve some maturity yet transcends any defiled reaction to their repeated mistakes. It is known as "Difficult to Practise" because both (helping and non-reacting) are hard to master. Thus:

> "Since they (have to) accomplish the good of beings and guard their own minds, it is a difficult training for the bodhisattvas; therefore it is known as 'Difficult to Practise'."

PARTICULAR MASTERY   This level is achieved through the elimination of ten factors, such as association with worldly people for purposes of gain and so forth. Therefore:

> "To hanker after acquaintances, a dwelling, places filled with distractions etc..."

PARTICULAR PRACTICE   Although bodhisattvas on this level practise all ten pâramitâ in general, it is said that they place particular emphasis on that of concentration meditation.

PARTICULAR PURITY   As previously explained, three causes make the roots of virtue of these bodhisattvas particularly great and pure:

> "To take an example, fine gold, first polished by a skilled goldsmith and then set with amberstones will be incomparably beautiful; it cannot be outshone by other pieces made of gold alone. Likewise for the roots of virtue of bodhisattvas on this 5th level, which are tested by the combination of wisdom and skilful means. They could never be outshone by the roots of virtue of bodhisattvas on lower levels."

PARTICULAR REALISATION   Bodhisattvas on this level realise the non-separation of (mind) streams[1]. They are aware of ten samenesses. Thus: "undifferentiated streams and..."

---

1. **streams**: (Tib. *rgyud* Skt. *tantra*) This word refers to the continua of events which make, on a gross and relative level, individual's lives and minds and the apparent continua of phenomenal reality.

PARTICULAR ELIMINATION COMPLETED   (see 2nd level)

PARTICULAR BIRTHPLACE   Most bodhisattvas on this level take birth as divine monarchs in the Tusita heaven. They are skilled in refuting the views of those holding distorted religious beliefs.[1] Therefore:

> "As a full consequence they become monarchs of the Tusita gods and are skilled in refuting aberrant fixations which are the source defilement behind all distorted religious belief."

PARTICULAR ABILITY   In one instant, a short moment, a small fraction of time, they can enter a thousand million profound absorptions etc. etc.

6th Bodhisattva Level

PARTICULAR NAME   "Revealed"

PARTICULAR ETYMOLOGY   Due to the support of *prajñâpâramitâ* there is no dwelling on (notions of) either nirvâna or samsâra. Thus, samsâra and nirvâna are revealed as pure. Hence the name of this level, "Revealed".

> "Since with the help of *prajñâpâramitâ* both samsâra and nirvâna have been revealed, it is called 'Revealed'."

PARTICULAR MASTERY   This level is achieved through 12 factors of training; learning how totally, perfectly to accomplish six things—such as generosity etc.—and learning how to eliminate six things such as longing for the śravaka or pratyekabuddha (state) etc. Therefore:

> "Through the utter perfection of generosity, right conduct, forbearance, diligence, concentration meditation and prajñâ, there is awareness etc."

---

1. *tirthika* some translations refer to these simply as "non-Buddhists", others as "heretics" etc. The term itslef is quite respectful, indicating good people with sincere religious convictions which are, unfortunately, deluded. Thus they are "those on the threshold; on a rung of the ladder" since their spirituality makes them potentially ripe for the truth.

PARTICULAR PRACTICE Although bodhisattvas on this level practise all ten pâramitâ in general, it is said that they place particular emphasis on that of *prajñâpâramitâ*.

PARTICULAR PURITY As explained previously, three causes make the roots of virtue of bodhisattvas on this level extremely pure and powerful:

> "...to give an example; when a skilled goldsmith decorates fine gold with lapis-lazuli, it becomes peerless and cannot be surpassed by other works of gold. Likewise the roots of virtue of 6th level bodhisattvas, assured by wisdom and skilful means, are both total purity and lucid clarity; they cannot be outshone by those of bodhisattvas established on lower levels."

PARTICULAR REALISATION On this level is realised the non-existence of both the totally defiled and the totally pure. These bodhisattvas are aware that there are really no such things as total defilement or total purity, even though they may arise through the play of interdependent origination. Thus it is said: "...the meaning of no defilement and no total purity."

PARTICULAR ELIMINATION COMPLETED   (see 2nd level)

PARTICULAR BIRTHPLACE Most bodhisattvas on this level take birth as a divine monarch among the *sunirmita* gods. They are skilled in overcoming beings' vanity:

> "Through this full consequence, they become kings of the sunirmita gods. Unsurpassed by śrâvaka, they eliminate vainglory."

PARTICULAR ABILITY In one instant, a short moment, a small fraction of time, they can enter a hundred thousand million profound absorptions etc. etc.

7th Bodhisattva Level

PARTICULAR NAME   "Far Gone"

PARTICULAR ETYMOLOGY   This level is known as "Far Gone" since it connects with the "one and only path" and one has come to the far end of activity[1].

PARTICULAR MASTERY   This level is achieved through eliminating twenty factors, such as belief in entity[2], and through cultivating the opposite qualities such as the three gates of total liberation[3] etc. Therefore:

"...belief in self-entity and beings...." and "...awareness of the three gates of total liberation.."

PARTICULAR PRACTICE   Although bodhisattvas on this level practice all ten pâramitâ in general, it is said that they place particular emphasis on that of skilful means.

PARTICULAR PURITY   As explained previously, three causes make the roots of virtue of bodhisattvas on this level extremely pure and powerful:

"...to give an example; when a skilled goldsmith decorates finest gold with all sorts of precious gems, it becomes most beautiful and cannot be excelled by another pieces of jewelry in this

---

1. Oral traditions vary in their explanations of quite what does and does not happen at different bodhisattva levels. There is also a question of things being eliminated on a gross level but still existing either subtly or as a potential, not to mention the obvious problem of describing that which is indescribable. One explanation for this name is that the 7th level is approaching the 8-10th levels. These latter are known as the "pure levels" because the age-old "I" and "other" perceptual reflex is no longer present. They constitute the "one and only path" taken by all the Buddhas; the path into which all other individual journeys feed. One must recognise, from the 1st level onwards, and even from the 8th to10th levels, the ongoing presence of a continuum, heading towards enlightenment, even though delusions of self have been overcome. Fully overcoming the dualistic split is a major breakthrough, terminating the long deluded journey; hence "far gone".

2. At this stage one is working on such beliefs in their very fine and subtle forms.

3. Phenomena are devoid of independent entity, devoid of true happiness and devoid of permanence. These points are directly related to the three key Buddhist doctrines of no-self, suffering and impermanence.

world. Likewise the roots of virtue of 7th level bodhisattvas are extraordinarily great and pure; they cannot be excelled by those of śrâvaka, pratyekabuddha or bodhisattvas established on lower levels."

PARTICULAR REALISATION   On this level is realised the non-separateness (of everything). All the various characteristics of dharma—the sûtra and so forth—do not appear as separate.[1] Thus it is said: "...non-separation..."

PARTICULAR ELIMINATION COMPLETED   (see 2nd level)

PARTICULAR BIRTHPLACE   Most bodhisattvas on this level take birth as a divine monarch among the *vaśavartin*[2] gods. They are skilled in bringing about realisations (like those) of the śrâvaka and pratyekabuddha:

"Through this full consequence, they become kings of the vaśavartin gods. They become great, outstanding, dharma teachers with a genuine understanding of the Truths of the Realised."

PARTICULAR ABILITY   In one instant, a short moment, a small fraction of time, they can enter 10^{16} profound absorptions etc. etc.

8th Bodhisattva Level

PARTICULAR NAME   "Immovable"

PARTICULAR ETYMOLOGY   It is so called because it is unmoved by ideas which either strive after characteristics or strive after an absence of characteristic. Therefore:

"It is known as the Immovable since it is unmoved by both notions."

PARTICULAR MASTERY   This level is achieved through eight kinds of

---

1. In particular, they realise that the scriptures outlining the interdependent nature of relative reality and those decribing the ultimate void nature of everything form an indivisible whole.

2. These are said to hold sway over all six types of sense-dimension gods.

mastery, such as understanding the behaviour of sentient beings etc. Therefore:

"Awareness of the mind of every being, love due to clear cognition..."

PARTICULAR PRACTICE   Although bodhisattvas on this level practice all ten pâramitâ in general, it is said that they place particular emphasis on that of wishing-prayers.

PARTICULAR PURITY   As explained previously, three causes make the roots of virtue of bodhisattvas on this level extremely pure and powerful:

"...to give an example; were a fine piece of golden jewelry, made by a master goldsmith, to be worn on the head or the throat of a world emperor, it could not be surpassed by gold ornaments worn by other people. Likewise the roots of virtue of 8th level bodhisattvas are so utterly and perfectly pure that they cannot be excelled by those of śrâvaka, pratyekabuddha or bodhisattvas established on lower levels."

PARTICULAR REALISATION   On this level is realised the space-like and concept-free nature of every phenomenon. Therefore its bodhisattvas are not shocked and frightened by voidness—the unborn. This is known as *the achievement of forbearance concerning the unborn*. Through this forbearance of the unborn nature of everything, they realise the non-existence of increase and decrease and they do not consider the really defiled or the total pure as either respectively decreasing or increasing. Hence "...no increase, no decrease..."

It is said that this is also (the first of) the **states with four powers**[1]:

1. over not conceptualising,   2. over very pure realms,
3. over primordial wisdom and   4. over activity,

---

1. According to one scriptural tradition, these four powers are related to the very pure levels, i.e. the 8th-10th bodhisattva levels. As we discover, the first two are proper to level 8 and the other two are related to the following levels 9 and 10.

Of these four, bodhisattvas on the 8th level have realised the first two powers—those of not conceptualising and of very pure realms.

Other scriptural sources say that those on the 8th level have achieved **Ten Powers**:

1. over lifespan
2. over mind
3. over commodities
4. over action
5. over birth state
6. over prayer
7. over intentions
8. over miracles
9. over primordial wisdom
10. over Buddhadharma

PARTICULAR ELIMINATION COMPLETED   (see 2nd level)

PARTICULAR BIRTHPLACE   Most bodhisattvas on this level take birth as a divine monarch among the *brahmâ* gods, with power over an entire kilocosmos.[1] (They are skilled in) expounding the meaning of the *śrâvaka* and *pratyekabuddha* paths.

> "The full consequence is to take birth as a brahmâ god, lord of one level of the metacosmos. They are unsurpassed in the exposition of the doctrines of the Arhats and Pratyekabuddhas."

PARTICULAR ABILITY   In one instant, a short moment, a small fraction of time, they can enter as many profound absorptions as there are particles in a million metacosmoses etc. etc.

9th Bodhisattva Level

PARTICULAR NAME   "Excellent Intelligence"

PARTICULAR ETYMOLOGY   It is so called because it is endowed with such good intelligence i.e. clear and exact discernment. Therefore:

> "That level is Excellent Intelligence because of its good intelligence, clearly discerning."

PARTICULAR MASTERY   This level is achieved through 12 factors such as infinite prayers etc. Therefore:

---

1. In the ancient world view this represented a thousand planetary systems such as our own. A thousand of these made a second cosmic level and a thousand of those made up the metacosmos.

"Infinite prayers.. knowledge of divine languages and..."

PARTICULAR PRACTICE   Although bodhisattvas on this level practise all ten pâramitâ in general, it is said that they place particular emphasis on that of powers.

PARTICULAR PURITY   As explained previously, three causes make the roots of virtue of bodhisattvas on this level extremely pure and powerful:

> "...to give an example; were a fine piece of golden jewelry, made by a master goldsmith, to be worn on the head or the throat of a universal monarch, it could be excelled neither by the pieces of jewelry worn by the kings of the various regions nor by those worn by any of the inhabitants of the four planets (of that system). Likewise the roots of virtue of 9th level bodhisattvas are so adorned with great primordial wisdom (jñâna) that they cannot be excelled by those of śrâvaka, pratyekabuddha or bodhisattvas established on lower levels."

PARTICULAR REALISATION   Of the four powers (mentioned in the previous section), bodhisattvas at this 9th level realise the state of power of primordial wisdom (jñâna), since they have achieved the four perfectly clear discerning knowledges. What are the perfectly clear discerning knowledges? The daśabhûmikasûtra explains:

> "What are the four clear discerning knowledges? They are constant possession of perfectly clear discerning knowledge of dharma, perfectly clear discerning knowledge of meanings, perfectly clear discerning knowledge of definitions and perfectly clear discerning knowledge of teaching skill."

PARTICULAR ELIMINATION COMPLETED   (see 2nd level)

PARTICULAR BIRTHPLACE   Most bodhisattvas on this level take birth as a divine monarch among the brahmâ gods, with power over a megacosmos[1]. They are able to answer all questions.

"The full consequence is to take birth as brahmâ, lord of the

---

1. In the ancient world view this represented a million planetary systems such as our own.

intermediary level of the metacosmos. In (answering) questions arising from sentient beings' ways of thinking, they are unsurpassed by Arhats and so forth."

PARTICULAR ABILITY   In one instant, a short moment, a small fraction of time, they can enter as many profound absorptions as there are pure particles in a million "countless"[1] Buddhafields etc. etc.

10th Bodhisattva Level

PARTICULAR NAME   "Cloud of Dharma"

PARTICULAR ETYMOLOGY   It is called *Cloud of Dharma* because the bodhisattvas on that level are like a cloud which causes a rain of dharma teachings to fall upon beings, thereby washing away the fine dust of their defilements. Furthermore, like clouds filling space, their profound absorptions and their power of mantra pervade the space-like dharma(ta) they have achieved. Therefore:

"It is the Cloud of Dharma because the two, like clouds, pervade the space-like dharma(ta)."

[This is the interpretation of Maitreya and that found in the commentaries of his tradition. It is said in the mantrayâna that at the end of the 10th level, bodhisattvas receive empowerment from the Buddhas of the 10 directions and themselves become Buddhas. These two views are in fact the same. Different questions attract different answers, but there is no contradiction between the two.][2]

---

1. "Countless" — in the various systems of counting that were imported to Tibet from India, there are names for each multiple of 10, i.e. the equivalents of our words "hundred", "thousand", etc up to 10^{59}. In some systems there are names for multiples of 100, reaching further than figures 120 numbers long. These figures were used, among other things, in Buddhism to compare realities experienced by different sorts of beings—their relative lifespans etc. "Countless" signifies a figure beyond those having their own name, rather than something which was unable to be counted.

2. This point is in small print in the xylographic Rumtek text. It refers, perhaps, to the teaching ability of 10th level bodhisattvas, which is taught in the "Changeless Nature" as being the same as the Buddhas'. Is the shower of teachings they rain down precipitated from the timeless space of enlightenment or does it occur through their developed power

(continued...)

PARTICULAR MASTERY (Unlike for the previous levels) there is nothing mentioned for this level in the *abhisamayâlaṅkâra* but the *daśabhûmikasûtra* says:

> "O Children of the Victors! Up to the ninth level, bodhisattvas have thoroughly analysed and do thoroughly analyse immeasurable aspects of knowledge with an investigatory intelligence..."

and so forth, teaching that this level is achieved through an empowerment of primordial wisdom (jñâna) of omniscience due to *ten thorough masteries*. This 10th level is the *level of empowerment with omniscient primordial wisdom (jñâna)*. Why is it so called? Because, as the *daśabhûmikasûtra* explains, the bodhisattvas on the 10th level are empowered, through lights, by the Buddhas of the ten directions. Further details can be found in that sûtra. The *ratnâvalî* also says:

> "Because the bodhisattva is empowered by rays of Buddha light."

PARTICULAR PRACTICE Although bodhisattvas on this level practise all ten pâramitâ in general, it is said that they place particular emphasis on that of primordial wisdom (jñâna).

PARTICULAR PURITY As explained previously, three causes make the roots of virtue of bodhisattvas on this level extremely pure and powerful:

> "...to give an example; were a fine piece of golden jewelry to be made by a god skilled in craft and who studded it with finest gems and then were it to be worn on the head or the throat of an empowered divine king, it could not be surpassed by any other jewelry of gods or humans. Likewise the roots of virtue of 10th level bodhisattvas are so adorned with great primordial wisdom (jñâna) that they cannot be excelled by those of any

---

2.(...continued)
of mantra/dharani and meditation? There is no contradiction in these two explanations, as the whole journey of the bodhisattva is one of approach to a natural state of enlightenment — an uncreated nature — and not the creation of skills rooted in causality. The powers of mantra (dharani) etc. come through the removal of obstacles to a natural flow.

beings, śrâvaka, pratyekabuddha or bodhisattvas on the 9th and lower levels."

PARTICULAR REALISATION   Of the 4 powers (mentioned in the previous section), bodhisattvas at this 10th level realise the state of power of activity, since they accomplish the welfare of beings just as they wish, through every type of emanation.

PARTICULAR ELIMINATION COMPLETED   (see 2nd level)

PARTICULAR BIRTHPLACE   Most bodhisattvas on this level take birth as the King of the Gods, Maheśvara, with power over a gigacosmos.[1] They are skilled in teaching the pâramitâ to all beings, śrâvaka, pratyekabuddha and bodhisattvas.

> "The full consequence is to take birth as Lord of the Śuddhavâsin Gods, as the supreme Maheśvara and mighty lord over domains of inconceivable primordial wisdom (jñâna)."

PARTICULAR ABILITY   In one instant, a short moment, a small fraction of time, they can enter as many profound absorptions as there are pure particles in a thousand million million "countless" Buddhafields etc. etc. Furthermore, in one instant they can manifest from just one pore of their skin countless Buddhas in the company of incalculable numbers of bodhisattvas.

They can manifest as all sorts of beings — as gods, humans etc. According to whatever is necessary for the training of those to be trained, they can teach dharma by adopting the physical form of Indra, Brahmâ, Maheśvara, universal guardians, monarchs, śrâvaka, pratyekabuddha or tathâgata. In the *madhyamakâvatâra* it says:

> "In one instant they can manifest, from a pore, perfect Buddhas in the company of countless bodhisattvas and also gods, humans and semi-gods."

This completes the explanation of the 10 bodhisattva levels.

---

1. In the ancient world view this represented a billion planetary systems such as our own.

5. The Buddha Level

This corresponds to the stage which is the Phase of Completion. When the vajra-like profound absorption arises, it eliminates simultaneously the obscurations to be removed by (the phase of) cultivation, i.e. defilements and the cognitive obscurations which remain, comparable to the pith.[1] The achievement of this level is described in the *bodhisattvabhûmi*:

" These levels are accomplished over the span of three countless cosmic æons. During the first great countless æon, one traverses the level of practice motivated by aspiration and achieves the state of Joy Supreme. Further, this is all achieved through constant effort; the achievement will not take place without it.

In the second great cosmic æon, one transcends Joy Supreme and works through to the 7th level, Far Gone, to achieve the 8th level, Immovable. This is precisely the way it happens since bodhisattvas of pure intention will definitely make these efforts.

In the third great cosmic æon, one traverses the 8th and 9th levels and attains the 10th, Cloud of Dharma. Some apply themselves to this most diligently and thereby reduce many sub-æons of progress into one. Some even reduce many æons' work into one. But there are none who reduce the countless æons into one. It should be known in this way."

This was the nineteenth chapter, explaining the spiritual levels,
from this Gems of Dharma, Jewels of Freedom

---

1. Refer to the seventh point (particular elimination) for each bodhisattva level, where these obscurations were compared to the skin and the flesh of a fruit.

Part 5

Chapter Twenty:

The Kâya of Perfect Buddhahood

When the phases and levels have been completely traversed as described above, one will become a perfect Buddha[1] within the three embodiments[2] (*kâya*). Therefore it says, in the *bodhipatha-pradîpa*:

"Buddha and enlightenment are not distant."

"Buddha" is described by the synopsis:

The embodiments of a perfect Buddha are described through seven points: their nature, etymology, aspects, presentation, definite number, characteristic properties and particularities.

---

1. The word "perfect" has a technical meaning here. The terms "buddha" and "enlightenment" are sometimes applied to bodhisattvas from the 1st level onwards, on account of their tremendous liberation, purity and insight compared to that of worldly beings. To make the distinction betwen them and fully-enlightened beings, qualifying adjectives such as "totally pure and perfect" are placed before the words enlightenment or Buddha.

2. The profound and indescribable nature of enlightenment, "which resembles nothing in our world" (*mahayanottaratantra*), poses some problems when it comes to translating *kâya*. Kâya (Skt. = Tib. *sku*) literally means "body" or "embodiment"—of Buddhahood—but, as we discover in this chapter, the dharmakâya is formless and the other two kâya manifest like rainbows or mirages in beings' minds, in terms of their own subjective realities. It is not as though enlightenment has fixed bodies somewhere. Its wisdom, compassion and so forth are embodied in the subtle ways in which the absolute manifests, as described in this section.

1.   The Nature of a Truly Perfect Buddha

A truly perfect Buddha is the best possible purity and the best possible primordial wisdom (jñâna).

1A   THE BEST POSSIBLE PURITY

This means that all the defilements and the cognitive obscurations have been being eliminated during the phases and the levels and that, subsequent to the vajra-like profound absorption, they are completely eliminated, with no trace remaining.[1] Other obscurations, such as those impeding various meditative absorptions, are subcategories of the two main obscurations and so disappear with the elimination of those two.

1B   THE BEST POSSIBLE PRIMORDIAL WISDOM (JÑÂNA)

There are different views on this point. Some say that Buddhas have concepts as well as jñâna. Some say that Buddhas do not have concepts yet they have jñâna, which knows everything clearly. Some say that the continuum of jñâna is broken. Some say that the Buddha has never possessed any such thing as jñâna. However, the authoritative texts of the sûtra and śâstra speak of the jñâna of the Buddhas. Of the sûtra, we find in the *prajñâpâramitâ samcayagâthâ*:

"Therefore if you want to penetrate the supreme jñâna of the Buddhas, trust in this, the mother of the Victors."

The *prajñâpâramitâ* in a hundred thousand verses says:

"A totally pure and perfect Buddha has secured jñâna which knows everything without any obscuration."

It also says, in the 21st chapter of the same work:

"There is the jñâna of a perfect Buddha. There is the turning of the wheel of dharma. There is the bringing of beings to maturity."

Many statements on jñâna are also to be found in other sûtra. Of

---

1. i.e. unlike in other levels of purification, not only is the superficial manifestation of delusion removed but also all potential for its remanifestation.

the śāstra, we find, in the *mahāyāna-sūtrālaṅkāra*:

"You should know that just as when one sun ray shines, all the others are shining too, so it is also with the jñāna of the Buddhas.. The mirror-like jñāna is immovable, the basis for the other three jñāna, of identity, discernment and activity."

Buddha-jñāna is also mentioned in other śāstra. The opinion of those who say that the Buddhas possess jñāna is based on these authoritative texts.

the way in which the Buddhas possess jñāna

In brief jñāna is twofold—the *jñāna of sublime awareness of how-it-is* and the *jñāna of sublime awareness of multiplicity*.[1] Of these, the jñāna which is sublimely aware of how-it-is is absolute sublime awareness. As mentioned above, at the very end of the vajra-like profound absorption there is complete familiarity with Thusness, from which every single conceptual objectification has been severed, thus dispelling all intellectual interference. Consequently the primordial space (dharmadhātu)—uncomplicated by intellectual speculation—and primordial wisdom (jñāna)—uncomplicated by intellectual speculation—are of one taste, indivisible. Being so, they are inseparable, like water poured into water or butter poured into butter. They are like saying that one *sees* space even though there is nothing there to be seen. They are the great prajñā, supreme awareness of the non-manifest and foundation of every precious quality. Therefore it is said:

"Like water poured into water, like butter mixed into butter, the knowable, free from complication, and the jñāna, free from complication, inseparable from it, are totally fused. It is this which is called 'dharmakāya' and this which is the essential nature of all the Buddhas."

And

---

1. Respectively *yathābhūtaparijñāna* and *yathāvad vyavasthānaparijñāna*.

"People talk of *seeing space*. Think about it and consider how they *see* space. The Tathagâta taught that this is how to see phenomena. Such seeing cannot be expressed by any other example."

The jñâna which is sublimely aware of multiplicity is omniscience with respect to conventional, relative reality. All potential for obscuration has been destroyed by the vajra-like profound absorption and so there is great wisdom (prajñâ). Through its power, every aspect of the knowable, throughout the three periods of time, is seen and known, as clearly as if it were a fresh ju-ru fruit in the palm of the hand. The sûtra speak of the Buddhas' sublime awareness of the relative in these terms:

"All the various causes of a single eye in a peacock's tail are unknowable by one who is not omniscient yet such knowledge is within the power of the Omniscient One."

Furthermore the *mahayânottaratantra* says:

"...with great compassion he knows the world;
    having seen everything in the world..."

When Buddhas know and see as described above, it is not as though they perceived things as real. They see and know things as illusions. Thus it says, in the *dharmasangîtisûtra*:

"An illusionist is not himself duped by his conjurations and thus, through his clear knowledge of what is happening, does not become attached to his illusory creations. Similarly to this example, those skilled in perfect enlightenment know the three types of existence to be like an illusion."

The *pitâputrasamâgamanasûtra* says:

"By remaining conscious of the fact that conjurations are but illusions, a magician will not fall under their spell. I pay homage and praise you, the All-Seeing Ones, who regard all beings in such a way."

(jñāna of multiplicity: the view that buddhas do not possess it)

Some hold the view that truly perfect Buddhas do possess the jñāna of how-it-is, sublime ultimate awareness, but that they do not possess sublime awareness of the relative, the "jñāna of multiplicity." Their point is not that there is something there to know and that the Buddhas are not aware of it, but rather that, since there is nothing relative there to be aware of in the first place, there can be no jñāna which is aware of it.

Relative or *conventional* reality means that which appears to immature beings due to the influence of ignorance accompanied by defilements. It also includes the subjective experience of the three types of realised beings, due to their ignorance, which is without accompanying defilements. An example of such subjective experience would be the blurs and dancing shapes that appear to someone who suffers from an eye disease. Subsequent to the vajra-like profound absorption, a Buddha has totally eliminated ignorance and so "sees" Thusness in the way one "sees" nothing whatsoever. Thus (they believe) a Buddha partakes in no way of the illusion of the relative, just as a person cured of an eye-disease no longer sees blurs or dancing shapes.

Therefore relative appearances occur due to the power of ignorance and only exist in relation to what is worldly. In relation to Buddhahood, they have no existence and so there can be no Buddhajñāna which is sublimely aware of them.

Were the Buddhas to have a mind which contained relative appearances, then, by definition, Buddhas would themselves have to be deluded due to the manifestation of such deluded fields of experience. This is in contradiction to the scriptures which state that the great Victors are constantly in a state of meditation etc., as it says, for instance, in the Play of the Vast:

"Totally pure and perfect Buddhas are at all times in meditation."

(jñāna of multiplicity: Buddhas do possess it)

Those who hold the view that Buddhas do possess jñāna of multiplicity declare, because (being aware of the relative) is only an ancillary[1] activity, it will not alter the (Buddha's awareness) and therefore does not contradict the scriptural authority which states that he is always in meditation etc.

It is not correct to assume delusion simply because illusions are apparent to the mind. Although the illusory objective realities of others' awareness are apparent (to the Buddhas), this in no way misleads them and they are aware that those are simply delusions. Furthermore they dispel them, using them as a cause for the higher rebirth, purity and liberation of beings. So how could there be delusion? Thus:

"Through awareness of it being merely delusion, that which is not deluded can be perceived with certainty."

Yet others say that there is no great logical harm in holding the relative as a valid object, provided one does not cling to it as being real. The absence of harm comes from the fact that although it is the Buddhas' phenomenal reality, they are not deluded.

Those who hold the view that Buddhas do possess multiplicity jñāna consider "multiplicity jñāna" to be the subsequent primordial awareness that Buddhas possess. Thus they say:

"First there is sublime awareness of how it is; undeluded, meditation and without mental process. Then there is sublime awareness of multiplicity; the appearance of delusion, subsequent knowledge and mental process."

Those who hold the view that Buddhas do not possess multiplicity jñāna quote, as their authority, the *anantamukhasādhaka nāma*

---

1. **ancillary**: the word here is *rjes.tob.* which normally means "post-meditation" or "inter-meditation" (see meditation pâramitâ chapter). In most contexts this term refers to worldly experience in between formal meditation sittings. To understand the use of this term here, one needs to reflect upon the evolution of the perception of worldly reality from that of immature beings who meditate to that of bodhisattvas, and then to follow the evolution through the bodhisattva levels (see previous chapter). The profound meditation instructions of the Kagyü lineage dealing with the relationship between relative and ultimate reality are also helpful here.

dhâranî which says:

> "Having reached true and perfect Buddhahood, the Tathâgata neither knows nor has in mind any phenomenon whatever. Why is this? Because there exists no objective reality whatsoever to be known."

Furthermore it is said:

> "Some non-Buddhists say that you speak of going to liberation (yet) when you have arrived at peace there is nothing left, like something burnt away."

This concludes my review of the debate around this issue.

(the Geshe-pa's[1] position on Buddhajñâna)

The actual pure and perfect Buddha is the dharmakâya. The very term *dharmakâya* – "embodiment of dharma" – is applied to the exhaustion of all delusion and thus it is a nature (defined) only *a contrario*. It is expressed in this way merely in terms of conventional reality. In fact, dharmakâya itself is unborn and uncomplicated. It says, in the *mahâyâna-sûtrâlankâra*:

> "Liberation is simply the exhaustion of error."

Thus a Buddha is the dharmakâya and, since the dharmakâya is unborn and uncomplicated, there can be no possession of jñâna. One may say that this contradicts the sûtra which speak of two jñâna. In fact, it does not, for just as visual consciousness is triggered by the presence of the colour blue and one says, "I see blue," so the primordial awareness (jñâna) which is the dharmadhâtu is primordial awareness of how-it-is, whereas the jñâna of multiplicity is the relative aspect (of that same primordial awareness) when it is triggered by what manifests to beings. This explanation is taught as being a very convenient one.

---

1. Gampopa is referring here to the academic teachers of the earlier part of his life, who belonged to the Khadampa tradition. As he points out a little later in the text, this intellectual justification of the term jñâna and the explanation given to him later on by his guru, Milarepa, are compatible with each other.

(Jetsun Milarepa's position)

One talks of "jñâna" yet in itself it is uncontrived awareness, beyond all such terms as "is" or "is not", "eternal" or "nothing"; it is quite beyond the scope of the intellect. Therefore, no matter which terms are used to express it, there is nothing to refute. It is whatever it is. Some would-be scholars once asked Lord Buddha himself (about this topic) but his reply was:

"Do not think there is any one-sided reply to this! Dharmakâya is beyond the grasp of the intellect. It is unborn and free of conceptual complication. Do not ask me; look into the mind. That is the way it is."

Thus the very essence or the very nature of a Buddha (can be viewed as) the most perfect purity and the most perfect primordial wisdom (jñâna). As is said in the *uttaratantra*:

"Buddhahood is indivisible yet one can categorise (it) according to its qualities of purity: the two characteristics of jñâna and freedom from impurity, comparable to the sun and to the sky."

Also, it says in the *mahâyâna-sûtrâlankâra* :

"Those who, through vast purification, have absolutely triumphed over all the defilement and cognitive obscurations, along with their latent potentials, constantly present for such a long time, and who possess the supreme good qualities through perfect transmutation: those are Buddhas."

2. Etymology of "Buddha"

Why *Buddha* ?[1] The term *Buddha* – "awakened plenitude" – is

---

1. The Sanskrit words *budh bodh Buddha* etc. come from a stem which has a root meaning of emergence from constraint, giving two main meanings — 'to awaken" and 'to flourish". No doubt an Indian in former times would have these two meanings triggered subconsciously on hearing those words and, for instance, on hearing the word *Buddha* would imagine someone awake and fully-flourished. No single root syllable in Tibetan

(continued...)

applied because they have awoken from sleep-like ignorance and because the mind has expanded to embrace the two aspects of the knowable[1].

3.   Aspects

Buddhahood can be divided into three aspects[2], the three *kâya*: the *dharmakâya*, the *sambhogakâya* and the *nirmânakâya*. It says, in the *suvarnaprabhâsottamasûtra*:

"All the tathâgatas possess three kâya: the dharmakâya, the sambhogakâya and the nirmânakâya."

One might remark that some scriptures speak of two kâya, others of four kâya and some of even five kâya. Although they are discussed as such, they are all covered by this categorisation in terms of three kâya. Thus the *mahâyâna-sûtrâlankâra* says:

"One should be aware that all the Buddhakâya are included within the three kâya."

4.   Presentation

The dharmakâya is what Buddha really is. The 8,000-verse version of the *prajñâpâramitâ* says:

1.(...continued)
conveyed these two meanings and so they chose the bisyllable *sangs.rgyas*, which means "awakened plenitude", to translate the word *Buddha*. In English we have a different problem, inasmuch as we have adopted the Sanskrit term *Buddha* but we have neither the same subconscious images triggered by this word as an Indian would have done 2,000 years ago nor the "awakened" and "plenitude" images that a Tibetan has on hearing *sang.rgyas*. The main value, for the Western reader, of this point of the chapter is to introduce these images and thereby replace the vague notions which are normally evoked by the word "Buddha."

1. As-it-is and multiplicity.

2. These divisions exist in terms of intellectual analysis. Within enlightenment itself there are no divisions, no separate areas. This point is strongly affirmed in the *uttara tantra sastra*. These would be like different images people see in a mirror, according to their position. They are valid observations from each person's relative point of view. However, the mirror itself does not have one image stocked here, another there etc. Its unique nature gives rise to its relative aspects.

"Do not view the tathâgata as the form kâya. The tathâgata is the dharmakâya."

One can also quote the *samâdhirâjasûtra*, which says:

"Do not view the King of Victors as (being) the form kâya."

The two form kâya are a consequence of:

- the power of transmission[1] of the dharmakâya,
- the subjective experience of beings and
- former prayers[2].

Were the form kâya solely due to the power of transmission of the dharmadhâtu[3], the logical consequence would be that everyone would be effortlessly liberated, since the dharmadhâtu pervades all beings. (Were that the case) alternatively it would follow that all beings would come face to face with the Buddhas. However, since this is not the case, the (kâya) do not come solely from the dharmadhâtu's blessing.

Were the form kâya solely due to the subjective experience of beings training on the path, Buddhahood would be dependent upon error, since to perceive something which is not there is an error (of perception). Also, since beings have been perceiving erroneously since beginningless time, then all of them should already be Buddhas. This not the case either and the form kâya are not just the subjective projections of beings training.

Were the form kâya solely due to former prayers, then has a true and perfect Buddha achieved power over prayer? If he has not, then he has not reached omniscience either. If he has, then since

---

1. *byin.rlabs* often translated as "blessing", means the power of transmission. When, in vajrayâna Buddhism for instance, one prays for blessing, it is not for some vaguely uplifting spiritual experience but for the power to realise the wisdom inherent to mind's true nature. Here, dharmakâya is the fundamental, pure nature of mind which has the capacity to give rise to experience of the two form kâya.

2. i.e. former prayers of the Buddhas — when they were bodhisattvas working through the paths and levels.

3. Note that the text changes from speaking of the dharmakâya's power to that of the dharmadhâtu. These two are the same, in essence i.e., they are two facets of the same, indivisible, thing. *Dharmakâya* stresses the wisdom, *dharmadhâtu* stresses the voidness.

his prayers are unbiased and for the benefit of all beings, then the logical consequence would be for each and every being to be liberated. This is not the case and thus the form kâya do not come solely from former prayers.

Therefore the form kâya are a consequence of the combination of these three factors.

5.   The Reason for a Definite Number, i.e. Three Kâya

This number is determined by necessity, inasmuch as there is dharmakâya as own value and the two form kâya as value for others.[1]

the own-value of dharmakâya

How does the dharmakâya represent own value? Once dharmakâya has been achieved, it is the basis for all other qualities, such as the (four) fearlessnesses, the (ten) powers etc.[2], which gather as if they had been summoned. Furthermore, even if one has not achieved dharmakâya itself, those who aspire to dharmakâya, have a little realisation of it, a partial realisation or almost complete realisation of it, will have just a few qualities, many qualities, a great number of qualities or an immeasurable amount of qualities respectively.

The qualities arising from aspiration to dharmakâya are those of the profound absorptions, clear cognitions and all the superb qualities up to and including the Highest Worldly Point[3].

The qualities emerging from a little realisation of dharmakâya are all the qualities of purification, clear cognition, supernatural ability

---

1. **value**: The Tibetan syllable *don.* is charged with meanings: it signifies "value" and "benefit". It signifies that "which has meaning" or "is the meaning of". It also signifies a point of reference of experience, such as the perceived object of a sense. With so many meanings revolving around a central idea conveyed by the English word "point", it is impossible to translate this term adequately. For instance, in this particular case *don* implies that the dharmakâya is that which has meaning for oneself, meaning within itself; that which is experienced by oneself; that which is the ultimate benefit for oneself.

2. See Changeless Nature; chapter on enlightened qualities.

3. The Highest Worldly Point is the 4th of the stages of the Phase of Integration.

and so forth of realised śrāvaka arhats.

The qualities emerging from a partial realisation of dharmakāya are all the qualities of purification, meditation, clear cognition and so forth of realised pratyekabuddha arhants.

The qualities emerging from almost complete realisation of dharmakāya are the qualities of purification, profound absorption, clear cognition and so forth of bodhisattvas of the (ten) bodhisattva levels.

the value for others

The two form kāya are presented in this way—as value for others —inasmuch as there is the sambhogakāya which appears to pure disciples[1] and the nirmānakāya which appears to impure disciples[2].

Thus there are definitely three kāya.

6.   The Characteristic Properties of the Three Kāya

i. dharmakāya

The term "dharmakāya" simply means the exhaustion of all error—the disappearance of what is of a delusory nature—once the meaning[3] of voidness, the dharmadhātu, has been realised. However, as such, *dharmakāya* is simply a term representing a conceptual convention. In real essence there is nothing of it whatsoever which really exists—neither as dharmakāya nor as characteristic properties of dharmakāya nor as anything which could serve as a basis for properties (of dharmakāya). Since it is like that, that is how my guru Milarepa explained it. Dividing it into its various aspects, dharmakāya (can be explained as) possessing eight characteristic qualities: being identical, profound, permanent, homogeneous, right, pure, lucid and linked to sambhogakāya.

---

1. i.e. bodhisattvas of the ten levels. Note that the word disciple is used literally here: those still training.

2. i.e. those of the Phase of Accumulation and the Phase of Integration.

3. Again this word *don*: meaning, point, value, benefit.... (see above)

6iA   IDENTICAL This means that there are no differences of dharmakâya from any one Buddha to another.

6iB   PROFOUND It is profound because it is difficult to realise, since it is nothing to do with conceptual complication.

6iC   PERMANENT Being uncreated, it is without a coming into being or a cessation and without beginning, middle or end.

6iD   HOMOGENEOUS It is indivisible, its space (voidness) and its primordial wisdom (jñâna) being inseparable.

6iE   RIGHT It is without error, since it transcends the two extremes of underestimation[1] and over-assertion[2].

6iF   PURE It is free from the pollution of the three obscurations, i.e. defilements, the cognitive obscuration and impediments to meditation.

6iG   LUCID CLARITY By not thinking, it is focussed upon non-conceptual suchness.

6iH   LINKED TO SAMBHOGAKAYA It is the basis for (manifestation of) the sambhogakâya; the very expression of vast[3] qualities. The *uttaratantraśastra* says:

"Beginningless, centreless and endless, indivisible, without the two, free from the three, stainless and non-conceptual—such is realised to be the nature of dharmadhâtu, when seen by the yogin resting in profound meditation."

The *mahâyâna-sûtrânkâra* also says:

"Identical, the nature kâya, subtle and linked with sambhoga-kâya."

---

1. Ignorance of its nature and qualities.

2. To take one's limited conceptions, of it being something, as real.

3. **vast** is a sort of codeword in mahâyâna Buddhism. It refers to the infinite range of qualities associated with the phases and levels of bodhisattva development. Its counterpart is the word **profound**, which refers to the one void nature of dharmadhâtu.

ii   sambhogakâya

The sambhogakâya[1] also has eight characteristics, those of: entourage, domain, form, marks, teaching, deeds, spontaneity and absence of an own nature.

6iiA ENTOURAGE The entourage with which it is spontaneously experienced is composed solely of bodhisattvas abiding in the ten bodhisattva levels.

6iiB DOMAIN The domain in which it is experienced is that of the utterly pure Buddhafields.

6iiC FORM The way in which it is experienced is in the form of illustrious Vairocana etc.

6iiD MARKS The marks with which it is physically endowed are the 32 marks of excellence and the 80 adornments.

6iiE TEACHING The dharma through which it is perfectly experienced is uniquely that of the mahâyâna.

6iiF DEEDS The enlightened activity which forms its deeds is to predict (the future enlightenment) of the bodhisattvas etc.

6iiG SPONTANEITY Those deeds and so forth are all accomplished without any effort, occurring spontaneously as in the example of the supreme gems (wish-fulfilling gems).

6iiH ABSENCE OF OWN NATURE Even though it manifests various sorts of form, they are not its true nature; they are like the colours picked up in a crystal.

Thus the *mahâyâna-sûtrâlankâra* says:

"Perfect experience: in every domain a complete entourage; the place; the marks; the form; the perfect use of dharma teaching and its deeds. These are the various characteristics."

---

1. **sambhogakâya**: "the embodiment of perfect experience". This term is sometimes translated as "perfect enjoyment" and this has been misunderstood more than once. It is true in the sense of enjoyment meaning "having access to" but nothing to do with the relative notion of having a good time. This noble term is applied because the sambhogakâya is solely the domain of experience of bodhisattvas in the ten levels. Their access to the enlightened mind takes places through the purest and most <u>perfect</u> sense <u>experience</u>—meaningful visions, hearing profound teachings etc.—all against a background of their genuine experience of voidness. The Tibetan text exploits this idea of experience, or enjoyment, in the points which follow.

Also, in the *abhisamayâlaṅkâra* it says:

"The one endowed with the 32 marks and 80 adornments is known as 'the perfect experience kâya of the Buddha', since it makes use of the mahâyâna."[1]

iii   the nirmânakâya

The nirmânakâya[2] also has eight principal characteristics — those of its basis, its cause, its domain, its duration, its character, its role of encouraging, its maturing function and its liberating function.

6iiiA BASIS Its basis is the dharmakâya, (from which it emanates) without there being any shift.

6iiiB CAUSE It arises from tremendous compassion which aspires to benefit every single being.

6iiiC DOMAIN Its domain embraces both the very pure lands and quite impure ones.

6iiiD DURATION It endures, without interruption, for as long as the world endures.

6iiiE CHARACTER Its character is to manifest forms as the three types of emanation:

▸ *creative emanations* endowed with outstanding skill in and mastery over a given art or craft, such as lute-playing etc.,

▸ *birth emanations* which take birth in various inferior bodies in specific types of existence, e.g. as a hare and

▸ *supreme emanations* who manifest (the 12 deeds:) descent from Tusita heaven, entering the mother's womb etc. and eventually entering great Peace. As it says, in the *mahâyâna-sûtrâlaṅkâra*:

"Always manifesting the creative, birth and great enlightenment and nirvâna, the Buddha's nirmânakâya is a great means of liberation[3]."

---

1. "It is perfect since he only ever uses the mahâyâna and the profound true meaning to teach—unlike nirmânakâya which, given the nature of its disciples, has to use teachings other than mahâyâna and has to resort to expedient truths." [Khenchen Trangu Rinpoche]

2. **nirmânakâya** — "emanated form"

3. For sentient beings.

As is said in the *uttara tantra*:

"Through emanations of various natures, he manifestly takes birth, descends from Tusita (1), enters the womb (2) and is born (3). Skilled in all arts and crafts (4), he enjoys the company of his consorts (5), renounces (6), undergoes hardships (7), goes to the seat of enlightenment (8), vanquishes the armies of negative forces (9), attains perfect enlightenment (10), (turns) the wheel of dharma (11) and passes away (12). In all places, quite impure, he shows these deeds for as long as worlds endure."

6iiiF ROLE OF ENCOURAGING The nirmânakâya makes ordinary worldly beings long for and work towards whichever of the three types of nirvâna corresponds to their mentality.[1]

6iiiG MATURING FUNCTION The nirmânakâya brings to full spiritual maturity those who are already engaged in the path.

6iiiH LIBERATING FUNCTION The nirmânakâya frees from the fetters of existence those who have reached a full maturity in virtue.

Thus it says, in the *uttaratantra*:

"It causes worldly beings to enter the path of peace, brings them to full maturity and it is that which gives rise to predictions."

These are the eight characteristics of the nirmânakâya. The *abhi-samayâlankâra* says:

"The kâya that acts simultaneously and in all sorts of ways to help beings, for as long as existence continues, is the unceasing nirmânakâya of the Accomplished One."

7.   The Three Particularities

The Buddhakâya have three particularities; those of identity, permanence and manifestation.

7A   THE PARTICULARITY OF IDENTITY

The dharmakâya of all the Buddhas is identical, being inseparable from its support, the dharmadhâtu. The sambhogakâya

---

1. i.e. śrâvaka, pratyekabuddha or bodhisattva.

of all the Buddhas is identical since its noble disposition[1] is the same. The nirmânakâya of all the Buddhas is identical because their activity is common. Therefore the *mahâyâna-sûtrâlankâra* says:

"These are identical, because of their support, intention and activity."

7B   THE PARTICULARITY OF PERMANENCE

The dharmakâya is permanent by its very nature since it is the very identity of the ultimate; that which is without coming into being or ceasing to be. The sambhogakâya is permanent through being continuous, inasmuch as the experience of dharma it manifests is uninterrupted. The nirmânakâya is permanent insofar as its deeds are permanent. Although its manifestations disappear, it shows itself over and over again. Although that which manifests in correspondence to a certain need will cease, there is a functional permanence since it arises appropriately, without delay[2]. The *mahâyâna-sûtrâlankâra*:

"Permanence of nature, of uninterruptedness and of continuity."[3]

7C   THE PARTICULARITY OF MANIFESTATION

Dharmakâya manifests through the purification of the cognitive obscurations clouding the dharmadhâtu. Sambhogakâya manifests through the purification of the affective defilements. The nirmânakâya manifests through purification of karma obscurations.

This was the twentieth chapter, on the result, perfect Buddhahood, from this Gems of Dharma, Jewels of Freedom

---

1. Compassionate intention to help others.

2. i.e. it is always there, ready to manifest as soon as there is need, as soon as a mind is open enough to experience it.

3. This refers to dharmakâya, nirmânakâya and sambhogakâya respectively.

Part 6

Chapter Twenty-One

Non-Conceptual Enlightened Activity to Benefit Beings

First one develops bodhicitta, then the path is practised and finally the fruition, Buddhahood (is achieved). As all these goals have been pursued solely in order to eliminate beings' sufferings and to assure their happiness, one may wonder how in fact there can be any benefitting of beings when Buddhahood is attained, since Buddhas are without either conceptual activity or effort[1]. There does however occur a spontaneous and uninterrupted benefitting of beings, even though Buddhas do not think or make effort. If one wonders how this can happen, the answer is given in the synopsis of this chapter:

---

1. This would be a valid question for most ordinary people, for whom activity would imply thought and effort.

"Enlightened activity is summed up in three points: the noble bodies of the Buddhas, without thinking, accomplish the benefit of beings and likewise do the magnificent speech and the noble mind."

Examples of this non-conceptual benefitting of beings — physically, verbally and mentally — are given in the *uttaratantra*:

"Like Indra, the drum, clouds and brahmâ, like the sun and the precious jewel is the Tathâgata; also like an echo, like space and like the earth."

1.   Examples of the way in which the noble forms of the Buddha non-conceptually accomplish the good of beings

The quotation "Like the manifestation of Indra" gives an example of how the non-conceptualising kâya can bring benefit to sentient beings. In the example, Indra, Lord of the Gods, dwells in his palace called "House of Victory", in the company of a host of young goddesses. The palace is made of beryl so pure and lustrous that Indra's reflected image appears on the walls and can be seen from the outside. Were humans living on earth to be able to behold this image of Indra and his divine enjoyments in the heavens above them, they would long and pray to live like that. With such a goal in mind, they might make sincere efforts to be virtuous and, through their virtue, they could be reborn in such a state after death.[1] The vision which inspires them takes place without any intentional effort on the part of Indra.

In a similar way, those who have entered the path of highest good and who cultivate faith and similar virtues will see the forms of the perfect Buddhas adorned with their special marks and signs; they see them walking, standing, sitting, sleeping, teaching the dharma, meditating and accomplishing all sorts of miracles. As a

---

1. There are several versions of this story. In some, it is explained that when the general karma of an area is good, the people can see some of the divine worlds, high above them in space. This almost magical play of reflections in Indra's palace not only enables the people to appreciate his way of life but also gives them an understanding that he has reached that state through his own former virtue. With this tantalising incentive before them, they feel inspired to do likewise. In other versions of the example, it is our earth which, through its gem-like clarity, reflects the divine worlds.

result of seeing such things, they will experience faith and yearn to attain such a state. In order to become like that, they will practise those virtues which are its cause: bodhicitta and all the other necessary practices. As a result, they will eventually become Buddhas. The manifestation of the Buddhas' form kâya takes place without any thinking and without any movement.[1]

> "Just as, on the clear surface of beryl, there appears the reflected form of the Lord of Gods, so on the clear surface of beings' minds there appears the reflected form of the King of Victors."

2.   Examples of the way in which Buddhas' pure speech nonconceptually accomplishes the good of beings

The quotation "like the divine drum" gives the example for how the Buddhas' speech can accomplish the welfare of beings, without forethought. In the example, there is the sound of a drumbeat[2] in the realm of the gods. It resounds as a result of the gods' former good actions. The drumbeat does not think or intend, yet its sound conveys messages such as *All conditioned things are impermanent!* which stimulate the gods, inclined to neglect virtue in the present.

> "Just as in the divine realms and through the power of their (the gods') former virtue, the dharma drum, without any thought, without any effort, location, mind or form, stimulates all the carefree gods, over and over again, with the words "impermanence", "suffering", "no self" and "peace" and also the four seals which are the sign of the Buddhas' teachings: "All conditioned things are impermanent," "All phenomena are devoid of self entity," "All tainted phenomena incorporate suffering" and "The whole of nirvâna is peace..."

As in the example, it is without any effort or deliberation that the speech of the Buddhas transmits to those who are ready the

---

1. i.e. the Buddhas do not intend to so inspire people and their emanations are not like projections which have a source in one place and an appearance in another place. Reflection on this point helps one understand that Buddha is therefore the essence of everyone's mind.

2. There is not any drum to be seen or found, only the sound of a drumbeat.

teachings that suit them.

> "...likewise, without effort and so forth, the omnipresent embraces all beings, without one exception, with the speech of the enlightened ones, teaching the dharma to those who are ready."

In the above way, the speech of the Buddhas accomplishes the welfare of beings without any (need for) thought.

3.   Examples of the way in which the perfect mind of the Buddha non-conceptually accomplishes the good of beings

3A   LIKE A CLOUD

For example, during the monsoon the clouds gather effortlessly in the sky and their rain, as it falls upon the earth without any deliberation on its part, causes the growth of perfect crops and causes many other things to happen:

> "Just as the clouds, during the monsoon, cause an effortless mass of water—the condition for plentiful crops—to fall upon the earth..."

In a similar way, the activity of the Buddha mind, without any deliberation being needed, pours down the rain of dharma onto beings training in virtue and it ripens their crop of wholesomeness:

> "...similarly the clouds of great compassion cause, without any need of deliberation, a rainfall of the sublime teachings of the victorious ones to..."

Thus the Buddha mind accomplishes the welfare of beings without any need of thought.

3B   LIKE BRAHMÂ

In this example, Brahmâ, Lord of Gods, manifests his presence in all the heavens yet never leaves his own brahmâ-heaven. In a similar way, without ever moving from the dharmakâya, the Buddha manifests the twelve deeds and other similar emanations to those training in virtue, thereby bringing them benefit.

> "Just as Brahmâ, without ever moving from the brahmâ heaven,

effortlessly shows his manifestations in all the other heavens, so also does the Victor, without ever moving from the dharmakâya, effortlessly show his emanations everywhere, to those whose karma makes them ready."

3C   LIKE THE SUN

In this example the sunrays, without any need for deliberation, cause the lotuses and an infinity of other kinds of flowers to blossom, simultaneously. In a similar way, without any thought or effort, the rays of the Buddhas' teachings cause the lotuses which are the minds of infinitely different types of disciples, with their varied aspirations, to open towards that which is wholesome.

"Just as the sun, without any deliberation, through the simultaneous radiations of its sunbeams, brings the lotuses to full bloom and ripens other plants, so also do the sunrays of the tathâgatas' sublime teachings, without any need for deliberation, pour into the lotuses of beings training in virtue."

Taking this example of the sun another way, just as the reflection of the sun appears simultaneously on all surfaces sufficiently clear and smooth, so also does the Buddha appear simultaneously to all disciples of sufficiently pure inner disposition.

"In all the water vessels which are those pure disciples, simultaneously appear countless reflections of the Buddha sun."

C4   LIKE A WISH-FULFILLING GEM

In this example, just as a wish-fulfilling gem does not think yet effortlessly produces whatever is requested by the person who prays to it, likewise the goals corresponding to the various motivations of the śrâvaka and other disciples are accomplished because of the Buddha:

"Just as a wish-fulfilling gem, without thought and simultaneously, completely fulfils the wishes of those who are within its sphere of influence, so also, on account of the wish-fulfilling Buddha, will those of various motivation hear different kinds of teachings. However, these happen without any deliberation in (the

Buddha's mind).

Similar to the above, there are three more examples[1]—those of an echo, of space and of the earth—showing how beings can be benefitted by the Buddhas without there being any need for deliberation on their part.

This was the twenty-first chapter, on non-conceptual enlightened activity, from this Gems of Dharma, Jewels of Freedom

---

1. In the *uttaratantra*.

Index